Louis ...., was shortl...... .... the *Guardian* First Book
Award and won the Somerset Maugham Prize. Her novel *Special*
was published in 2002 to wide acclaim, and her most recent
book, *The Wreckers*, was sho............. ... ...
Association Gold Dagger Awar....

From the reviews of *The Bicycl....*

'Everything you ever wanted to know about the bike, its history
and uses'   *Sunday Times*

'You can keep the internet. You can keep the computer and the
mobile phone. In the bicycle, humanity has its most perfect
invention of the past 300 years and in Bella Bathurst the bike has
found the best and brightest booster so far'

BORIS JOHNSON, *Mail on Sunday*

'Excellent ... a curious tour around a timely topic ... As this
beautifully written and gently erudite work easily proves, cycling
is ideal for many things, and will doubtless draw more converts
to agree that "there's no lovelier form of transport"'

BRIAN SCHOFIELD, *Sunday Times*

'Lovely, lively, anecdotal anthology of good stories about cycling'
The Times

'This charming, gently erudite history embraces every aspect of
the bicycle, from its bone-shaking origins to today's sleek
machine'   *Sunday Times*

By the same author

The Lighthouse Stevensons
Special
The Wreckers

BELLA BATHURST

The Bicycle Book

I want to ride my bicycle
I want to ride my bike
I want to ride my bicycle
I want to ride it where I like

QUEEN, 'Bicycle Race'

Harper
Press

HarperPress
An imprint of HarperCollins*Publishers*
77–85 Fulham Palace Road,
Hammersmith, London W6 8JB

This Harper*Press* paperback edition published 2012

1

First published in Great Britain by Harper*Press* in 2011

'Bicycle Race' words and music by Mercury © 1978,
Reproduced by permission of EMI Music Publishing Ltd/
Queen Music Limited, London W8 5SW

A catalogue record for this book
is available from the British Library

ISBN 978-0-00-730589-6

Typeset in Minion by G&M Designs Limited,
Raunds, Northamptonshire
Printed and bound in Great Britain by
Clays Ltd, St Ives plc

MIX
Paper from
responsible sources
FSC™ C007454

For Fog
Beloved friend, teacher and fellow traveller,
1997–2010

CONTENTS

INTRODUCTION

'The gross and net result of it is that people who spent most of their natural lives riding iron bicycles over the rocky roadsteads of this parish get their personalities mixed up with the personalities of their bicycle as a result of the interchanging of the atoms of each of them ... you would be surprised at the number of people in these parts who nearly are half people and half bicycles.'

FLANN O'BRIEN,
THE THIRD POLICEMAN

A bicycle undoubtedly has its downsides. It won't shelter you from the elements, or protect you from the fury of your fellow traveller. It lacks the romance of a sailboat or the simplicity of your own two feet. It will not give you the same sensation that sitting in £180,000-worth of over-charged horsepower does. It is miserable in the wet. No other form of transport ever takes it seriously. It is sliced up by cabs and menaced by buses. It is loathed by motorists and loved by the sort of politicians who would never dream of actually using it. It can't transport you from one end of the world to the other in time for Christmas. It doesn't have a particularly distinguished industrial history. It gets stolen, on average, every minute and a half. It delivers you at the end of your journey covered in a light film of sweat and toxic diesel particulates. It requires a lot of silly clothing. And, of course, it is occasionally fatal.

And yet cycling obsesses people. They take it up for practical reasons – health, economy, twelve points on their driving licence – and before they know it they're gleaming with zeal and talking slightly too fast about fixies and resting BPMs. Things that they hadn't thought about since they were children start to preoccupy them – the stuff of bikes, the speed of them, their grace or style or character. It doesn't take long before the daily commute to work becomes a journey to be looked forward to, an adventure instead of an ordeal. There are conversations with colleagues about bikes and the experience of cycling; new connections are made. On the road, they start silently checking out fellow converts. Looking for short cuts and alternative routes, they ride past bits of the city – intriguing, come-hither bits – they never knew existed. In their houses, items of bike kit start to multiply. Tyres and lights now take up as much space as hats and coats. They persuade themselves that lugging a muddy vintage steel-framed roadster up three flights of stairs at night is a reasonable way to get fit. Cycling starts to become as much a way of life and a philosophy as it does a form of transport. It spreads from work to weekends to holidays. They nominate themselves for sponsored rides and charity marathons. They stop thinking in miles and start thinking in kilometres. Almost by mistake, they find themselves in possession of a whole fleet of bikes: one for work, one for speed, one for the wet, one for annoying other people who know about bikes. They realise that one of the major advantages to cycling is the ability – more than that, the *need* – to consume their own bodyweight in spag bol and chocolate cake every day. Instead of road-tripping it round America as in the old days, family holidays are now spent hurtling through the Austrian Tyrol like two-wheeled von Trapps. They arrive at work early every day now, radiant with sweat and self-satisfaction. At home, they talk about getting rid of the car. In the evenings, they admire their newly altered profile in the mirror; the helmet hair, the buns of steel, the bloody knees. After a while they find themselves making unexpected judgement calls – can one cycle elegantly in a pencil skirt, what is the optimum number of children per bicycle, how wet is too wet, is Kent too far, perhaps an Étape might be nice. They discover that the thing about cycling isn't that it's healthy, or environmentally friendly, or fast, or convenient, or politically correct. The thing about it is that it's fun.

Part of that is the straightforward childlike joy in riding a bike, the urge to yell, 'Whheeee!' on the way downhill. There's a huge pleasure in going places cars can't go, in dodging and weaving, in a bike's simple agility. It makes previously unknown districts more accessible and familiar ones more difficult. It reinvents familiar geography, opens up towpaths or riverbanks or favoured rat runs across town. It offers the little tremor of happiness from bending urban by-laws back to suit the individual, and the constant delight in going straight to the front of the queue. It allows one to feel smooth and charged and graceful in a world full of blocks and obstructions. It has the peculiar attraction of being healthy, dirty and risky all at once. It offers the interesting discovery that getting to and from work need not necessarily mean the abandonment of sanity. It can be companionable or solitary, competitive or amicable. And, like the horse or the sailboat, it feels somehow as if it's exactly the right pace for a human to travel.

And so the bicycle – old, and cheap, and slightly comic – has become the twenty-first century's great transport success story. Since the millennium, its use in Britain has doubled and then doubled again. Thousands now cycle to work, and more take it up every day. It has allowed the reinvention of the British landscape, opening up miles of Forestry Commission land to mountain bikers, and in doing so has given us back both the countryside and our sense of ourselves. It's introduced thousands of people to racing and to the world of European pro-touring. It's offered those of middle-aged mind and limb a chance to see themselves renewed. It has connected people through events and races and just hanging out. It has become the fastest and most reliable form of transport for people all over the country. In trial after trial, it is the bike which reaches its urban destination faster than the car, the bus, the tube or the pedestrian. It represents the power of self-reliance and the triumph of straightforwardness. Cycling has recycled itself. It is an ancient idea, and its time has finally come.

🚲 🚲 🚲

I started writing this book because I wanted to read something good about cycling and bikes, and there didn't seem to be that much around. There were books, certainly, but none of them were written for people like me. There were route guides or sports science manuals or conspiracy theorists poring over Lance Armstrong's doping record or biographies of individual heroes. There were instructions on mending a puncture at 10,000ft or nerdy accounts of club cycling. There were breathless records of difficult trips and books hung just on the cycling-related pun in the title. But there wasn't anything for the sort of cyclist who liked cycling, and reading, and stories, and who had long ago given up any desire to experiment with exogenous EPO.

This, then, is not designed to tell the reader how to differentiate between brands of derailleur or explain why riding a bicycle is good for your health. There is plenty missing. I've left out most of the political and environmental debate (provision of facilities, zero emissions etc.) because it is either obvious or it is already well served by innumerable blogs and forums. I haven't included anything on track cycling on the grounds that if you need a velodrome to do it then it is out of most people's reach. There's nothing on folding bikes, Moultons or recumbents because they look ridiculous and can't corner. I cannot tell you about your VO2 max or how to lace a wheel. I don't know how to stop your bike getting nicked and or how you become an Iron Man. I've picked and chosen quite shamelessly from all the available information on the basis of what I felt was interesting and useful. Because almost all cyclists feel a strong sense of ownership of both the bicycle and the experience of cycling, there will almost inevitably be some I can't satisfy, and who will wish I'd included less of some stuff and more of another. That, I'm afraid, is an occupational hazard of writing about a subject about which so many people feel so passionately. The other occupational hazard, common to all non-fiction, is discovering that half the best stories come to you after the book is published. People write in, talk to you at book events, offer fabulous heaps of gold-mine material. Sometimes you get to include some of that material in future editions. Even if you don't, there's always the pleasure in knowing that the subject has inspired readers to dust off their own untold stories.

My own background is straightforward. I ride a bicycle every day in London, I do as much mountain biking in Scotland as I can, I've done long tours abroad, I've taken part in sportives and audaxes, and that's it. Like thousands of other cyclists around the country, I also use every other form of public and private transport available – cars, cabs, trains, planes, buses, the London Underground. I'm not a cyclist because I hate cars or can't understand the pleasure of driving – I'm a cyclist because I reckon there is no lovelier form of transport.

歲 歲 歲

ONE

Framebuilding

Far away in a corner of Lincolnshire, there are men looking at the sky. They stand in a row in a car park and they stare at the clouds. They stay like that for quite a long time. In order to see the sky more closely, most of them have got cameras with huge white lenses of the type generally used by paparazzi photographers to take covert shots of celebrities' deodorant marks. The lenses are the size and shape of ships' foghorns, and are so heavy that they require a whole separate entourage of kit to support them – sandbags, tripods, vans, wives. Despite their supporting role, the wives do not seem to be that interested in either the cameras or the sky. Instead they sit patiently, sharing out home-made pasta with other wives or lying back on deck-chairs soaking up the flatland sun while the men swing their lenses from ground to cloud and back again.

When the men have looked at the sky for long enough, they go and stare at a wall instead. Directly opposite the car park is a wooden perimeter fence a couple of metres high. With a small stepladder, it is easy enough for the men to press their lenses to the gaps or for the taller ones to see over the top. Anyone passing down the road from the nearby town can see a long line of men wobbling on their ladders with their noses pressed to the planks. It looks like a convention of trainee window cleaners, or maybe peeping toms – very British, but a little bit sinister too.

It's midsummer in the countryside, and this is the sort of scenery to make you believe in England again. Somewhere nearby, there are canals, bright expanses of poppies and the occasional heart-lifting lilt of a lark's call. Once in a while a hare lollops out of the high fields of green grain and tears off into the distance, pursued by invisible demons. In the distance Coningsby's church tower sails over the surrounding fields and the proper old-fashioned bell still tolls the hour. Even so, the men with long lenses have not picked a particularly restful place to sit back and picnic. Every twenty minutes or so there is a low rumble from somewhere far away. The men take it as a cue to start twiddling dials and taking urgent meter readings. The wives get up suddenly and run for the cars. The rumble moves closer, resolves itself into an approach from east or south and alters from a mutter to a roar. A small black dot appears over the tree tops. It is moving very fast. The sound has sharpened and is suddenly so huge that you have no choice but to stop whatever you're doing and turn towards the source, so huge it blots out everything except itself. And then for a second a vast black triangle slides over the sun. It is very low now, low enough to see every detail. The men with the lenses click silently, their movements frantic. Indifferent, almighty, the triangle heads towards the runway. Even with your hands over your ears, the sound of it is now so overwhelming it makes your vision go fuzzy. Its passage makes your heart squeeze tight with fear and excitement, and when it has gone it leaves a stinking rip in the summer air.

This is RAF Coningsby, home not only to the surviving RAF Battle of Britain planes (a Lancaster bomber, several Spitfires, a couple of Hurricanes and a Tiger Moth), but to the British contingent of Eurofighter Typhoons. The Lancasters and Spitfires alone would probably bring the planespotters in their droves, but the combination of nostalgia for World War Two and anticipation for the thrills of World War Three is almost irresistible. During particularly busy periods, including training days for the Battle of Britain displays, the car park and the whole surrounding area is full of people all busily destroying what remains of their hearing. Each man has his camera and a little notepad on which to keep track of dates, times, radio frequencies and serial numbers. If you like fighter planes, this place is Mecca.

So it's fortunate that Dave and Debbie Yates are keen on engineering in general. Their smallholding is about half a mile from the end of Coningsby's runway, and life for them is punctuated by the roar of approaching bombers. They moved here four years ago from the North East, and have set the whole place up as a smallholding. In the winter, they train spaniels as gun dogs. And in the summer, Dave makes bicycles.

Dave Yates is famous for his frames. In his time, working either as part of larger manufacturers or for himself, he has built the basic skeletons of over 12,000 bikes of every shape and size. Most of his time is spent here in the workshop either putting together bespoke frames for clients or repairing their old favourites. The rest of his time is spent teaching the secrets of framebuilding to others. It's a rare skill. Once, there were thousands of small-scale framebuilders all over the country, producing a few steel-framed bikes a year for their local markets. But few individual framemakers managed to survive cycling's long decline in popularity, and fewer still were prepared to teach what they knew to a new generation. Dave is one of only a handful of those who kept the faith. And after half a professional lifetime working for small-scale companies in the North East, he and Debbie came south and set up here.

His workshop is over in a discreet corner of the farm well away from the main house. One half contains a lot of light industrial machinery – mills, lathes, obscure bits of componentry – while the horizontal bit is a light, comfortable space including three workbenches, a stack of Reynolds 531 and 521 tubing, a jig and several shoulder-height canisters of oxyacetylene gas. Despite the midsummer fields outside, the workshop has a very particular smell to it, a potent combination of metal, fire and instant coffee. For nine or ten individual weeks during the summer months, Dave takes two students (more would be impossible, since so much of his time involves working with things that might explode) and guides them through the construction of their own frame. That frame can be any shape or size as long as it is made from steel, can reasonably be made from scratch in five days and is not something silly like a tandem.

Partly because he's rare and partly because he's good, there is usually a waiting list of about two years for a place on one of Yates' courses. He has the patience of a born teacher, unflappable, generous with what he knows and truly passionate about his subject. As the week progresses, he begins to remind me of Gimli the dwarf in *The Lord of the Rings*. Not because he's unusually small, but because there does seem to be some irresistible connection between fire and metalwork and dark, bearded Northern men. Besides, no one works with one element for the whole of their professional lives without taking on a few of its characteristics. His father worked in the Swan Hunter shipyard on Tyneside, and Dave took his passion for bikes first into teaching metalwork and then into framebuilding. 'I loved making things, I loved fiddling about with things, I loved building things. But I never had a point where I thought, I want to be a framebuilder, I want to make my living at this. It was just natural that I got stuck into bikes because it was there that there were things needed doing.' In his younger days, he did a lot of racing around the North East, got his pro licence, went to France for a bit. 'I was never good. I was good, but I wasn't *good*. Because I had a switch up there' – he points to his forehead – 'which …' – there is a long pause – '… I wasn't a winner. I didn't want to win at all costs.'

There are two types of people who usually sign up to his courses, he says. There are the experts who have been studying the science of bicycles for a long time and who want to build something to an exact specification. And there are people like Graeme and me, who like bikes but not to the point of perversion. Graeme Symington, who teaches cycling maintenance and road safety courses in Sheffield, knows much more about frames and framebuilding than I do. He wants to make a big solid classic porteur-style bike, bombproof in its construction but elegant as well. I want to make a classic lugged-frame road bike – a 1950s sort of frame but with modern gears and componentry. Both ambitions are judged to be well within the scope of a week's work, even though Graeme's metalworking experience is minimal and I have none at all.

Obviously, the different demands we're making from our bikes will dictate their eventual shape and weight. Graeme's porteur will be a copy of the strong, elegant bikes once used by messengers and delivery boys to haul newspapers or shoeshine kit round the streets of Paris or Rome. They needed to take big loads at both front and back, so they had to be very stable. They also had to be capable of dealing with all weathers and of surviving for years with minimal maintenance. Graeme intends to use his for commuting, for cycle training in schools, and for 'coping with runs to the shop, where it needs to carry shopping for a family of three'.

Porteurs – and their long-distance equivalents, roadsters – are the spiritual ancestors of hybrids, the bikes which most adults now start out on when they return to cycling. Roadsters were the classic old Edwardian bikes used both for jaunts in the countryside, long-distance touring and city errands. They were big, roomy, comfortable bikes, well made and designed to be ridden slowly but steadily all day. They wouldn't set the world on fire, but nor would they leave anyone looking like Quasimodo at the end of the day. The modern hybrid still has the roadster's practicality, but has borrowed elements from two other bicycle types. The better ones should have a bit of the sturdiness and adaptability of a mountain bike while keeping the speed and responsiveness of a road bike. In practice, a lot of the cheaper, less well-made ones just have the weight of a truck and that's it. The advantage to them is that they can be loaded with panniers and racks and baskets for groceries and whatnot, and their upright riding position helps to make the rider visible. The downside is that they're dull. Most people treat them as the two-wheeled equivalent of an estate car; the bike you use to get to and from work, do the shopping, take the kids to nursery. Practical and useful, but totally anonymous. Which is fine, because the other very useful thing about hybrids is that they make riding anything else feel thrilling. If you've spent five years riding round town on a heavy bike festooned with laptop bags, then the first time you get on a road bike you're going to feel like Chris Hoy. All that time spent hauling around a lump of cheap badly-adjusted chromoly might not necessarily do you any anatomical favours in the long term, but, in the short term, it'll do your glutes and your confidence a power of good.

Meanwhile, I'm after something more lightweight. A classic road (or racing) bike is not a thing to be laden at all, but a thing made of air designed for speed and hills and huge distances. It isn't practical in the sense of either transporting big loads or being a particularly comfortable ride, but if both bike and cyclist can be made to match each other, then a good racer is unquestionably a thing to make the soul sing. And building a steel-framed racer here will

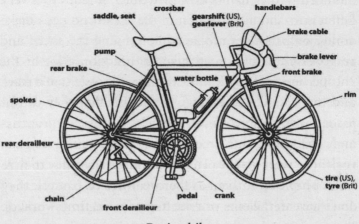

saddle, seat crossbar handlebars
gearshift (US), gearlever (Brit)
brake cable
pump brake lever
rear brake front brake
water bottle
spokes rim
rear derailleur
tire (US), tyre (Brit)
chain pedal crank
front derailleur

Racing bike.

inevitably be a nod to the classic road bikes of the past. Over the past few decades, the drive for faster and lighter bikes has pushed the majority of manufacturers towards newer, stiffer materials. Steel is regarded as a heavy, spongy, tolerant substance which has enormous tensile strength but which is far too slow and unresponsive for modern racers. And so, apart from a few specialist events such as Italy's annual L'Eroica audax, the majority of modern road bikes long ago left Reynolds 531 behind and took to aluminium, titanium or carbon fibre instead. The bikes used by pros in the Tour de France will be made from woven carbon-fibre weighing at or around the UCI (Union Cycliste Internationale – cycling's governing body) minimum of 6.8kg. Anything lighter than that is judged to be too expensive to develop and too unstable to ride. Producing carbon-fibre bikes simply isn't possible for small individual framemakers like Dave Yates. Since the fibres are moulded rather than brazed or welded, it requires a very different set-up to manufacture. Dave can and does make or repair aluminium and titanium frames, but for teaching purposes he likes to stick to good old-fashioned steel.

If I'd wanted a fast bike purely for the city, I could have gone for a single-speed or a fixie. They're the beautiful pared-down essence-of-bikes which have become increasingly fashionable for urban cyclists in the past few years. For those who live in places without many hills, they're ideal. They don't have racks or panniers or baskets, they don't have derailleurs or cassettes or (sometimes) brakes. They're just a frame, a set of wheels, and a prayer. Single speeds have one gear and a freewheel, fixies have one gear and no freewheel – in other words, the pedals will always be turning while the bike is in motion. Both are light, elegant and good for posing. In most cases they're not about logos and branding, but about riding something bespoke. Hence the occasional double-take sight of someone blazing down the Marylebone Road on a white frame with gold rims or swanking around Hoxton on a frog-green number with hot pink tyres. Most are made of steel, which keeps the price down, but because they come without any of the bells and whistles associated with most bikes, they're still very light. Messengers and fakengers like them because they need almost no maintenance at all apart from a squirt of lube once in a while, and everyone else likes them because they look beautiful and they get you where you want to be, fast. But since I want to climb hills – proper, grown-up hills – then I need a bike with gears: a racing bike.

Once in a while, Dave gets someone who wants to make either a BMX or a mountain bike. Out there on the open market, a really good MTB with suspension at both front and rear can set you back more than a top-of-the-range modern road bike will, and an amazingly fancy one can cost you five figures or more. The money goes on the geometry. The sheer complexity of fitting suspension at both front and rear, and then in making that suspension strong enough to take anything that earth and wood and rock can hurl at it, and then in making it light enough to carry with ease, and then just for good measure making it simple enough so you don't need a degree in aeronautics to repair it all comes at a price. The sheer pounding that a heavily used downhiller takes means that it's no use stinting on materials: anything cheap or badly made will get destroyed by the first tree stump it meets. It isn't that uncommon to hear downhillers complaining of getting through two or three front forks within the space of a single competition, and since the hydraulics in a good-quality fork can cost hundreds if not thousands of pounds, it's not a sport for the parsimonious or faint-hearted.

The bikes Graeme and I want to make are less demanding, and the parts are a lot easier to come by. So our first job is to come up with a series of measurements. To get a proper, comfortable ride on a bike, you need to know how heavy you are, how long your torso is, how long your arms are and what your inside leg measurement is. As a very rough rule of thumb, most men have proportionately longer torsos and shorter legs, while with women it's the reverse. The length of your torso dictates the length of the top tube, the length of your leg dictates the length of the seat tube and the length of your arms will eventually dictate where and how you arrange your handlebars. Your weight will determine what type of materials you use. Clearly if you're 6ft 3in., 13 stone and use your bike for doing the school run, it's no good welding a couple of metal twigs together and hoping for the best. And so the next job is to pick out the parts we'll need for our frames. There are four main tubes in a classic diamond-frame road bike: the head tube (the short, thick post running down from the centre of the handlebars to the top of the front wheel forks), the top tube (or crossbar), the down tube (which runs from the head tube to the bottom bracket) and the seat tube (which runs from the bottom bracket to the saddle). The forks flare out from the head tube to enclose the front wheel. At the back there are the two chain stays on either side of the rear wheel, and the seat stays, which run from the top of the seat tube to the centre of the rear wheel.

Within those basics, there are a lot of possible variables. The angles will vary substantially from person to person and from bike to bike, and each type of bike has a different geometry. Mountain bikes, for instance, will have long head tubes with slacker head angles to help absorb shock. Road bikes will have a short head tube with a steep angle – usually between 73° and 74° – and an equally upright seat tube. The more upright both head tube and seat tube are, the more responsive but less comfortable the ride. The sharp angles mean that the rider has to reach forward over the top tube, reducing his resistance to the wind. The more curved the angle of the forks, the more comfortable but less efficient things will be. Road and track bikes are usually designed to be ridden with the saddle higher than the handlebars – in other words, when you're riding it, your bum will be higher than your hands. Which is aerodynamic, but uncomfortable.

According to Dave, the first and most important thing in framemaking is to find out what the bike will be used for. 'The primary requisite is that the frame fits the rider and is suitable for the purpose. So if you want a touring bike, there's no earthly use in making an audax bike. You can do anything on anything – you can tour on a racing bike, you can race on a touring bike, but you'll do neither very well. So you have to get the frame to fit the customer and the purpose. If you're going to build a track frame to ride in Manchester, the position of the track frame is completely different to a touring frame you'd make for riding around the world. With a track bike, the priorities are speed and efficiency. A track bike is not much good for anything other than riding on a track or short trips on the road. A touring bike, other extreme, you want something that's comfortable to sit on all day, that will carry a load. A good racing bike, you steer with your backside and you think it round corners. You don't have to physically steer it, it just goes. It's an extension of the body and everything flows. When you're racing at a high level, the bike is absolutely critical – the rider has to have complete confidence in it. And if there's anything not quite right, it will affect his performance. That's the trick in building a good frame – in getting inside a rider's head, seeing what his or her vision is and translating that into something that's going to do the job.'

Will a well-made bike make you a better rider? 'No. But it will stop you being a worse rider. There are some people who will never be good racing cyclists. I've seen many riders with the right physical attributes, but nothing up there. They haven't got the confidence, they haven't got the drive to succeed. I've seen riders that wanted like nothing else on earth to succeed and flogged themselves almost to death. But they would never do it because they haven't got the physical attributes – the lung capacity, the heart capacity, whatever. You've got to have those physical attributes, and if you haven't got them, you'll get to a level and that's the size you'll stay. And the best frame in the world won't make a blind bit of difference. A good bike will stop you being any worse. If you put a good rider on a bad bike, he won't ride to his full potential. If you put a rubbish rider on a good bike, he'll still be a rubbish rider.'

He gets quite a few gear freaks, the cycling equivalent of the planespotters outside Coningsby, who love the names and numbers more than they love the ride. 'A classic example is a customer who came to me in the early eighties wanting a frame built. He had a drawing – "Can you make that?" I looked at it. "Yeah, I can make that, who's it for?" "It's for me." "It's not going to fit you, it's far too big for you." 'But that's what I want." "Why do you want this?" And he said, "That's Eddy Merckx's bike. That's the dimensions of Eddy Merckx's bike." I said, 'Yeah, but Eddy Merckx is 6ft 1in. and you're 5ft 4in."' He laughs. 'Not quite, but there was a disparity. So I made it and I sprayed it and he built it up, and I saw him for years riding round on it looking completely ridiculous – it was far too big for him. It was too long and too big. But that's what he wanted.'

Anyway. Since the four main tubes are those which dictate the basic geometry of a road bike, they come in a variety of different shapes and sizes. The simplest and strongest will be a straightforward plain-gauge steel tube, same idea as a metal curtain pole. Next up will be single-butted tubes, which have one end thicker than the middle, thereby making the frame stronger at the point of connection. And finally there will be double- or triple-butted tubing, stronger at the ends and lighter in the middle. The strength in plain-gauge tubes will be the same throughout their length, whereas the strength in single- or double-butted tubing will be concentrated at the joints. To join these tubes together, there are two alternatives: welding or brazing. Welding raises the temperature to the point where the steel melts and joins to its neighbour. It produces practical but ugly joints – the cheap hybrids and mountain bikes you see with big gobby lumps of steel at the seams will probably have been TiG (or tungsten inert gas) welded. Brazing, on the other hand, uses another metal inserted between the two steel tubes to make a connection. It's less heat and energy intensive and therefore less likely to damage the alloys. With brazing, you can use two methods. Either there are lugs, separate, ready-made joints which are then connected to the tubes with brass filler; or there is fillet brazing, where the joints are filed to a perfect fit, filled completely with brass and then sanded down to form a seamless connection. Fillet brazing looks beautiful but requires both time and skill, so Graeme and I are both sticking to lugs. Because over the years Dave has built up a good set of contacts among bicycle-makers, he's already got a ready-made supply of new- and old-style lugs and tubes in stock. Having picked out the components we want, Graeme and I stand there for a moment or two, daunted.

To begin with, everything is divided into a series of sub-assemblies which will then be joined together on the jig at the end of the week. First job is to file a careful mitre to the bottom of the seat tube and then to connect it to the bottom bracket (the big joint through which four tubes meet and the crank axle for the pedals passes). Having given us the necessary briefing on the uses and abuses of oxyacetylene gas, Dave gives both of us a pair of welding glasses, fits the tube and the bracket into the jig, gives it a daub of flux (to prevent the steel from oxidising), sparks up the torch and passes it over. The brass is a long, thin rod which is held very exactly over the joint until it reaches melting point. The aim is to get the brass to melt neatly and without lumps or gaps into the space between bracket and tube. This is not easy. If you don't hold the flame over the lug and the brass for long enough then nothing will happen, and if you hold it for too long you'll burn away the steel of the tube. The intention is to get both the heavy lug and the light brass to the same temperature so that the braze will run seamlessly between them. Both Graeme and I are so nervous before trying it for the first time that our hands shake slightly as we hold the rods.

The gas hisses faintly, and half a mile away the plane-spotters steady their lenses. The lug begins to glow and the air above it shimmers. The brass bubbles, and at a point only Dave can see coming, it melts, vanishing into the gap as we pass the stick round the bracket. Dave stands over us, watching, instructing, telling us to pull away if we get too close to the tube or linger for too long in one place. Inevitably, it takes a while before we work out what the melting point looks like and how fast to move the stick around the join. But when it does go right, it is a moment of purest magic. One metal suddenly liquefies and slips sublimely in between the other as the torch flares round the circumference. When the steel cools, they are joined as solidly as if they had been born like that. All three of us become so absorbed in the work that for several hours we do not even notice that half of Britain's air-defence capability has just passed overhead.

Next is to bounce up and down on the fork blades. There are many types of curve you can give a fork, and all of them will do something to the way the bike rides at the end of the process. In theory no curve at all would send every bump and pothole from the road straight into your arms, while a very pronounced curve may make the ride too squishy and unresponsive. In practice, it's possible to have an entirely straight fork with enough offset to give a comfortable ride. By fitting the blades into a ready-made curved jig and then leaning down on them with our full weight, it's possible to bend them into a couple of EU-approved banana curves, giving a bit of shock absorption but not enough to slow the ride down much. The two fork blades then get slotted into the fork crown and brazed in, and after that the drop-outs (the pieces which hold the wheels and rear derailleur in place) are attached to the chain stays. All of them are comparatively small joints but tricky, since the steel is thinner and lighter, and the risk of burning a hole consequently that much greater. The slot in the chain-stay must be perfectly angled and mitred, and we seem to end up pushing a lot of brass down what looks like a very deep hole. Once the metal cools, pedants – including me – then get to spend hours filing the join down so it looks more attractive, a detail which, when the bike is completed, will be noticed by no one except other pedants and dachshunds.

Then we join the head tube and seat tube to each other. To connect the two, the end of the seat tube must be perfectly filed down and mitred. If it isn't – if there's too much stress on one part of the joint but too little on another – then it's the joint most likely to crack or fatigue. At this point, my choice of lugs comes back to haunt me. The ones I picked out have frillier edges than normal, and therefore need more careful brazing. Moving round them with the torch, learning the way the heat sucks the brass towards it or pushes it away, remains endlessly fascinating. We mill the end of the head tube down to the right size, stick it in the top of the fork crown and braze them together. Even at this stage, the whole thing has begun to look less like a series of GCSE metalwork assignments and more like a bicycle.

And then there is the moment when, after three days and a lot of coffee, all the different bits and joints are put into the main jig and brazed together. This is the moment of truth, the point at which everything either comes together into one priceless diamond-frame or disintegrates into a load of unrideable parallelograms. The different components might all look great on paper, but no one can really tell you how harmonious it's going to look when it's all connected or, more importantly, what kind of ride it's going to be. Once it's all been brazed together, it's left overnight in the jig to cool and settle. The following day, we take it out, poke the fork stem up through the head tube, examine our handiwork and agree unanimously that it looks like a bike. The forks are curvy, the bottom bracket proportionate and the top tube so straight you could hang pictures with it. Once in a while, I glance at the point at which the seat stays attach to the top of the seat tube. In mass-produced hybrids, the join is usually done with a big clot of weld. But in old-style racers, there should be a couple of sharp, cleanly pointed ends, like one-sided spears. Having managed to get those brazed and filed down so they come to a perfectly curved point just below the saddle is a moment of deep private satisfaction. One of the last tasks is to swap to silver solder in order to fit in the bottle bosses (the two little holes in the down tube which take the cage for a water bottle). Silver has a lower melting point than brass, and thus the flame has to be held higher and moved away quicker than with most of the brazing. But silver is good for the smaller tasks where a really clean finish is required, and for joining things to the centre of butted tubing where the steel is lighter and potentially more fragile.

At the end of the week, both Graeme and I have frames. Once they have been shot-blasted and all the excess brass removed, they look as clean and professional as half the frames hanging from the rafters in bike shops all over Britain. A few months later, painted an unrestrained blood-red with gold outlines round the lugs and then fitted out by Rob Sargent in Finsbury Park, I have something I think is properly astonishing. It rides like a dream. It accelerates up hills. And, believe me, there are very few kinds of smugness greater than the smugness of being asked where you got your bike and being able to say, 'I made it myself.' Back in Sheffield, Graeme has a similar experience. 'It is a bike that I can't ride without people stopping and asking about it (might be because it's painted bright yellow). I tell far too many people that I built it myself, an immodesty that I put down to my enthusiasms rather than my vanity.' Sitting in the Coningsby café during our lunch breaks, we had stuffed ourselves with dreams of all the places our fabulous new frames would take us. I wanted to try my bike out in the hills and glens of the Scottish Borders and then see how it did in France. Graeme was mulling over the idea of a full-scale north-to-south trip down through America. But the truth of it was that it didn't matter where we were going to take them, or why. What mattered was the dream itself. As Graeme said later, 'There is magic in framebuilding.'

I'd felt the same. Watching Dave with a brazing torch and a stick of brass was as close as I'll ever come to watching an alchemist at work. Not merely because there's something occult about watching that flame scorch its white-hot pathway across the steel, but because at the end of it all we've been part of the transmutation of those materials from disparate parts to unified whole. And because in the process Graeme and I both learned so much about what a bicycle is and how it works. As Dave says – slightly more prosaically – making a bike is really just plumbing. But it's definitely magic plumbing.

You Say You Want a Revolution

To get to the place where Dave Yates is now, to be able to calculate so cleanly the angles and weights that separate a mountain bike from a tourer or a BMX from a racer, takes more than just experience. It takes history. Every part and every angle of a bicycle has an ancestry, a time when something else was tried and found either to fit the purpose or to form a mechanical dead end. It doesn't really matter if the aim of the framebuilder was to produce a bike that was light or durable or speedy – in order for Graeme and me to have built our dream machines, someone somewhere long ago had to do the R&D. The loss of a second or a gram or a millimetre of travel will always have been achieved by one man's trial and another man's error.

And, perhaps because the history of the bicycle is relatively short and well documented, much of that history is still contentious. For as long as there are bicycles in the world, there will be people squabbling about who invented them. The truth is that it was a collaborative process – not quite invention by committee, but more a cumulative uncovering of basic mechanical principles. The British contribution was threefold: an Englishman came up with the tangential wheel and leather saddles, a Scotsman came up with crank pedals and another Scotsman working in Northern Ireland came up with pneumatic tyres. For the sake of European harmony and a quiet life, it's easiest to agree that the French invented everything else.

On the other hand, if you go to Germany they will tell you unequivocally that the bicycle came straight down the line from the draisienne, or velocipede, a heavy, wooden two-wheeled contraption without pedals or steering mechanism invented by a civil servant in 1817. In his professional life, Baron Karl von Drais was Master of the Forests in the Duchy of Baden. In his private life, he was an enthusiastic amateur inventor. His first project – a horseless carriage – had failed, but his new running machine met a more generous reception. Made out of wood and iron, it looked like a big old-fashioned version

1818
draisine
Karl von Drais
Germany

1830
two-wheel velocipede
Thomas McCall
Scotland

1860
pedal-bicycle
Pierre Michaux
France

1870
high-wheel bycycle
James Starley
Germany

1885
safety bicycle
John Kemp Stanley
England

1960s
racing bike
–
USA

Mid 1970s
mountain bike
–
USA

of the pedal-less bikes that children now learn to ride on. Though its front wheel was moveable, it weighed a minimum of 20kg and the only way of guiding it was to lean from side to side while pushing it along with the feet. Its unreliable trajectory meant that city riders couldn't help straying onto pavements, while its huge weight often left them with painful ruptures of the groin. The combination of heavy fines, hernias and public ridicule was not a winning one. Even so, great claims were made on the velocipede's behalf. Its popularity spread, and soon much of Europe knew about the new fashion. In February 1869, three young men on velocipedes announced that they had managed the 53-mile run from London to Brighton in only 15 hours, a feat which would have been more impressive if someone had not shortly afterwards walked the same route in 11½.

Some time later, a blacksmith from Dumfriesshire named Kirkpatrick Macmillan was arrested in Glasgow for dangerous driving. In June 1842, Macmillan was found riding along a pavement on a velocipede, knocking down a child in the process. More unusually, he claimed to have made the journey from Old Cumnock, 40 miles away, in only five hours. The secret, he claimed, was in the adaptations he had made to his machine. By adding cranks and pedals to the front axle, he had produced something which could be powered by the legs and balanced by its own velocity. Now, instead of shunting himself along, he could pedal continuously, and in doing so reach much greater speeds than were ever possible on the velocipede. His appearance had produced great interest among the locals and a visit from the *Glasgow Herald*. While conceding that Macmillan's invention was 'ingenious', the reporter was not that impressed. 'This invention,' he wrote, 'will not supersede the railways.'

But Macmillan did nothing to broadcast his new device, and in the end it was the French who successfully reinvented the wheel. Pierre Michaux in Paris, also a blacksmith, once again added cranks and pedals to the front axle of a wooden velocipede. More importantly, he published and exploited the design, and by doing so moved the bicycle one step closer to being. This time, the idea caught on. 'Boneshakers', as they were nicknamed, became popular among young Parisians and then throughout Europe, though, as their name implied, they weren't a comfortable ride. Since the wheels were wooden, every jolt and bump from the road surface was transmitted directly through the frame. Mounting required a running vault into the saddle, and since the whole thing weighed at least 30kg, any misjudgements could be permanently disabling.

Still, the impact on nineteenth-century society of the new contraptions was extraordinary. Charles Spencer, an early advocate of cycling, ran a gymnasium in London where novice riders could go to practise. One interested spectator recalled his reaction when one day in 1869 a man arrived at the gymnasium with a packing case containing 'a piece of apparatus mainly consisting of two wheels … Mr Turner took off his coat, grasped the handles of the machine, and with a short run, to my intense surprise, vaulted on to it, and putting his feet on the treadles, made the circuit of the room. We were some half-dozen spectators, and I shall never forget our astonishment at the sight of Mr Turner whirling himself round the room, sitting on a bar above a pair of wheels in a line that ought, as we innocently supposed, to fall down immediately he jumped off the ground. Judge then our greater surprise when, instead of stopping by tilting over on one foot, he slowly halted, and turning the front wheel diagonally, remained quite still, balancing on the wheels.' Track standing, or remaining stationary on an upright bike, was evidently a Spencer speciality. His 1877 guide to *The Modern Bicycle* moves briskly on from the vaulted mount to riding without using hands or feet. Once the difficulties of riding side-saddle had been mastered, it was time to try staying still. 'Of course, this is a question of balancing, and you will soon find the knack of it. When the machine

An early cycling class.

inclines to the left, slightly press the left treadle, and if it evinces a tendency to lean to the right, press the right treadle; and so on, until, sooner or later, you achieve a correct equilibrium, when you may take out your pocket book and read or even write letters, &c, without difficulty.'

As the popularity of boneshakers spread, so the design began to progress organically, first to iron or steel instead of wood and then towards the great 'high wheelers' of the 1870s. Back in England at the Coventry Sewing Machine Company, James Starley and his colleague William Hillman took the design one stage further. Their new Ariel model was made entirely out of steel instead of wood and iron, a change which knocked a good 40lb off the weight of the machine. As well as an optional 'speed gear', Starley's other great innovation was the tension wheel. Now, instead of spokes being laced straight from hub to rim, they were laced at an angle, thereby significantly improving the wheel's strength and setting the standard pattern for all wheels since. To prove the Ariel's efficacy and its excellent value at £8, in 1870 Hillman and Starley decided to ride all the way from Paddington station in London to Coventry, a distance of 96 miles. 'Mr Starley's weight gave great velocity to his machine,' one reporter noted, 'a speed of at least 12mph being attained.' The two cyclists reached home as the clock struck midnight, and apparently slept solidly for three days afterwards. Mr Starley's weight was also the driving force behind another of his inventions. Since he was a large man with a substantial backside, the old saddles of wood or iron pained him. As he said, 'There's a lot of me to get sore.' Arriving in the factory workyard one day, he got off his bike, plonked himself down on a pile of sand lying nearby, got up, examined the indent he had made and announced to his watching workers, 'That's how a saddle should be shaped – to fit the bum! Get a cast of that and make me a saddle of stout leather.'

As bicycles became lighter, so the front wheel got larger and larger. Since every turn of the cranks directly corresponded to a revolution of the wheel, the early riders had to maintain a very high cadence in order to move forward. The only way of lowering the cadence while maintaining reasonable forward momentum was to increase the size of the wheel the cranks were attached to. And so began the era of the Ordinary (or penny farthing). Huge and highly strung, Ordinaries were not for everyone. Like veloci-pedes, they were tricky to control and rapidly became notorious for flinging their riders off at odd moments. Most of the new guides to cycling devoted at least a chap-ter each to the complicated subjects of mounting, dismounting and how to fall off so you only broke the minimum number of bones. As Mecredy and Stoney, the authors of *The Art and Pastime of Cycling*, advised, 'If you find you are unable to dismount because of the pace and steepness of the gradient, go for the nearest hedge or hawthorn bush, and just as you approach, throw your legs over the handles. You are sure to be hurt, but you may escape with only a few scrapes and bruises, whereas to hold on means more or less injury. If no hedge or hawthorn bush is near, throw your legs over the handles and put the brake hard on, and you will shoot forward and alight on your feet, when you must make every effort to keep on your feet and run as hard as you can, for your bicycle is in eager pursuit, and a stroke from it may place you *hors de combat*.' If fractures didn't deter people, then maybe impromptu tattoos would. Since many paths and tracks of the time were covered in coal cinders, riders who did fall off and graze themselves found that the coal dust got into the cuts. If the cuts weren't cleaned immediately, the dust would tattoo itself in beneath the healing skin forever. 'Some of the best racing men have been sadly disfigured about the face, elbows and knees this way.' Such a potent combination of cost and personal hazard meant the market for the new Ordinaries was restricted mainly to the rich. Even at the tail end of the 1890s cycling craze, a new British-made bicycle could cost three months of a schoolteacher's salary.

In the end, it was a simple mechanical innovation which made the difference. By fitting a chain drive to the rear wheel instead of cranks to the front, James Starley's nephew, John Kemp, brought the cadence down to a point where wheel sizes too could be equalised. His first design, introduced in 1884, has a 36in. front wheel and a curved down tube and crossbar. Otherwise, it looks more or less identical to a modern bike and proved so successful it became cycling's Model T – an affordable, high-quality, mass-market product which very probably converted thousands of people to the pleasures of cycling. The bike could deliver letters, take the children to school, convey newsboys from place to place. It could be used by policemen and butchers, telegraph boys and teachers. It belonged to everyone, not just to the rich. Quick, silent, unobtrusive and requiring far less skill or maintenance than a horse, the traditional diamond-frame suddenly seemed the ideal way to negotiate the streets. Just as significant was John Boyd Dunlop's notion of fitting rubber tyres filled with air to his son's trike. In 1889, the first Dunlop pneumatic tyre was tested on London's streets to thigh-slapping ridicule and the confident prediction that it would never catch on.

As the popularity of cycling increased through the 1890s, so the price began to come down. Manufacturers now offered hire purchase arrangements, and the bicycle's obvious advantages for middle- and working-class commuters brought it to the point of near-ubiquity. Back in 1869, *Scientific American* had foreseen the results of such popularity. 'The art of walking is obsolete,' it claimed. 'It is true that a few still cling to that mode of locomotion, are still admired as fossil specimens of an extinct race of pedestrians, but for the majority of civilised humanity, walking is on its last legs.' In America, over two million bicycles were sold in 1897 alone, and in the UK the numbers of both small- and large-scale framemakers rose from 22,241 in 1895 to 46,039 in 1897. Small framemakers found the demand so overwhelming they couldn't keep up. Metalworkers of all descriptions took to producing frames, setting up their own little workshops in sheds and back-yards at home. Larger manufacturers included shipbuild-ers and munitions factories – places, in other words, which already had the tools and raw materials available, and which found knocking together a few bike frames on the side an easy transition to make. The bicycle's leisured competitors did not do so well. In the US, by the late 1890s, the sudden passion for bicycles had led to a fall in sales of pianos by up to 50 per cent.

Back at home, the new interest in cycling brought with it an equal interest in matters of dress and diet. For men, woollen garments were thought best, topped off with a Norfolk jacket. Other more radical innovations were less popular. One outfitter offered a wind-cutter, worn strapped to the chest and shaped at an angle like a snowplough on a train. Different types of hat were suggested, including golf or cricket caps which could be worn with a wet cabbage leaf inside for refreshing evaporation on hot summer days. To disguise scrawny legs, stockings with extra-thick knitting on the calves were offered. For racers, good, stodgy, protein-rich meals topped off with strong liquor were recommended. When in 1875 David Stanton set out to ride 100km round the Lille Bridge track, he supported himself with a combination of brandy-soaked sponge cake, mutton and tea. A couple of years later, Charles Spencer was advising racers that 'The daily use of the cold bath, or tepid if necessary, cannot be too strongly insisted upon ... and the avoidance of all rich viands, such as pork, veal, duck, salmon, pastry, &c, &c. Beef, mutton, fowls, soles, and fish of a similar kind, should form the principal diet.' To ensure continuing vitality, it was also advised that 'The mouth should always be kept shut. The nose is the proper organ to breathe through, and is provided with blood vessels to warm the incoming air, and with minute hairs to catch particles of dust, germs of infection, and other extraneous matter ... To ride with an open mouth, besides giving one an idiotic appearance, is apt to cause severe cold, neuralgia,

&c.' Many guides advised against riding uphill. In *Cycling as a Cause of Heart Disease* of 1895, physician George Herschell threatened a terrible fate. Should the rider persist in heading upwards, it was almost certain that their heart would be unable to cope. 'A time will come when it will be unable to contract effectively at all. The rider will lose consciousness, and possibly die then and there.'

As bicycles became easier to ride they became more widespread, and as they became more widespread so too did conflict with other road users. Then as now, there were many who felt that two-wheeled traffic should not be granted the same status as four-wheeled. Since in its early stages the cycling craze was limited mainly to the young and rich, pedestrians did their best to stop them either by fair means (setting the law on them) or foul (stabbing umbrellas through passing spokes). The main complaint was that they frightened the horses and, since the majority of road freight then went by horse, it could legitimately be claimed that cyclists were disrupting the commercial life of the country. In Leeds in 1893 a cyclist passing a solicitor on a carriage failed to ring his bell. The solicitor struck out with his whip, lassoed the man round the neck, dragged him to the ground and ran over him with the carriage. When fined £30 for the assault, he was unrepentant: 'I should do it again and let you take your luck, even though it killed you. To us gentlemen who drive spirited horses, you cyclists are a great nuisance.' In 1882, one 'respectable gentleman' was fined 40 shillings for riding 'furiously' through London at 10mph, and when a female horse-rider became entangled with a group of racers on the Great

North Road, she took her complaint to the police. Fearing that the sympathy of the public would lie overwhelmingly with the rider and that legislation would surely follow, the National Cyclists' Union (NCU, later the CTC) took the extraordinary step of pre-emptively banning all forms of mass-start road racing from 1888 onwards. Time-trialling (individual timed races against the clock) became the only alternative. Even these were organised and conducted in an atmosphere of secrecy similar to that surrounding the acid raves of the 1990s. Would-be participants were given codes and passwords and told to turn up at some distant corner of the country wearing strange clothes at odd hours of the night. The ban was not finally repealed until the 1950s, a fact which partly explains Britain's isolation from the rest of Europe's racing world and its relative lack of pro-level champions.

But neither legal nor practical obstacles deterred the new enthusiasts. The bicycle was quick, silent, straightforward and ideal for covering city-sized distances. It had grace and style and the thrust of modernity behind it. It could be adapted for speed or designed to take heavy burdens. It coped easily with the relatively shallow gradients of most urban hills. And always it trailed behind it an indefinable sense of boyish joy that nothing – not even the clogging stress and grime of the great industrial towns – could ever quite suppress.

It also had another unexpected result: it began to be seen as a tool of socialist revolt. Together with a group of disaffected colleagues from the *Manchester Sunday Chronicle*, Robert Blatchford founded the penny weekly

NATIONAL·CLARION·CYCLING·CLUB

Fellowship is Life

Lack of Fellowship is Death

SOCIALISM·THE·HOPE·OF·THE·WORLD

the *Clarion*. Blatchford was a journalist and writer whose beliefs had been strongly marked both by his time in the army and by his experience of the Manchester slums. Writing under the pen name of Nunquam (short for Nunquam Dormio, or 'I never sleep'), Blatchford's real brilliance was to ally strong campaigning journalism with cycling. The *Clarion* was distributed by cyclists, and the National Clarion Cycling Club was founded by Blatchford's colleague Tom Groom to spread the word. Socialism and bicycles were, Groom considered, perfect bedfellows. 'Little troubles keep him (the cyclist) sympathetic – punctures, chains that break, nuts that loosen, lamps that won't burn etc. Runs in the country and glorious sights prevent him from becoming narrow and bigoted ... The frequent contrasts a cyclist gets between the beauties of nature and the dirty squalor of town make him more anxious than ever to abolish the present system.'

The Clarion Scouts used their days off to paper their local areas with leaflets, pamphlets and copies of the *Clarion*, 'nailing down lies and disposing of fables, improving the landscape by sticking up labels'. In some areas disputes arose between those who felt that the business of the NCCC should be to bring about the downfall of capitalism, and those who were much more interested in riding a bicycle as fast as possible. Despite an early move to prevent racing on the grounds that competition in any form clearly represented an attempt by bourgeois ruling forces to divide the proletariat, time-trialling did become an integral part of the NCCC. Trials would be organised most weekends, though it was, as always, conducted according to firm socialist principles: the National Racing Secretary Alex Taylor considering that 'Our biggest asset lies in our being a working-class organisation ... The knowledge that he is riding for a principle ... gives new energy to tired legs.' Even so, Robert Blatchford ended his life in disgrace with many in the movement, partly due to his support for conscription during the Boer and First World Wars but mainly for the much greater crime of writing for the *Daily Mail*. And the *Clarion* itself ended up a victim of war as readers either defected to other, redder publications, or stopped reading altogether. Besides, world politics had intervened. By the 1920s, socialism as an ideal had either been replaced by communism as a reality, or by the usual watery British pragmatism. In 1908, the aims of the NCCC were defined as 'Mutual Aid, Good Fellowship and the Propagation of the Principles of Socialism as advocated by the *Clarion*'. At some point, the words 'propagation of' were quietly replaced by 'support for'. Socialism, in other words, was a whole lot less fun than socialising.

Other attempts to push cycling into one niche or another also failed. In the US, the League of American Wheelmen, or LAW – founded in 1880 and hugely popular in its time – was permanently tainted by its decision to prohibit the admission of black members. The decision was taken as a direct result of the success of one rider. Marshall Taylor's father worked as coachman to the Southards, a white family in Indianapolis. The Southards had a son, Daniel, of Marshall's age, and since the two boys played together, they also learned to ride bikes at the same time. The Southards paid for Marshall's first bike, and he grew up with a good grounding as a cyclist. Unfortunately, the result of his connection with the Southards was predictable: his family and friends found him too white and white society found him too black. His best escape vehicle from both was the bicycle. He went to work for a local bike shop, performing tricks and stunts outside to lure customers. The job earned him both a new cycle and a new name, Major, after the military costume that he wore. His boss entered him in races which Major almost always won. The clubs and leagues that organised the races began to take notice. Some clubs (those on the east and west coasts) were happy to let a rising star compete. Some realised that the controversy generated by a winning black rider in an overwhelmingly white peloton had an electrifying effect on audience figures. But a small number of organisations wanted nothing to do with Major. In 1894, the LAW (then the main cyclists' association with a membership of around 100,000) voted to ban black riders, including Major. He could still take part in LAW races, but only as an outsider. Despite an atmosphere of dangerous hostility, Major's talent won out. He became World Sprint Champion in 1899 and made a

Major Taylor. Despite becoming World
Sprint Champion in 1899, Major found
the discrimination against him so
intolerable that he gave up racing in
his own country.

triumphant tour of Europe. Back at home in the US, he found it harder and harder to appear competitively. Hotels, bars and restaurants would refuse to serve him, and Taylor eventually found the climate against him so intolerable that he gave up racing in his own country. Though the LAW's membership declined sharply at the beginning of the twentieth century (partly as a result of their segregation policy), it took a further century for the prohibition to be fully repealed.

Meanwhile, the world itself was moving on. By the 1930s, the days when bicycles were competing only with horses and trains were long gone. Motorised transport had increased and diversified enormously. This was no longer a case of a few stately cars poop-pooping down the dusty roads preceded by flag-waving flunkeys; in the decade after 1945, the numbers of cars on the road increased threefold. In a world where an Austin Seven or a Model T cost £175 and a bike £5, it was evident that two wheels had lost to four. The national highways were now full of trucks, military vehicles, private cars, taxis, buses, ambulances, police cars and motorbikes. Even then, the bicycle still somehow held on. In 1950, 11 per cent of all journeys were made by bike, and there remained twelve million regular cyclists in the UK. To get some idea of how awe-inspiring a figure that is, it's worth remembering that in 2010 only 3 per cent of all UK journeys were made by bike, and that was double on the previous decade. Even more peculiar, throughout that entire period the bicycle industry managed to remain healthy. In 1976, 15 per cent of UK households owned a bike. By 1986, that figure had risen to 25 per cent and by 1995 to 33 per cent. People were still buying bikes, they just weren't using them much beyond the age of ten.

Meanwhile, back on the roads, the consequences of a complete non-policy were predictable. A 1937 Ministry of Transport survey found that a third of all road accidents involved cyclists; 1,421 cyclists were killed on the roads that year. Bicycles were not merely old-fashioned, they were fatal. Unfortunately, riders couldn't always look to cycling organisations to support their cause. In an echo of its curious act of self-sabotage in banning mass-start racing in the 1880s, the main cyclists' organisation, the CTC, chose to oppose the establishment of a national network of cycle paths during the 1930s on the grounds that it might interfere with their right to use roads. By the time the future of travel was being considered in the 1950s, 1960s and 1970s, 'transport' was taken to mean only 'things with engines'. The first motorways were built and the London Underground expanded. Tram systems came and went. Beeching axed half of Britain's railway network, and cars, instead of being a temptation, became a necessity. London's population rose steadily through the millions. In the committee rooms of Westminster there were inquiries into the high cost of rail fares, working parties on round-abouts and Royal Commissions on buses. And the motorist reigned supreme. Until, almost without anyone noticing, something interesting began to happen.

ڶڶڶ

THREE

Feral Cycling and the Serious Men

Here lies the body of Jonathan Hay
Who died defending his right of way.
He was right – dead right – as he strolled along;
But he's just as dead as if he'd been wrong.

QUOTED IN GEOFFREY BOUMPHREY,

BRITISH ROADS

At the Earl's Court Cycle Show, the Serious Men are out in force. They are walking the aisles between the stalls, eyes a little narrowed, intent. They're looking for something, even if they don't necessarily know what it is. It could be anything – a chain ring, a new brake, even an ordinary ding-dong bicycle bell – as long as it gives them the edge, the thing which will raise them from middle-aged, middle-weight mortality to the Olympian heights of which deep down they know they are still capable. And somewhere amid the coloured rims and the briefcase panniers in matching purple leather, it's got to be here.

This, for the hard-core urban cyclist, is retail heaven, pure, gasping bike porn. It's porn because it's desirable and illicit and a little bit sad, and because most of these men have a private file on their laptop full of tubular things they'd like to stroke after everyone else has gone home. And because it's porn and because they know it, the Serious Men also know that it's essential to compensate for that knowledge by pretending to their peers that the difference between Shimano and Campagnolo is right up there with the difference between protons and electrons. For the next three days, lots and lots of cyclists come to worship here, to feed the European economy and to celebrate the fact that bicycles really are adults-only now. Most of them are dressed in normal weekend wear – jeans and trainers, the occasional hardy pair of shorts – but if you look closely, they always have one or two items of cycle gear flagged up like a password. Some have got the right sort of jacket, others are wearing the distinctive quasi-Edwardian combo of plimsolls, thick black leggings and thin plus fours. There are a few with stripy Bianchi caps and others with copies of vintage Arcore jerseys. Others have done no more than roll up the legs of their jeans or forget to take off the second bicycle clip. Quite a large number of them have long-standing hair issues: either it's in the act of being misplaced or it's gone completely. Others have accepted the inevitable and are now modelling the new Fall of Saigon-style helmets as a substitute.

Beside the bikes out on the floor are more men, arms folded, waiting in line to give each bike an experimental lift by its crossbar. That casual heft upwards is the urban cyclist's equivalent of dogs and lampposts, part territorial signature, part statement of intent. When demonstrated outside on the street to a bike one is sizing up or to the ride of a rival, it says two things: one, that the lifter knows enough about bikes to know that weight = cost of materials = amount of money spent = devotion to the cycling cause, and, two, that it will really piss them off if the rival's bike is lighter than theirs. And so round the bike stands the Serious Men go, lifting crossbars with the same air of familiar authority that perhaps a hundred years ago they would have slapped the rump or checked the pasterns of an attractive yearling. The gaze of the stallholders follows them around, hopeful and assessing. They know perfectly well the Serious Men have money and that they're prepared to spend it. The trick is to find exactly where, and how.

The Cycle Show is held annually at Earl's Court and is as good a place as any to gauge the state of the nation's relationship with bikes. In 2008 during the financial crisis, this place had a conspiratorial quality to it, a sense that here among the long-converted there was some kind of answer to the mayhem beyond the doors. There were relatively few people and those who did appear had probably been riding bikes for twenty years or more. Then, things were still transitional. Many of the stalls still carried with them a sense that cycling was something esoteric, a throwback to a past time. There was a residual air of both apology and of defiance. This was the old campaigning face of British cycling, used to being shoved into the gutter, laughed at, written off. The stalls weren't particularly professional and only a few places had really bothered to put on a show. The point was really just as much to hang around drinking smoothies and congratulating yourself on having got out of the petrol market before oil exploded in everyone's faces.

Two years later, there's a different feeling. It's more professional. More time and money have been spent, more businesses are emerging. The feeling now is that the bicycle market is a serious contender with proper money to be made and proper middle-aged incomes to be tapped. The big brands have arrived, and are putting on a show. As you walk in there's a fenced-off area with a cycle track. It's been done up as a kind of fantasy landscape, with a few plastic trees, a tiny little MTB area and a circuit with a lot of corners.

At present, various bikes are being test-ridden. For a second, if you squint very hard, it almost looks like Amsterdam. The number of people flogging different sorts of cycle-related clothing has increased enormously; lots and lots of tasteful jackets, half a mile of black and white merino-base layers, a lot of labels involving the word 'wicking'. There are coloured wheels and kit for triathlons. There are bullhorn bars, fancy bidons, courier bags and enough hi-visibility gear to start a building site. There are a couple of places selling assorted bits of bicycle knick-knackery (bar ends, novelty saddles) which, no matter the angle you examine them from, still somehow manage to look like sex toys. There are jackets and helmets, socks and trouser clips, bibs and shorts. There is a very great deal of Lycra. Above all, there is an atmosphere of purpose, a sense that here among the children of the new cycling revolution there are vital things to be done and said and bought, a feeling that critical mass either has been reached or is very close to being reached. None of these cyclists (except perhaps the women) looks marginal any more.

By the Condor stand, where the bikes have been placed in alcoves and spotlit like exhibits in a gallery, the men stand in worship, hands behind their backs and weight on one hip. Beside the most attractive bikes, a little crowd forms. Someone strokes a crossbar, someone else gives a tyre a friendly pinch. The lights give the paint on the frames an impression of infinite depth and sparkle so the green is as green as the Emerald City. The saddles are black or retro leather, and so spare in shape they look like medieval arrowheads. In the eyes of the men are such expressions of longing that the discreet price tags beside the bikes begin to seem less like statements of fact than taunts. With that, the eyes say, you could go as fast as carbon fibre, you could go as fast as a car – maybe you could even go as fast as Armstrong. With that, you could ride right off the edge of the city and into the sky. Some of them tap the tyres one more time and then move on, regretful. Others just stay, wandering in circles round and round the different bikes, gazing.

It is only when you get outside the Exhibition Centre that you come down to earth. This is London. Here on the streets of Earl's Court there is no brave new world where the bicycle reigns supreme, and no matter how hard you squint it never looks like Amsterdam. There are certainly a few cyclists moving to and fro, but they are dwarfed by the numbers of cars, buses, motorbikes and vans. There are HGVs with busted mirrors and mothers driving battered Polos distracted by squabbling children in the back. There are van drivers with lunchtime sandwiches smearing their dashboards and couples in estate cars arguing about parking. There are dispatch riders on motorbikes overtaking bendy buses and skinny blonde women driving obese black SUVs. There are black cabs and delivery lorries, a Civic-full of ladies, minicabs and Transits. It's the usual London streetscape, the same mixture of bricks, wind and barely suppressed impatience as probably existed a couple of hundred years ago. The cyclists who are here only slip in and out of an existing scene. In this particular area, there are no cycle lanes (unless a desultory sketch of a figure of eight in the gutter can be called a cycle lane) and no special pleading. There's nothing here that acknowledges the bicycle or even the motorbike. If you want to cycle, then you have to do so on four-wheeled terms. The same picture extends out past the SW postcodes, through the centre, the north and the west, out past the river to the suburban hinterlands. If you try cycling in Bristol or Birmingham, Manchester or Glasgow, the geography might vary significantly but the logistics don't. Bristol and York both pride themselves on providing for cyclists. Cambridge and Oxford have been getting students and tutors to and from lectures by bicycle for decades. Lincoln and Ipswich both look as if they were rolled out on the flatlands with nothing but cyclists in mind. But, in practice, cyclists still play second fiddle to cars in every city in Britain.

But there are perks to being the transport system's perpetual underdog. For a start, it means that officialdom's efforts are concentrated elsewhere, so planners and people with parking tickets generally leave you alone. It also means that cyclists tend to find routes away from the main arterial roads, and thus end up with their own private transport network. Cycle through Bloomsbury, or along the many hidden canal towpaths which still join England's cities together, or near Richmond Park, and you'll find yourself joining if not quite a movement of population on a Chinese scale, then something astonishing. There are bicycle traffic jams by Tottenham Court Road and bicycle gridlocks on Parkway. In winter, you could sit near the major cycle lanes and watch more flashing lights pass by than in the sky near Heathrow.

And because cycling is currently set up to favour the rebellious and the broke, it means that cyclists can never be homogenised into a single grey entity. One of the lovely things about riding round a city – any city – is watching other cyclists and savouring their strangeness. There is not and never has been one single urban type, and there never really could be. The figures are rising – between 2001 and 2008, the numbers of people in the UK who cycle regularly rose from 2.3 million to 3.2 million and the numbers of cyclists in London doubled – but all that rise seems to have done is to increase the diversity. Wait near a frequently used route and watch the cyclists streaming past during the morning and evening rush hours. After a bit the scene begins to appear like the Eastern Bloc countries after the fall of the Berlin Wall; many different groups jostling for dominance, a total restructuring of social politics, lawlessness, occasional outbreaks of violence, lots of exceptionally bad clothing. For every rider blazing with gadgetry, there's another on a bike which looks as if it was cobbled together out of old chair legs and office stationery. There are packs of Ridgebacks all racing each other to the junction, there are old ladies on things which look like two-wheeled shopping trolleys, there are men in suits and pillocks on Bianchis. There are government-issue cyclists who are either very afraid of breaking the law or very afraid of being caught on camera while breaking the law, and there are those for whom the law is an entirely optional concept. There are those who ride like they belong on a bike and there are those who ride like they'd rather be in an armoured vehicle. There are those who have helmets, those who don't, and those who sport different headgear entirely – woolly bonnets, Santa hats, things with built-in headphones. There are businessmen on space-age racers going at the same pace as girls on silver single-speeds. There are those for whom The Look evidently matters more than either The Bike or The Ability to Ride That Bike. There are people who look like they know what they're doing, and those who are obviously bluffing. There are guys on lowriders, slung out half reclining like Dennis Hopper on a Harley, and those who have evidently forgone the stern mistress of style for the stairlift of practicality. There are those who cycle in skirts, there are those who cycle in overcoats, there are those who wouldn't dream of cycling in anything other than six-inch red stilettos. There are fluorescent commuters on their spanking new hybrids and lardy boys twiddling along on folding bikes like elephants on beach balls. There are tourists on Boris Bikes and lots of kids of seventeen trying to get home on a BMX without being seen by anyone who knows them, and there are ladies who are Doing Their Bit for the environment. There are those who cycle with a child at either end, and there are those who prefer to load the bike like they do in Cambodia. Just like London itself, everyone is represented; every age, every class, every race and religion.

Cycling here is not like cycling in either the Netherlands or India. It does not rely, as in Holland, on the knowledge that the cyclist has a legal and moral right to be there, or, as in India, on the assumption that by getting on a bicycle the cyclist has proved himself so existentially inferior that he has no rights at all. It relies instead on the principle that you must fight your own corner. Once on a bike, you realise very quickly that everyone else on the road is cleaving to an irrefutable truth: that whatever form of transport you happen to be using at that moment – car, bus, own two feet – is the only possible right one, and all other forms should cede to it instantly. You must therefore make it clear to all other road users that you too would like to arrive at your destination safely and promptly, even if you have to dance on the grave of every rule in the Highway Code to do so. Still, after only a few short weeks, it doesn't even occur to you that the experience you have just had and the way you have therefore learned to cycle is the exception, not the rule. If you were to behave like you do here in Berlin or Amsterdam or Shanghai, you would be regarded – and rightly so – as a complete idiot. For better or worse, you have joined the ranks of Britain's feral cyclists.

Which leads on to another interesting discovery. What really bothers many cyclists is not other vehicles, but other cyclists. General traffic begins to fade from main event to mere backdrop. You realise that you have a much more pressing issue to deal with in dropping the guy on the white single-speed and making sure he stays dropped. Or riding down the man who just overtook you on a vastly inferior piece of kit. Or – most satisfactory, this – knowing the city better than the person you're racing, taking a nifty shortcut and emerging a few hundred yards ahead of them at a crucial stage in the game. If you get five cyclists lined up in front of the lights, they may not acknowledge each other's existence, they may never make eye contact with anything other than the pavement, but there's a reasonable bet that four out of them will be working out how to annihilate the fifth. And if you can arrive at work having maintained the purity of your trajectory and having been overtaken by nothing but cars, then it will cheer you up for the whole day.

There were many reasons behind cycling's miraculous resurrection – the introduction of the Congestion Charge in London, a succession of scares about rising fuel costs, terrorism. On the day of the July bombings in 2005, the Evans Cycle franchise announced that they'd sold over four times as many bikes as usual. Some were sold because, with half the city's transport links in ribbons, there was no other way of getting home, and some because what had happened that day had frightened many people so badly they were never going to go back underground. But beyond the bombings or the Congestion Charge there was something else – a more profound swell of enthusiasm for bicycles and their benefits. Government policy had nothing to do with it; for the past ten years, local and national initiatives on cycling have trailed well behind the deeper trends.

Unfortunately, as politicians are now beginning to realise, by marginalising cycling for decades they have managed to turn a bunch of mild and herbivorous middle-class individuals into a bunch of fit, trained and highly assertive lawbreakers. Since cyclists were faced with a landscape which either took no interest in them or appeared keen on actively eliminating them, they had to work out how to stay safe. The solution for many was to develop a style of cycling based on a combination of mountain biking, road racing and BMX skills with a dash of gymnastics thrown in for good measure. Proper observation of the rules of the road had absolutely nothing to do with it; the law ignored them, so they would ignore the law. Or, rather, every time they got on a bike, they made the law anew on a case-by-case basis. It wasn't like being a driver where you had to pass a test and where the way you behaved was strictly regulated by the nature of roads and other road users. If you were a cyclist, you could make a decision every time you got into the saddle about whether to cycle furiously or easily, about whether this trip was going to be about taking on the fixie at the roundabout or restricting your sense of competition to giving three taxis the finger. Some might stop at one red light because it's a crossroads, but they almost certainly won't stop at the next and definitely not when they're racing someone else. They would never ride on the pavement except when it would be ridiculous not to. Some days, they'll ride straight over pedestrian crossings, other days they won't. Plainly, explaining to the courts that today you broke the law because you felt like it but yesterday you didn't break it because you couldn't be bothered is not a realistic defence. But it does make you feel a lot more alive.

There is, of course, a more sinister flip side to all this. Alison Parker is a partner at Hodge Jones Allen, a London law firm specialising in personal injury. She exudes reassurance and competence, and has the kind of unforced gravitas that comes from doing and knowing your chosen subject very well for a long time. A sizeable proportion of her clients are cyclists. 'You cycle yourself, presumably?' Yes, I say. 'Well, I absolutely don't, and I wouldn't cycle in London – I consider it to be completely suicidal. I wouldn't do it, I just wouldn't do it. Probably because I see too many incidents. The problem is that when a cyclist comes into contact with a very large vehicle, they are absolutely bound to come off worse.'

We meet at a restaurant near her firm, and on one of the paper table mats Parker sketches out the four classic accidents to befall urban cyclists. First is the cyclist coming down on the inside of heavy traffic. The lane of waiting traffic parts to allow a car to turn right, the car goes straight into the cyclist. Second is on a roundabout: the cyclist sticks to the outside while the car takes the inner route but then pulls across the path of the cyclist when they reach their exit. ('Go round on the inside and indicate outwards. Or get off and walk round the roundabout – that's my advice.') Third is people opening car doors directly into the path of a cyclist – either the passenger door in stationary traffic, or the driver's door in a line of parked cars. Fourth, and most notorious, is the HGV making a left-hand turn. There's a cyclist on the inside by the curb, the HGV swings out to the right, the cyclist rides into the gap and is then crushed by the HGV as it turns to the left. Of the thirteen cyclist fatalities in London during 2009, nine were killed in this way by HGVs. Sight lines on HGVs are notoriously poor – a cyclist or a pedestrian has to be several yards in front of the cab before they become visible – and the drivers are simply unaware that there's a cyclist anywhere close. 'The advice is NEVER to go into that gap. It's safer just to hang back.' Eight of the nine HGV fatalities during 2008 were women. As cyclists, women are more cautious and law-abiding than men, and more prone to tuck themselves into corners at junctions where drivers can't see them.

The combination of physical risk and environmental smugness is a potent one, and when they first take up cycling many commuters go through a phase of almost radioactive self-righteousness. After all, if you feel you own the moral high ground *and* you're doing something a little bit scary at the same time, then you might well reach the mystical god-like state called Always Being in the Right. Big mistake. After a couple of years, the best urban cyclists mellow, realise they didn't personally invent cycling and get on with reaching their destination. The bad ones just keep arguing until someone breaks their jaw. 'As a pedestrian in London,' says Parker, laughing, 'I really hate cyclists! They never bloody well stop at zebra crossings, and I'm more likely to be road-raged as a pedestrian than I ever am when I'm behind the wheel of a car. There are some very arrogant and cavalier cyclists in London who would happily mow you down. I think cyclists, particularly in cities, do have a mindset that everyone's against them.' After all that, it almost comes as a relief to hear Parker has an even riskier group of clients than cyclists. 'I've always thought that motorcycling is a bit like smoking – if someone had realised when they were invented how incredibly dangerous they are, they would never have been allowed, a bit like cigarettes. It's too late now. You're on two wheels, you've got no stability, no protection at all round your body, and you're sitting on 1,000cc of engine, and doing 80mph – I mean, how dangerous is that? I just find it mind-boggling every time I think about it. Stay on four wheels, or on two wheels where you're travelling at a speed where you're much more in control of what happens if you come off.'

武 武 武

Muratori's Café is at the junction of Farringdon Road and Margery Street opposite the Royal Mail's Mount Pleasant sorting office. It's an old-style kind of café – a London greasy spoon with warmth and Formica but without the reek of grease. There's wood panelling on the walls and tabloids on the benches, and once in a while someone emerges from the kitchen with a comment or a joke to refill each cup with tea. Outside the huge corner windows, the view is of rain and wet cyclists. Muratori's has been a cabbie's refuge for years, and this particular afternoon – slimy, cold, early Feb – the place is half full.

The following lively exchange of views is interesting not because it's unexpected, but because, for an hour or so, it's salutary to imagine what it must feel like to be a cabbie driving in circles round London's endless frustrations. Cabbies have always felt an enormous sense of ownership about any city they work in. They're part of the place; London would not be the city it is without them. And since they feel they belong to these streets, then one of two things happens. Either they're completely secure in that knowledge and very laid-back about everything, or they're monumentally pissed off at all the things on the road that they feel don't have as much right to be there as they do.

BB: *So have you ever cut up a cyclist?*
Les (*taxi no. 30839*): No!
Unanimous shouting from everyone round the table: No! No, no, no!
Les: Seriously! Because the last thing I want is a cyclist bashing my cab.
Keith (*taxi no. 30729*): Because we know we're on a loser. Even if you do nothing wrong, you're on a loser.
BB: *That isn't most people's experience. Most people have been cut up by a cab at some point.*
Mickey (*taxi no. 54316*): Yeah, OK, but let's say that happens, come up and talk to me, don't bang on the wing mirror and when I get out, cycle off. I've seen a cab and when the guy got out, the cyclist rode round and round tormenting him because he knew any time the guy got near him he could just cycle off.
Keith: They're so aggressive, aren't they? They bang your bonnet, bang your wing mirror and then they cycle off, they won't stay around to argue. That's what really pisses me off.

BB: *Do you think all cyclists are the same?*

Keith: Yeah. You can generalise with cyclists.

BB: *So you don't discriminate between people who are cycling for work, couriers, and other cyclists?*

Keith: They're all the same.

Les: You do meet the odd one with the lights on and the yellow stuff all over and the backpacks and everything, and they generally stick to the rules. But the ones who are riding around with next to nothing on, just a bit of Lycra, zooming about delivering stuff, they will take the mickey, no doubt about it. I don't go out of my way to get in their way, but I just find it's hard to avoid them sometimes.

BB: *They're just doing a job, same as you.*

Les: I understand that, but if they come up the side as they do, if you look at any of our cabs, there'll be little scrape marks along the paintwork. Now, if I go in the garage for that, they'll go, £50 mate. I'm not going to get that back off them, never in a million years. And that happens every day.

Paul (*didn't give his driver number*): You know what it all boils down to? There's no punishment. They don't think the law applies to them.

Steve (*over at table in corner*): There's a place where all the paramedics go, the guys who deal with all the bad accidents and things, and their entertainment when they're sitting waiting for a call is watching the traffic lights to see how many cyclists stop. They say they actually take a tally. Nine out of ten don't bother.

Les: I don't understand why they've always got to push to the front.

BB: *Because if you don't, you're invisible and you're stuck behind some trucker's exhaust.*

Les: Yes, but I still don't think, well, I've got to commit suicide, push myself in front of a lorry, just because I'm breathing a bit of crap. I'd sit a few yards back.

Keith: There should be some sort of registration for them. I know it's difficult and it should be free at first, but they should be registered. Because every cyclist, that's one less car on the road, and that's great. But you still can't have them all banging and breaking things.

Mickey: If they knock off your wing mirror, scratch the side of the cab, smash your back light, there's nothing you can do. There's no comeback. They just ride off. There's no way of recognising them again. The old cabs used to have a diesel cap on the back. Many times, they just hold onto that and get dragged along by a cab rather than cycle.

Les (*reflectively*): There's a lot of anger, isn't there? A lot of anger coming out of people. See, most cab drivers know we're not going to get anywhere quickly. So we don't drive fast. We know – I've had twenty-nine years' experience of knowing I'm not going to get anywhere. We'll get there eventually, but there's no point in rushing.

BB: *But the point is, you* can *get somewhere quick on a bike.*

Keith: See, that's the trouble. That's their mindset – I can get past that, I can go faster, I can get across town. But they've still got to realise they've got to stop at a red light.

BB: *If every cyclist suddenly stopped at every red light, would you start respecting them?*

Les: Well, I don't know …

Keith: Get 'em off the roads. Cycle lanes, whatever, just get 'em off the roads.

Les: License them.

Mickey: Round 'em all up and nuke 'em! (*general hilarity*).

Paul (*looking out of the window at a couple of cyclists coming across the junction towards the café*): Hang on, watch that – watch that! He's coming up to the red and … (*the cyclist stops*). Well, he's done it safely, but nine times out of ten they don't. Look! Look! Guy's just gone straight through. He's gone through a red light. Look! He's overtaking!

BB: *He's allowed to overtake!*

Keith: Yes, and he's wearing a dirty jumper. And that ain't right (*gales of laughter*). We don't like cyclists, do we? We hate 'em.

Mickey: Last summer, June or July it was, there was a naked cycle ride. I was amazed, I was sitting there and there must have been a thousand of them.

BB: *So if all cyclists cycled naked, would it make you like them better?*

Keith: Yes. Definitely. They shouldn't be allowed to cycle unless they're naked.

After an hour or so I put away my Dictaphone and get up.

Keith: There you go, then. Sorry about that. Tell you what, though, we hate bus drivers more. Bendy buses. Oh, we really dislike them. So you're not top of the list. And motorbikes. They're third.

In fact, this turns out not to be a comprehensive list. The next time I took a cab, I asked the driver what he thought of other road users. In addition to cyclists, motorbikes and bus drivers, he added Post Office vans, dustbin lorries and anyone driving a Mercedes.

🚲 🚲 🚲

On a cold clear day in mid-November, Patrick Field is spreading the gospel at Speakers' Corner. Field is in his late fifties, bundled up in a couple of well-worn jackets and a fleece hat – no helmet, no hi-vis, and what looks like a home-built bike with a plain blue lugged frame, drop bars and CDs slotted between the spokes. The only obvious concessions to safety are a very powerful front light and his red jacket. Clearly, here is a man who knows his stuff. Field has been cycling and thinking about cycling for a very long time. In addition to running the London School of Cycling, he's known as something of a two-wheel guru, writing articles, appearing at conferences and teaching the rules of good behaviour to everyone from complete beginners to experienced racers. He knows the city very well, and he has a lot of strong opinions about it. The feelings are obviously reciprocated. At some stage London has imprinted itself on him so completely that, if you look carefully, you can prob-ably find the route from Kingston to Stratford mapped through the lines on his face.

Anyway, for today the plan is to find out about how to cycle. Not how to cycle with government approval, or how to cycle by trial and error, but how to cycle realistically.

After Field has given my bike a quick check, we set off along Upper Brook Street to practise positioning. Field echoes Alison Parker: what, he asks, is the most common type of accident for cyclists? Parked cars – hitting the open door of a parked vehicle. To avoid doing so, 'Your default position should be the middle of the leftmost lane of traffic.' The important thing is to take a nice smooth line. If you know you're just about to have to swing out back into the road to avoid a line of parked cars, the best thing is not to tuck yourself too far into the kerb to start with, to look behind you to see what's coming and to make it plain either by indicating or by your trajectory what your intentions are. But here we run into another familiar issue – the way men and women behave on bikes. 'Girls tend towards, "I'm not really here, don't worry about me, I don't want to be a nuisance." That's dreadfully dangerous because these drivers have all got busy lives and they're distracted and they haven't had enough rest, and if you're doing your, "Oh, don't worry about me" act, then you can't be surprised if they don't notice you at all. The other side of the coin is what we can call the male problem, and that's, "Well, fuck you, I'm going to ride my bike." It's like making an enemy out of everyone else on the road. And I think that's quite English, in a way – no one's ever told these poor boys that they can be powerful without being furious. No one's ever encouraged them to be a powerful friendly cheerful adult – "Yes, I do own the road, let's share it."'

The best thing to do is to learn to take what's yours – the full six feet, the car-sized space on the road. You cycle at least a metre out from any parked cars, but you don't tuck too far back in when the cars disappear. And once you start realising that you need exactly the right amount of road – not too much and not too little – then in all probability you'll stop being scared as well. 'The truth is that you're not as desperate as everybody else, because you're on a bike and if you need to hurry, you can. You can actually be generous and kind and friendly and helpful. But under-neath, you can only be generous with this commodity because you've owned it – "This is my space, and I'm happy to be generous with it." But if you're only letting other people take from you, then you're in trouble. So at the beginning, I try and encourage people to be more tough-minded than you need to be later on. You can relax into a smaller place when it's appropriate because you know that when you need a big space you can take it right back. And, anyway, why would you want to pick a fight with someone who's fifty times more powerful than you?'

Part of the trick, Field says, is to be visible. Many rookie urban cyclists assume that the best way to be seen is to festoon themselves with lights and colours in the hope that if they dress in head-to-toe electric yellow, the traffic will be dazzled enough to get out of the way. Unfortunately, if everyone who cycles wears the same thing, then everyone looks anonymous, and as soon as they start being anonym-ous they become invisible. True visibility has very little to do with wearing fluorescent vests and everything to do with the way in which you cycle. You could be lit like the Post Office Tower but if you cycle in the gutter, then no one's going to see you. 'What people take notice of is what attracts their attention. So your job is not to be a plastic cone, your job is to be a person. And if the hi-vis jacket helps you to be a person, that's beautiful. But the jacket on its own doesn't make you noticeable. What people see is your personality. So whatever helps you to express your personality is going to help.' The most conspicuous cyclists I can think of, I say, do not own any item of cycling paraphernalia at all. Field nods. 'If I'm driving my truck and I come up behind you and go' – he gives my bike an ostentatious once over – '"That's interesting, why a basket on the back, oh yes, leather boots, that's an interesting idea", or I come up behind you and go, "Get out the fucking way, you should be on the pavement", that's really up to me. But in both cases, you're safe because I'm thinking about you. And, of course, there are wonderful pragmatic and humanitarian reasons to want to be popular, but if you have to choose between being popular and being safe …'

Field's favourite role models are 'Knightsbridge matrons. I think they're becoming extinct because the Russians have priced them out of Mayfair and Belgravia. They don't have to be good at riding a bike, they're just good at being themselves. And you see them coming, and they're not nasty about it – they probably would be in a shipwreck, but that's another story – they're just, "Hello! Thank you!"' First rule, says Field, is to be able to ride a bike to a minimum standard. Next is to understand the rules of traffic, which, he says, were devised to be simple, 'because stupid people need to be able to understand them'. Traffic is formal, and it works on the principle that no one wants to crash because crashing is painful and expensive. And 'because they're nice people like us and well socialised and with responsibilities and families and all kinds of stuff, but even the gangsters, even the idiots whose parents didn't love them enough, they don't want to run over random people. They might want to run over their enemies, but they don't want to run over you or me. So if you give them a chance not to run you over, they won't.'

We keep going, down Rotten Row, over South Carriage Drive and into Knightsbridge, cycling at a reasonable pace to keep warm, moving from busy main roads down quieter side streets. When we get to a convenient place to pull over, Field gives me a few more tips on safety. How you treat a red light, he says, depends on how you're feeling about both yourself and the rest of society. 'I tend to always stop at red lights. And the reason I like doing it is because I can show off that I can still have my feet on the pedals and my arms folded, and I'm a very vain old man, but I like doing it because I know I don't have to. It's like an ostentatious show – you know, I'm making a social contract with you people, I'll follow these stupid rules, but if I do run a red light, I have to be in a hurry. The ones who make me laugh are … you know, I'm waiting at a red light, and these kids go past, desperate to move, as if their bike will explode if they stop. And then thirty seconds later, fat granddad overtakes them and I'm not even breathing heavy. The people who can't stop at red lights aren't happy – they don't have the psychological resources to be themselves, so they're infected with this anxiety, this, "I've got to get going." I'm not saying I've stopped at every red light even today, but it's my default, to stop.'

But, I say, there may be too many cyclists out there who have now learned to love cycling in a place where reds are considered optional. The rest of the world would still like us to stop. If possible, for good. Field is dismissive. Why try and fit into a system if that system is already faulty? 'There's an authoritarian optimism – if we're really obedient, then everyone will treat us well. But when Tesco wanted to smash the Sunday trading laws, what did they do? They opened on Sundays. They challenged the law. If you want to get rid of the law, you break it. So obedience doesn't make people respect you. That's just stupid.' As for the howls of protest from motorists, he reckons they're just looking for an excuse to be angry. 'What pisses motorists off is that they're pissed off already. I've had a bus driver blowing his horn at me because he wanted me to go through a red light so he could go through a red light. The idea that, oh, I would respect cyclists if they stopped at red lights – people who say that don't respect cyclists. And they're looking for an excuse not to.'

He instructs me on taking a circuit of Sloane Square. It's all stuff I've done before but not thought about in a systematic way – enforcing my priority, looking over my left shoulder to make sure no other two-wheelers are taking the corridor between the parked cars and me, riding like I had a right to be there. The important thing with cycling in the city, he says, is to be generous. Riding a bike is 'about negotiating conflict, it's about understanding what other people want, making sure they know what you want and resolving any problems that arise from that. And your abilities are your ability to be small or to be big, your ability to change your shape – these are all like stereotypically female characteristics.' He has a technique for dealing with aggression. It's an original one, but it makes sense. 'Go through the traffic spreading love. In a way that's much crueller to the idiots as well – if they come up to you going, "beep beep blah blah", and you start swearing at them, very quickly it's all getting a bit out of control and unstable. But also you're giving them exactly what they wanted – to export a bit of their disappointment about the way their life turned out. Whereas if you go, "Are you having a bad day?" (*in a caring voice*) and you just pitch it at exactly the right point where they can't tell whether you're being sympathetic or taking the piss so they don't know how to respond, you actually give them a chance to grow. Which is a bonus.' He smiles.

'It's so nice,' he says reflectively, 'to have something that's completely under your control. You know, if bin Laden is blowing up the Blackwall Tunnel as we speak and there's going to be a traffic jam from London to Birmingham, it's not really going to be a big problem for us. We can carry on.' With that, he presents me with my Dictaphone. 'It says on the screen here, oh, for God's sake, shut up, you boring old bastard.' I cycle northwards, wondering if I should have a flashing front light. After a bit, I stop wondering. It goes on flashing. Like the city it belongs to, Field's version of cycling is a pungent mixture of pragmatism, tolerance, experience and moral politics. If you start cycling in most British cities, experienced cyclists will often tell you to think and behave completely defensively. Field doesn't do that. Defence plays a part, but so do openness and a sense of being permitted to take up exactly as much room in this world as you need. It's a novel concept. Or, rather, it seems a novel concept on the streets of London. But in other parts of the world, there are places which are much better than this – and much, much worse.

殗 殗 殗

FOUR

The Great Wheel

At some point during your early education you learn the world's countries. Africa is hot, Antarctica is cold, America is powerful and the Falklands are ours. And the Netherlands are flat. There may be other details – canals, dope, clogs, tulips – but the one overriding reality is that in all of its 16,000 square miles it doesn't have two lumps to rub together. Even so, it's only when you actually arrive in the Netherlands that those old facts come alive. Looking out of the train window at the countryside – fields of potatoes, barns, cows – you finally grasp what 'flat' actually means. Flat means not a hummock, not a summit. Flat means a country of angles and rules, a place where a road or a canal could, if it so wished, go right over the horizon and straight on till morning. Flat means there are no fast or slow bits, no freewheeling, no challenging a gradient. Flat means that you don't need gears. At all. Ever. Flat means that in order to climb anything more than stairs, you have to leave the country. For anyone used to a countryful of curves, flat is really, astonishingly, completely flat.

Of course, the Netherlands are flat because the ocean is flat, and in this part of the world earth replicates water.

This is a borrowed land, a surface taken field by field from out of the sea, a place that only exists at all as a great collective act of faith. 'God made the world,' as the saying goes, 'but the Dutch made the Netherlands.' Almost a third of the country is below sea level, protected by a system of dikes and embankments. Half of it wouldn't appear on a map at all if the Dutch hadn't spent several millennia putting it there. That they did so – and that two-thirds of the population still lives, so to speak, underwater – is testimony to the Dutch love of heavy engineering.

Spending time in the Netherlands feels remarkably similar to how things must have felt in Britain during the heyday of the Victorians. There's the same sense of flexibility to things, the sense of great practicality married to infinite possibility. After all, if you have a country with no hills and almost no natural features, then you can start from scratch. You can have towns and cities, heaths and dams. You can build bridges, embankments, locks and level crossings. You can slap down an airport runway absolutely wherever you like. You can have fields the size of six football pitches and motorways without bends. You can have enormous wide roads covered in clever asphalt which makes less noise than the ordinary stuff. You can plough your fields with water, or you can make them harvest wind. You can have forests, and then you can chop down all your forests. And then, having noticed belatedly that everything looks weird and that you have no windbreaks, shade, oxygen or building materials, you can grow your forests back. When threatened, you can make your country an island, or drown out your enemies. You can have cycle lanes larger and better maintained than the average British B-road. You can have kids believing that a race down the slope of a subway underpass proves their prowess as a grimpeur. You can walk down the street one week and find it gone when you come to walk back. You can live in a mythical place where things – houses, shops, motorways – appear one week and vanish the next. The Netherlands may be notoriously stable and prosperous, but it also has to be the most changeable place in Europe.

And, in a country without summits, there can be absolutely no possible reason not to cycle. In fact, the only puzzle is why it took someone (or several people) so many centuries to get around to inventing the bicycle, given that this reclaimed landscape appears to have been designed specifically with two wheels in mind. But, strangely enough, the Dutch did not take to the bicycle immediately. In common with the rest of Europe, the middle classes caught the velocipede craze sometime back in the 1870s. For a while, it became fashionable to be seen making journeys into the countryside on the new contraptions. Unfortunately, in many rural areas, a lot of people who saw them didn't like them. Velocipedists found themselves under attack, targeted by locals who lay in wait and hurled stones or coal at them. Certain areas became notorious for attacks. Round Delft, where cyclists were blamed for putting the cows off their milk and making the horses run wild, they were forced to band together and ride in groups in order to pass safely.

Despite such deterrents, the Dutch cycle industry grew rapidly from the 1890s onwards. Since by then it was the British who had the strongest and best-developed market in bike design, Dutch framemakers either copied them or imported from England. In 1895, 85 per cent of all bikes bought in the Netherlands were from Britain; the vestiges of that influence can still be seen in the solid, gentlemanly shape of a traditional Dutch bike even now. Demand eventually became so strong that British manufacturers couldn't cope, and an increasing number of local framemakers stepped in to fill the gap.

By the turn of the century, the bicycle was the dominant mode of transport for most of the country. A network of cycle paths was established and the major cities began to incorporate bicycles into their traffic plans. The homegrown industry began to develop; in tandem with the independent framemakers – who, as in the UK, were often blacksmiths or metalworkers by training and therefore had both the skills and the materials to hand – big brands like Gazelle and Batavus started to emerge, churning out large numbers of good-quality bikes for a growing market. To the Dutch, cycling just made sense. It suited the size of the country and the fact that so much of it was urban. Bicycles became cheap and ubiquitous enough that almost every member of a family could have one, parents using them to commute or to fetch provisions, children to get to and from school. Since they didn't need elaborate gears, there were very few parts to get rusty, and since they didn't need to climb, they could sit down solid on the road. They could be left out in the rain for days without rusting and, since all bikes had dress guards, there was no chance of getting one's clothing messed up in the spokes. Almost all were designed to be ridden fully laden.

Jan Rijkeboer is the managing director of the Azor cycle factory in Hoogeveen, a rumpled man with a lived-in face and the sort of personality more at home with doing than thinking. The factory he runs has a homely feel with the radio on and a light summer breeze wafting through the open doors. Rows of unpainted steel tubing imported from Belgium and the Far East lie on racks while a man laces spokes into a wide rim beside a machine which tests each wheel to see if it's true. Pretty multicoloured forks in bright Mondrian colours dangle from a rack next to a row of shining mudguards. A man in a pair of frighteningly tight jeans laces brake cables into place. Next to him, someone slots chain guards into position and checks to see that the rack doesn't wobble. Everyone looks absorbed, industrious, locked into some private task. Plastic boxes of silvery nuts, bolts and washers lie next to a long pile of chains like necklaces in a jewellery box. In a corner at the back of the factory are several bakfiets, the cargo bikes used for carrying anything from children to furniture, the Dutch equivalent of a 4x4. A group of workers take their tea break out in the sun behind the plastic curtains at the back of the warehouse, smoking and gossiping.

Away from the intermittent whirr of machinery and drills, Rijkeboer explains how Azor got here. For many years, he worked for other framemakers, but when his previous employers went bust he made the decision to set up on his own. 'So I make drawings, I talk to people who deliver the goods, I talk to my wife and say, probably in the first year I am going bankrupt and we lose everything, my house, everything. But if I don't try it, I think I regret it the rest of my life.' Initially it was hard to break into a market dominated by the main brands, but little by little and proof by proof, Rijkeboer began to win his clients over. To begin with, he tried making cycles with good-quality frames but poorer quality accessories in order to save on price. But when things started being returned, Rijkeboer revised his original plan. Now he uses good-quality materials tested the Azor way. 'Sometimes you get here someone from Basta or big manufacturer of headlamps. I ask them, are these tested, and they say, "*Ja*, they are tested, they are tough." I say, "Are they tested on the Azor way?" They say, "*Ja, ja*." I say, "Do you know what it is, then?" "No, no, no." I tell them, "Should I show you, eh? OK." I get a headlamp and I throw them to the wall. And then when they break, I don't want them. They say, "We make the price low." I tell them, "No, when they are for free I even don't want them."' He laughs. 'The brake levers we put in the vice, and then I bend them the wrong way. If you bend them ten times and they do not break, then they are OK. And coat protectors, I kick them. *Ja*. I like to make new things, and when they sell, it's very nice. New things that run good, they are most beautiful, I think, when you see them in the wild.'

Given such stringent R&D, it's hardly surprising that a well-made Dutch bike is still supposed to last a couple of lifetimes or more. The best way to see this at work is obviously to go for a ride, so on a sunny day in early July I head out of Amsterdam towards the north of the country. Assen is a medium-sized town in Drenthe with a broad, wide canal leading straight into the centre of town, a TT track and the same comfortable, well-proportioned red-brick architecture that all of Holland is made from. As in every Dutch railway station, Assen has a bike rental shop which will hire you something for as long as you need it. The resulting Gazelle is heavy and strong with three gears and two baskets. Once it's in motion, it has roughly the same momentum and stopping distance as a medium-sized oil tanker. I set off northwards along the canal towpath past the lines of trees and barges spaced at regulation intervals and then up onto the main road out of town.

But that road does not look like it would look in Britain. In Britain, roads are solely and exclusively for cars. Out in the country they sometimes have short stretches of pavement, but more usually it's all just tarmac and road kill. Here, they have a much more elegant solution. First there's a pavement, then a cycle path, then there are trees, then there's a road. And the same on the other side. It all somehow fits in not because the buildings are any wider apart, but because the roads are thinner. And because there are paths specially for bikes already there, all sorts of things start to happen. The assumptions that one makes in Britain no longer apply; the whole way one cycles is suddenly called into question. Springing from the Dutch belief that cyclists have a legal and moral right to exist comes a whole series of equally bizarre notions: that you don't have to cycle defensively, that you are not just about to get wiped out by an HGV, that you do not have anything to fear. The UK has eight casualties per 100km cycled; the Netherlands has 0.8. And, since you don't have anything to fear, you don't have anything to prove. If you don't have anything to prove, you don't have to compete, either with motorists or with your fellow cyclists. Here, people cycle because they're interested in reaching their destinations. Everyone spins along at roughly the same pace – a steady, comfortable 20 to 25kph. Everyone rides as upright as if they were sitting at the kitchen table back at home, and everyone looks perfectly capable of pedalling halfway to Brussels if necessary. No one shows off or rides anything flashy or bangs the bonnets of transgressing vans. It is all very strange.

Groningen is a mid-sized city up near the German border, home to a large old university and a stately town square. In mid-July, the streets are full of couples and shoppers sitting outside the cafés and bars watching the street life as the students stride past. Down the side streets, the buildings are an artful mixture of new and old built up over decades, a mixture of red brick, stucco and shiny black pantiles. None of the buildings is more than three storeys high. Roses and hollyhocks grow by the doorways and buddleia muscles its way through the gaps between cobbles. In the market square a man with enormous white side whiskers like a Victorian policeman flips *poffertjes*, little round pillowy pancakes stuffed full of cream and served by the score. Over in the tourist office at the side of the square, they offer everything one would expect; handfuls of coloured wooden tulips, blue and white china in every desirable – and undesirable – shape and size, a large collection of clothes in patriotic orange, posters of Rembrandts and Vermeers, two or three model windmills. There are guidebooks and information, train timetables and flight times. There's all the stuff one would expect of a tourist office. The only thing there is no sign of is the one thing which to a foreigner makes Groningen notable: bicycles.

Back in 1972, Groningen was faced with the same dilemma as almost every other major city in Europe: in a place designed in the days when the main forms of transport were no wider than a horse or cart, how were they going to cater for a century full of cars? They could continue building roads, but roads are expensive and notorious for breeding more traffic. They could make the best of what they already had, but that included a medieval town centre intersected by a network of canals. They could build huge ring roads, but those would lead them nowhere. So they made a crucial decision: to turn away from cars and back to the bicycle.

And what was true of Groningen is true of the Netherlands as a whole. Faced with exactly the same set of incentives as the rest of the world – everlasting North Sea oil, a brutally influential car lobby, declining cycle use, variable public transport provision, rising traffic fatalities, a population boom, a partial road network already in place, the aspirational lure of cars and the fact that manufacturing them will always employ more people than framebuilding, etc., etc. – the Dutch took an extraordinary decision. They did something completely sensible. Perhaps it was because bicycle use never faded out to quite the same extent as it had in Britain. Perhaps it was a disastrous 1972 Dutch Economic Institute policy report which depicted a future Holland slashed from north to south by three-lane highways. Perhaps it was the sense that this, finally, was an engineering project too far. Or perhaps it was just because someone had finally noticed that cars had drawbacks as well as advantages. Either way, from 1972 onwards, there was a concerted effort all over the country not just to include the bicycle in transport planning, but to promote it. The cycle industry now employs around nine thousand people nationally and sells about one million bikes a year, half of which are imported.

In Groningen, most of the city centre was gradually closed off to private vehicles and a network of diversions established around the periphery. Business vehicles and buses could still travel into the centre, but most people either moved around on foot or by bike. Initially, the changes weren't popular. Local businesses complained about the changes until someone pointed out that they had brought greater prosperity and investment to Groningen, not less. Around 60 per cent of all trips in Groningen are now made by bike; at the moment only Shanghai has more cycle users, and that won't last for long if the Chinese continue motorisation at their current pace. It also now has probably the only station bike park in the world which could legitimately be considered a tourist destination in its own right. In an elegant underground space a bit like the old Penguinarium at London Zoo there is room for three thousand bikes, stacked up double almost as far as the eye can see. The park is completely full – there's such pressure on space that bikes which have been left for too long have little red tags placed round their back wheels in readiness for being moved on. There are rows and rows of cycles, painted or plain, laden with panniers or with bright plastic flowers wound round the basket and handlebars. It's like staring simultaneously into the future and the past.

Aside from all the pragmatic explanations for cycling's prevalence here – flat landscape, thin streets, car pollution etc., etc. – there is almost certainly a much more powerful one. Cycling in the Netherlands has no stigma. Once upon a time, when bicycles first arrived, it was the hobby of the rich, but by the turn of the twentieth century they had come within the reach of even low wage earners. Ever since, some sort of cycle – however cheap or gimpy – has been affordable for everyone. It isn't a poor man's form of transport, it isn't a rich man's hobby, it's not a child's toy or a machine for proving one's virility. It just isn't an issue. The main English-language bookshop in Amsterdam has three floors of books, and a transport section full of material on cars, trains, Spitfires and Fokkers, but not a single line on cycling – not a route guide, not a map, not even something on mending a puncture. Cycling here is so ubiquitous it's a non-issue. It doesn't belong to anyone, so it belongs to everyone. It's just a bicycle – as universal, unexciting and miraculous as a pair of legs.

🚲 🚲 🚲

If the Netherlands can show us one version of the future, India offers another. Looked at through the distant prism of global statistics from a search engine in the UK, India should be a cyclist's nirvana. The numbers certainly look right: 40 per cent of households own a bicycle and up to 35 per cent of all city journeys are made by bicycle. The four main manufacturers are churning out cycles made from Indian steel for Indian use by the million every month, Far Eastern imports arrive by the score and countless small assembly workshops still exist on every local street corner. During the monsoon months, when motorised transport often fails, it is those bicycles (plus the trishaws and passenger rickshaws) that keep the country moving through the rain. Seen like that, it looks very much as if India is showing the West which way to go.

Except that it isn't. Squint at the statistics from a different angle and things appear much less complacent. For India has fallen in love with the combustion engine – truly, madly, in love. Current estimates project that the number of motorised vehicles will rise by an average of 8.7 per cent every year between now and 2025 from a total of 49 million to 246 million. The country's capital, New Delhi, currently registers a thousand new car users a day, and India's largest manufacturer, Tata Motors, recently announced that they want to expand the number of drivers by 65 per cent in the next few years. In 2009, they launched the Tata Nano, the first Rs 100,000 (or just over £1,000) car yet produced anywhere in the world, and a good 30 per cent cheaper than its nearest competitor. At the same time, it's possible to buy a new motorbike for the equivalent of £300–£400, and employers often offer generous incentive schemes to their staff, advancing 70 per cent of the cost of a new motorbike as encouragement.

This passion for motorisation isn't necessarily due to a lack of alternatives. Almost all of India's great cities are well served by suburban and mainline train services and a good bus network, and several cities, including New Delhi, have space-age metro systems. Still, that's not the point. As elsewhere in the world, people here need cars for all sorts of reasons, almost none of which have anything to do with transport. As Indians point out, sitting on your backside getting angry in a traffic jam has been a venerable tradition for many years in London and New York, and if the West can do gridlock, then why can't the East do it, too? Besides, the scale is different. London has eight million inhabitants, Paris has twelve. Berlin or Palermo or Manchester are bicycle-sized, even if not always bicycle-friendly. But New Delhi has twenty million inhabitants and rising. The city is vast – too vast for humans or animals and so vast that it's easy enough to do 60 to 80km in a day just moving around the centre. And it's growing, keeping up with its own double-digit financial fortunes, spreading like bindweed before your eyes. On the periphery of Mumbai, the parallel city of New Bombay stalks box by concrete box all the way over the Western Ghats to Pune. In Calcutta, a tide of trucks and Ambassador taxis now seeps over a sizeable chunk of West Bengal towards the Sundarbans. To the south of New Delhi, the vast new suburb of Gurgaon slides onwards with the speed of a rising tide.

So it remains a complete mystery that a country developing so fast can spend most of its time going so incredibly slowly. At peak hours in the major cities, nothing moves. The traffic just sits, enveloped in a soft ectoplasmic blanket of its own fumes, and waits. It waits for someone to concede defeat, for the lights to change, for all the other cars and lorries and buses and bikes to miraculously teleport themselves out of the way so that drivers can continue their journey in majestic isolation. Since this doesn't happen, everyone just remains stationary while the sun beats down and a thousand thousand air-conditioning units breathe out their chemical halitosis. Thus, getting by car to a meeting or a station becomes a major strategic expedition, requiring planning, money, resourcefulness, cunning, psychology, ingenuity, fortitude and an almost zen-like capacity to let go all notions of time, space or worldly attachment. Catching a flight requires whole days on the road, great emptinesses of time spent staring out of the window at the softening tarmac while considering either the rise and fall of ancient civilisations or how much it's going to cost to get another ticket seventeen hours hence. It's just like London, only more so.

Besides, there's another, starker factor at play here. Though driving and road conditions vary widely across India, a rough Darwinism applies almost everywhere. Basically, the larger and bolder you are, the better. So at the top of the food chain are the lorries and the trucks. Then there are buses. Then there are jeeps and expensive four-wheel-drives. Then there are the foreign cars, the taxis and (depending on the city) the Ambassadors. Below them are the taxis and the auto-rickshaws. And finally, right at the bottom, there are the phyto-plankton of the transport system: primitive single-cell organisms like passenger rickshaws, cyclists, pedestrians and goats. There are the rulers, and there are the ruled; if you don't have an engine, you don't have a say. And in a fair fight between a car and a bicycle, the bicycle goes to the gutter every time.

And since cycling has no status, it also has no particular identity. There are forty-five million bikes in India, and most of them are identical. Here, a bike is a bike is a bike, it's made by Hero or Hercules or Atlas or A1, it comes in one form, and it's used purely by the poor to get from A to B. People don't usually aspire to bicycles; they aspire to cars or motorbikes or (at the very least) to reliable public transport. And so those who do cycle are in general those who do so in the absence of any better alternatives. Which may or may not be why India has the distinction of being the country with the highest proportion of road traffic accidents in the world – three times higher than in the developed countries.

止 止 止

The narrow streets and shadowy alleys of Old Delhi were built back in an age where no road needed to be greater than the width of a horse or a hand-drawn cart. Its medieval street layout is so narrow in places that two people can barely pass abreast, and sometimes even a scooter is too wide to get deliveries into the thousands of small stalls in the centre. Which makes them perfect for rickshaws and disastrous for cars. Even motorbikes are all wrong here, though their riders brazen it out, executing resentful three-point turns when the alleyways narrow. Because of both the street layout and the huge increase in the city's population, there are now ten times the number of rickshaws in New Delhi as there were thirty years ago.

Round the periphery on Esplanade Road within earshot of the amplified muezzins of the Jama Masjid, it is still possible to obtain anything and everything bicycle- and rickshaw-related. Out on the pavement, mechanics crouch, picking out single spokes from a sheaf by their side and pressing them individually into the rims. In the shops, traditional Indian bikes have been shoved to one side and bright plasticky mountain bikes have pride of place. One shop sells customised trishaws, the cheap mango wood still fresh enough to have kept its scent, while another does passenger rickshaws. Sitting in the shade at the backs of the shops, the owners wait like spiders, looking out over the street. Kirti Dhawan, aged thirty-seven, has been running a shop for twenty years. He's watched the changes in the market and is sure about what his customers want. 'The market for the old-style Indian bikes is negligible now. We don't have a single piece in our shop from that bicycle. Not a single piece. Because nobody buys them. They are good quality, but nobody wants that kind of thing – they want new, colourful, eye-catching bicycles, with big tyres. They want mountain bikes, even if they are more expensive.' Middle-class parents often buy their children a new bike every year or so, or use an import, wear it out and come back for another after eighteen months. No one, it seems, has much use for racing bikes – 'They hurt your back because you have to lean over.'

In the past, he says, many of his sales were to the families of young women needing a bicycle as part of a dowry. 'When people got married they would come here to get a simple bicycle about ten, fifteen years ago. If you could afford to, you gave a motorcycle as part of the dowry, but if you could not, you gave a cycle. A cycle plus a lot of jewellery. And people would buy this type' – he points to one of the standard-issue Heros – 'but now they have stopped. It was a very big part of our market, a very big share twenty years ago, but that sale has gone. It began to change in the past decade – people just stopped asking for dowry cycles.'

A few stops down the street, Ravi Guneja sells rickshaws and trishaws. Many drivers will pay outright for a new rickshaw, but those who cannot afford the full price will rent one off a middleman who may well have five hundred to a thousand in his fleet. He will usually take a cut of about Rs 50 a day from the drivers, irrespective of any fluctuations in their earnings. A diligent driver can earn up to Rs 500 a day, but the health of rickshaw wallahs is rapidly broken. 'I don't know why they are unhappy,' says Ravi, in between negotiations with a customer who has come in to order a new trishaw. He begins picking out the parts he wants – heavier or lighter axles, bigger or smaller wheels, higher quality wood, reflectors for the back (rickshaws do not have to display lights) and mirrors for the front. To get exactly the right measurements, he uses a piece of string tied with knots spaced along its length in the same way as people used to gauge their speed at sea. After protracted negotiations, the driver departs. 'A lot of them drink,' says Ravi, watching him leave as he stuffs each note of the deposit into the top drawer of his desk. 'Yes, it is very much physically hard work, but if you don't drink, don't smoke, if you have a good diet, then it won't affect you. But they practise all the vices. *All* the vices. Especially the drinking. It is their fault they are not healthy. But they are cheaper than auto-rickshaws and there are still places where only they can go, so they will always make money.'

So, I say, can I try one? For a moment, Ravi's eyes widen. Then they settle back to the same expression of imperturbable grandeur as before. He smiles. 'Go ahead!' I pick out a fresh trishaw – 75kg of prime bespoke Indian steel and mango wood – climb on, and set off towards Chandni Chowk. The heaviness is not surprising, but the feeling of instability is – riding over bumps, it feels as if the whole thing is going to topple to a stop. The trishaw also makes it clear that corners of any sort are not recommended, and that it only wants to go at one speed. That speed is not the same as the rest of India wants to go.

The passenger rickshaw proves equally entertaining. Made of much the same materials as the trishaw – give or take several extra kilos of optional ornamentation – it weighs 100kg unladen and anything up to 350kg with the addition of a well-fed fare. When I set off back down the street, the carriage tips abruptly as someone detaches himself from the crowd and leaps up into the passenger seat, shouting instructions. I ignore him; I'm having enough trouble maintaining the thing in an upright position to make any kind of response at all. The trishaw was all horizontals, but this is all verticals; the passenger seat is actually on the same level as the saddle, but it feels a lot higher. Whatever instability I felt with the cart is magnified a hundredfold. I go over a bump and very nearly come to a halt, convinced the whole thing, passenger and all, is going to topple slowly onto the pavement. My passenger, grandstanding for the growing audience, yells something at me in Hindi. Very slowly, very cautiously, I ride back up the road. Several spectators come up alongside, shouting encouragement. Pecking up and down in the saddle with effort, I note that none of my audience has had to break into a trot in order to keep up with me, never mind a run. Both this and the trishaw need a huge amount of strength to guide through all the old city's twists and holes. But it's not just that. There are so many cars and scooters here, so much on the pavement, so many people using the place as a workshop or a chai stop, so many schoolchildren and delivery lorries. And dragging the rickshaw's great dead-weight with the full rage of the waiting traffic behind makes one feel acutely vulnerable. Finally, I turn the corner back to the compound and come to a halt. A couple of the spectators applaud; my passenger leaps off and disappears. I climb off and return the rickshaw to its rightful owner. It's only later I realise I never collected my fare.

Outside the cities, things relax a little and the bicycle still threads its gentle way through the fabric of Indian life. The roads are older, less crowded, more easy-going. As I cycle southwards on a borrowed Atlas from Sultanpur, the highway becomes a thin corridor of noise and speed in an otherwise languid landscape, leaving eddies of sound in its wake. Step off onto a side road or a track and the sound recedes, the fumes vanish, time slackens down to a steady slow tick. It's the middle of February and still cold by Indian standards. The edges of the fields are bright with frangipani, and occasionally there's the vivid orange flash of marigolds. The bike itself dictates the speed of progress. It has one gear and one speed, and feels much the same as riding a donkey probably would: I could certainly try spurring it into faster action, but it wouldn't last for long and the results might backfire. It's happy ploughing south at a steady 12mph, adding the rhythmic squeak of one unoiled pedal to the general rural symphony. It feels so lovely to be back on a saddle again instead of walking or flying or being driven from place to place, gazing blankly through the glass at the glittering city like Iggy Pop's Passenger. Here, if you're threatened by a truck or a car, there's the whole of the countryside into which to fling yourself. Besides, here drivers use their horns to warn you of their approach, rather than as an order to sacrifice yourself to the pavement.

In Faroukhpur, I turn off onto a side road and find myself, after several unscheduled detours, taking tea with a farmer's family in their compound just outside the town. The farmer grows a mixed crop, and he's doing well. Not brilliantly, but comfortably. He loves his job, his family and his land. Two of his daughters already work in the city and his grandsons are at an English-speaking school. He looks round at his lovely blooming acres, the shady trees, the marigolds in blossom. In between the individual plants is the evidence of several generations of hard work. In a couple of years or less, all of it – guavas, peas, walls, home – will be buried under the Delhi metro. The first intimation of its arrival, the great concrete struts high above the road, are now no more than a few miles away. And in their wake come the shops and flats, the huge plastic baggage of the city. The city moves onwards, and those in its path understand that soon enough it will smother them all.

🚲 🚲 🚲

Several days later in Calcutta, I complete the two-wheeled trial. There is always something so extreme about Calcutta that the only possible response is a kind of open-mouthed stupefaction. After a bit, you move round the city in a state of overloaded amazement, tranced into tranquillity through permanent motion. Perhaps the best example of this is to be found on the roads. Getting around the city is always a full-on experience whichever form of transport you choose, but it's now rendered even more exciting by the unholy levels of pollution (the city recently voted down a motion to follow Delhi's example and convert all public vehicles to compressed natural gas, or CNG), and by the way Calcuttans drive. Indian driving habits have long been considered one of the seven wonders of the modern world by Western tourists, so there's nothing new about finding them notable. Still, there are moments when Calcutta's roads make Delhi seem like Brussels in comparison.

Since congestion on Calcutta's main roads at peak hours has reached gridlock, drivers have responded by taking a refreshingly freestyle approach to travel, casting aside outmoded notions like lanes or direction of flow and instead moving forwards by using any available empty section of tarmac. In other words, if the left-hand side of the road isn't working for you, then you simply cross the road and try the right-hand side – or, if necessary, the pavement. When you find yourself motoring towards traffic or pedestrians coming in the opposite direction, the usual driving codes then come into play: you stare them down, you hope you're in a better, bigger vehicle and you use the horn. To add extra interest, all the one-way streets in the city change direction at 1 p.m. So the road that you'd thought flowed southwards turns out to be hurtling north, and you suddenly find yourself staring straight down the barrel of a three-lane highway. In practice, there's a two-hour hiatus on either side of the one o'clock deadline during which time everyone treats the one-way streets as a free-for-all. Even the concept of 'streets' can occasionally be called into question. Returning one afternoon through the Maidan's wide boulevards, we discover that one of the city's most heavily used roads has vanished. Instead, three central lanes and part of a bus stand have been requisitioned and converted into an impromptu dining area. In place of traffic lights and the 15.09 bus to Ballygunge, there is now a marquee, a red carpet, enough seating for three or four hundred people and an attractive floral arrangement.

The city's response to the press of traffic has been to minimise or banish the non-motorised kind. Those who do insist on continuing to cycle – the very poor and the very young – are exiled to particular districts where, in the soft angular light of early morning, you still see them pedalling down the side streets with their loads of children or vegetables, ghostly reminders of a passing age. At the same time, the city's attempts at eliminating another old-fashioned form of transport have proved less successful.

Famously, Calcutta is the last major city in India to maintain a 20,000-strong fleet of hand-pulled rickshaws. In fact,
the rickshaws are so well known that they are probably by
now second only to Mother Teresa as a kind of pictorial
shorthand for the city. Introduced at the turn of the twentieth century by Chinese traders, initially as cargo vehicles
and later as a method of transporting passengers, they
became associated with degradation partly because they
were one of the first jobs that immigrants, forced off their
farms by famine or war, could take when they arrived in
the city. The work was unskilled; all you needed to lift a
rickshaw was strength and desperation.

The wars and the famines have moved on, but, despite
the best efforts of the communist government of West
Bengal, the rickshaws have not. The communists want to
promote Calcutta as a modern city, a forward-thinking,
go-getting kind of place, stuffed with glassy IT hubs and
splendid technological opportunities, and emaciated sixty-
year-olds in filthy lungis trotting slowly past those selfsame
IT hubs with a load of fat passengers don't really fit the bill.
And so, in an attempt at final elimination, the government
passed a bill phasing out hand-pulled rickshaws from
December 2006. In return, they offered the carrot of 'rehabilitation', and the stick of more forceful measures for
those who resisted. The pullers took to the streets, protest-
ing that 'rehabilitation' was only available to the few and
none of them had much desire to become human parking
meters instead. Besides, they pointed out, the ordinary citi-
zens of Calcutta maintained a more practical ambivalence
towards the hand-pulled rickshaws. Their image might be

troubling, but they're useful for short journeys and vital during the monsoon, when all other traffic ends up afloat. And so, for lack of any real incentive or alternative, the rickshaws continue, their licences passing illegally from father to son and their continuing presence keeping the landless families from falling the few fatal steps further.

Strictly speaking, the hand-pulled rickshaws have nothing to do with cycling, but they do offer a telling comparison. Borrowing one off a driver outside the New Market, I place myself between the shafts, bend down and lift. I think I'm expecting something of almost the same weight and substance as the Delhi trishaw, but the shafts rest lightly in my hands. And when I walk forwards down the street, the huge wheels turn easily, moving along without strain and passing over the potholes without lurching to one side. It doesn't take long to realise that the hand-pulled rickshaw has something no other type of rickshaw does: it has perfect balance. It has been engineered with such a precise centre of gravity that it appears to weigh almost nothing. Most of the structure – including the wheels, the seat and the canopy – is made of soft sheesham wood and bamboo, designed to be light and manoeuvrable rather than to take the heavy freight that passenger rickshaws and trishaws face. Everything has been minimised: the hood is no more than a lattice of steel covered with a dhoti, the shafts seem almost dangerously thin, and the carriage is just a bright scoop of leather. The whole thing balances on its two great coloured wheels as gracefully as a kite on a wire. It's still common to see the rickshaws being pulled along with a load of cargo, and they obviously have to be capable of taking at least two passengers of whatever weight and shape, but whoever first designed them for humans also did so with the aim of making them as bearable as humanly possible.

Noor Hussein has been driving a passenger rickshaw – the cycle type – for the past four years. He lives in a comfortable little compound within a Muslim bustee (or slum) in central Calcutta. Around each side of the compound is a small, single-room house for each family. In pride of place at the centre of the compound is a new Hero bicycle. The Husseins' house is shady and full of bright colours, with a pantiled roof and a bamboo screen acting as a porch and support for drying clothes. It has a tiny kitchen area in one corner, storage for crockery in another and a large, high settle at the other end which doubles as both seating area and bed for half the family.

Hussein became a rickshaw wallah four years ago when a career as a fruit seller finally grew too unproductive. His rickshaw is rented from a middleman to whom he pays Rs 40 a day irrespective of earnings, but on an average day he makes between Rs 100 and 150. Cycle rickshaw routes in Calcutta are restricted to certain areas, and the rickshaw wallahs work like taxis outside stations, picking up a fare, taking them along the permitted routes, dropping them and returning to the stand. The system means that, unlike the hand-pullers, they are always guaranteed fares, and their earnings are simply pegged to their energy levels. So who are the best fares? 'Schoolchildren – they are very light. You can't generalise about passengers, but anyone can be good – if we are good-natured, then it is a good job, and if not, then it is a bad job; it is up to us. People who are drunk are the worst passengers, because they usually don't want to pay.'

He takes me outside to see his rented rickshaw. His came with its previous owner's embellishments already in place, though Hussein likes their style and has added to them. On the back of the passenger seat is an awesome orange portrait of the Muslim actor Aamir Khan, recent star of *Ghajini*, at that point the highest-grossing Bollywood film of all time. Above him on the hood is a selection of magazine lovelies, and surrounding them is a frilly decorative edging of hi-vis tape. From the back of the seat hang long, spotty chains of red and green reflectors. The struts of the canopy are painted with bright flowers and the hood itself is an old PVC tablecloth covered in pictures of fruit. The wheels are new, the chain is clean, the pedals are green and the back of the seat comprehensively covers any Bollywood stars not already featured elsewhere. There are also six rear-view mirrors, three bells, two incense burners, five candlesticks and a pink fluffy thing around the front-wheel hub. It is unquestionably the finest tricycle I have ever seen. Posing astride it for photographs, surrounded by his neighbours, Hussein looks happy and proud. He works extremely hard, earns a regular income and his children are at a highly regarded school nearby; he is a man who has done his very best and the rickshaw reflects that.

But if cycling in India has now largely been shoved out to the margins, there are still a few people working on bringing it back to the centre. Perhaps the most striking example is Vinod Punmiya, The Man Who Raced the

Deccan Queen. On 25 March 2007, Punmiya, then a fifty-year-old Mumbai businessman, climbed onto his imported Trek and set off to cover the 140km distance between Pune and Mumbai. At the same time as he set off, the *Deccan Queen*, the high-speed train which connects the two cities, began its daily commute towards Mumbai. Every weekday morning, the *Queen* leaves at 7.15 and arrives reliably at Mumbai's Chhatrapati Shivaji Terminus three and a quarter hours later at 10.30, having touched a top speed of 105kph on the way. Punmiya was not aiming to race from station to station, but from suburb to suburb – which, at the Mumbai end at least, would significantly cut the mileage and mean he didn't get stuck in rush-hour traffic. Instead, he took the old and very battered highway across the Khandala Ghat, a route which would mirror, but not exactly parallel, the one taken by the train. He also travelled with an escort, including a car directly in front which cut the wind resistance down by around 40 per cent. Twenty-two minutes before the train arrived, Punmiya had made it to Dombivli.

Punmiya picks us up from the station in a newish Jeep, driving us high above the surrounding traffic the few streets back to his apartment. He is friendly, courteous and welcoming, quick to laugh but with a strong underlying intensity of focus. In many ways, he looks like what he is; a healthy, prosperous middle-aged man living comfortably in a quiet suburb of Mumbai with his gentle wife Indira and his son. The only incongruities are the carbon-fibre bike covered in sponsors' logos standing in the middle of the front room and a glass cabinet stuffed with trophies.

Even looking at them – even once he has shown me the framed certificate itemising his achievements and the album of photographs of him and Indira outside the Taj Hotel at the end of his four-day peace ride from Delhi to Mumbai, and the picture of him and India's current President, Pratibha Patil, standing behind the same bike at the Presidential Palace – it still seems unlikely that Punmiya breaks many land-speed records. It's only when I ask him if I can take some photographs and he returns in full Caisse d'Epargne Lycra that it all starts to make sense. Suddenly, he looks the real deal, with the small, tight physique of the congenital cyclist and a kind of indefinable rightness about the way he sits on a bike.

So how on earth did he come to be racing trains? There was nothing much in his early background to suggest any record-breaking ability. 'My family was rich,' says Vinod. 'There are four brothers and one sister – I am the second. I am very naughty, I am not doing study. I didn't like any subjects – I like cycling only.' Why cycling? Indira interjects, 'He likes the speed, I think, he likes to make challenges. And on a cycle you can run away from everything.' In 1987, he won the annual Mumbai–Pune race and was crowned King of the Ghats. At the same time, he was busy causing further divisions by falling in love with Indira. Her family were rich hoteliers, and were unimpressed when Indira declared her intention to marry a penniless racing cyclist disowned by his family with a day job in a photo-copying shop. Against the odds, they married, and Punmiya put the cycling to one side during the 1990s while he built up his jewellery business. When he took it up again, he was no longer interested in competing in normal races. 'Then I want to do something different. Then always I am doing the night training, first time beating the small, small scooters. Then I am beating the scooters. Then I take the (motorised) rickshaws, and I am faster than the rickshaws. Then faster than a car, then faster than a truck. Everything I am beating, I am thinking, "What machine is faster than me?" So I select the fastest train in the Maharastra – the *Deccan Queen*.'

His peers, and other members of India's elite racing fraternity, are sceptical about some of his achievements. They say he gave up ordinary racing because he was ostracised for cheating, allegedly climbing into his sponsor's ambulance halfway through a race, overtaking the peloton and then getting back on the bike. There's no doubt now that he's for real, but his contemporaries still question the point of it all. Do you know why you're so fast? 'I am following a car and doing cycling – I am always drafting.' Yes, but drafting only reduces wind resistance by a third or so – that still makes you pretty speedy. 'Yes. Very fast. I want to go more fast, but my wife is not allowing me!' They both laugh, joint participants in an ancient argument. 'My wife is not allowing me to do cycling, because it is very risky, behind the car, with the car, 100kph, 120kph. Any time, you can die. Because you have only one helmet and one T-shirt. If you fall at 100kph speed, you cannot do anything.' He smiles. 'Very risky. I like risk.' There is a pause, and Indira looks at him affectionately. She may hate the risks he takes, but she also participates fully, acting as his back-up team, physio and soigneur. The two of them are palpably and endearingly in love, and there is something invigorating about their pleasure in each other's company.

His friends continue to find his choice of transport mystifying. He has money now from the business. 'So,' says Indira, 'people make even more fun of him – "You have two big nice cars, why do you want to sit on a bicycle?"' 'If I have a big flashy car, then people will watch,' says Punmiya. 'If I have a big flashy bicycle, nobody cares. Even if you have something foreign costing ten lakh rupees [around £13,850], nobody gives it a second look.' Indira nods. 'It is true. When we go out to our native place in Rajasthan, there is also many tourists come over there. So we find them walking or cycling, and we – we are all in cars.' But does seeing him and his achievements encourage people? 'No,' says Indira, 'they don't. Nobody has taken to cycling after seeing him. People say, "You do it so it's OK, but we use our cars!"' Other members of India's racing elite may dismiss Punmiya as a self-promoting stuntman, but his wish to advance the cause of cycling and his idiosyncratic route to the top reveal more than just an enthusiasm for getting his picture in the papers. Besides, he's certainly not the first to come up with extraordinary ways of focusing public attention on cycling.

殳 殳 殳

FIVE

Watercycling to France

On 30 September 1920, a small crowd gathers in a semi-circle outside Richmond Town Hall in west London. It's an imposing but cheerful group: two or three policemen, several dignitaries, a doorman in full uniform, two or three recently demobbed officers and the Mayor, properly hatted and chained. Behind them are onlookers, a few more policemen and a number of children. In front, filming the whole thing for the movie theatres, is a Pathé news cameraman.

The focus of all their attention is a woman in her mid-twenties with a masculine cast to her face and a brisk demeanour. She is sitting astride an ordinary steel-framed step-through lady's bicycle mounted between what look like two long, flat planks of wood placed about half a metre apart and curved a little at the tips like skis. The planks have been braced in the centre and fastened to the frame of the bike so that the wheels can rotate freely, almost as if this was some kind of stabiliser arrangement for adults. The back wheel has been customised with small, flat paddles spaced at regular intervals along its length like a waterwheel, and the front is raised a little so that it is clear of the ground. Even though the bike is currently immobile, the young woman's choice of clothing is unusual; a smart white cap with a dark brim, a loose-fitting jacket with a nautical-style collar, an ankle-length pleated skirt and a stout pair of brogues. She smiles at the cameraman and waits as the Mayor steps forward. He is holding a small bottle of champagne at the base which he smashes hard against the head tube of the bike. At the second attempt, the bottle breaks, spraying the young woman, her long skirt and the Mayor with warm fizz. There is a very English moment when everyone laughs efficiently while pretending they are less wet than they actually are. Finally, one of the officers attaches the Union Jack to the handlebars and she is ready.

A short time later, the scene has changed. A much larger crowd of spectators has gathered by Richmond Bridge and

Zetta Hills (on the left) with an unnamed companion on one of her regular watercycling jaunts down the Thames.

is looking down excitedly at something on the river. Down on the water is the young woman again. She is still on her bike, but is now afloat. Some minor sartorial concessions have been made to this new water-borne state; she has rolled up the sleeves of her jersey and her long skirt has been exchanged for a marginally shorter alternative. Around her are various small launches and sculls, and the woman is shouting something to their occupants. Then, finally, she is off. Pedalling hard, she begins to cycle down the river, front wheel riding free of the water and back wheel sending up a fine white rooster plume of spray over her back. It is a splendid and astonishing sight.

The point of the two large planks is now evident. Like the twin hulls of a catamaran, they are buoyant, supporting the bike in the water. They have also been fitted with rudders which the young woman can move by turning the handlebars. A large rear mudguard has been added to reduce the splashing, but it isn't very effective; the faster she pedals, the greater the quantity of spray and the stronger the drag from the water. Once in a while, she breaks from her endeavours to eat a fortifying sandwich. But otherwise, she continues on towards London, skirt tucked into her knickers, upright and imperturbable, as if cycling down the middle of the Thames while dressed in Sunday best was the sort of thing one did every week.

In Zetta Hills' case, it probably was. That day in 1920 she cycled fifteen miles downriver, all the way to Temple Pier. Aquatically speaking, the adventure was probably insignificant; only a few months before, pulled south by currents, she had cycled forty-seven miles of the English Channel.

There was evidently something dauntless about Zetta. Born Lillian Hills in Folkestone in 1895, she had three real obsessions in life – the sea, swimming and showmanship. Her first (unsuccessful) attempt to cycle the Channel had been in 1913, aged only eighteen. After that, she worked as part of the amusements on Folkestone Pier giving swimming exhibitions before marrying a local man, Sidney Haimes, though marriage obviously did not keep her landbound. Zetta's ambition to cycle the Channel remained, and was given greater force by the appearance of a rival. A Mr Harold Ashton Rigby from Croydon made two successful attempts to cycle the Channel in 1920 and 1921. On the second attempt, the weather worsened as he reached halfway. He became too seasick to eat, and very nearly gave up his attempt. Struggling onwards, almost washed from the saddle by the waves, he finally rode into the harbour at Calais twelve hours after he had started.

Zetta's first attempt proved equally eventful. At its narrowest point the distance between England and France is only twenty-one miles, but the tides and currents pushed Zetta in a long, deep loop southwards. She had begun that morning at 7.15 from Calais pedalling hard, and had only four miles left to go when she found herself in real trouble. She had drifted close to the notorious Goodwin Sands, quicksands with their own eerie weather system which appear and disappear with the rising or falling tides. A thick fog came down, obscuring any sight of land and making it almost impossible to navigate. Even then, she kept going. Finally, after fifteen solid hours of pedalling, the front stay of the supporting frame gave way and Zetta was thrown into the water. The launch that had accompanied her all the way from France picked her up, revived her and took both her and the bicycle on to Folkestone. Undeterred either by the experience or its conclusion, she vowed to try again as soon as possible. Her second attempt – made shortly after giving birth to a son, also named Sidney – was successful. Having mastered La Manche,

Zetta Hills in later life, working as a sea lion tamer and motorbike stunt rider at Bostock & Wombwell's Travelling Circus. She is wearing one of her own customised drysuits.

Zetta then absconded. She left baby Sidney with her in-laws at a pub in Cornwall and ran away, first to the British Empire Exhibition as a swimmer and then finally, inevitably, to the circus.

Bostock & Wombwell's Menagerie was the most famous of late nineteenth-century travelling circuses, boasting a treasury of splendid and fantastical acts including a lion tamer with rheumatics, a gorilla, a band, and something described as a 'Royal Modern Musical Elephant'. Every few months, the troupe would roll slowly round the counties of England, pitching their tents on local village greens and unhitching the caravans from their pack camels. They would stay for a few weeks and then move on to the next village, playing for as long as there were audiences to watch. It was, of course, the perfect environment for Zetta. She had found another long-term partner – not her husband Sidney but a sea lion named Bonzo, to whom she was said to be strongly attached. Under her training, Bonzo had turned into the best juggling pinniped in the country and now had his own chorus line of attendant seals. When not looking after him, Zetta occasionally managed to retain her interest in two-wheeled transport. Undaunted by gravity, she was now appearing as one of Wombwell's stunt motorbike riders and making regular excursions to the Wall of Death. In 1929, after three and a half years with the circus, Zetta departed, leaving Bonzo behind her and fading from public view. All that was left was the short Pathé news clip, the watercycle and a whole lot of unanswered questions.

🚲 🚲 🚲

Over the years, many things have been claimed for the bicycle: that it changed history, that it brought the world closer to itself, even that it changed the shape of the global gene pool. Since the bicycle widened the potential radius that a healthy individual could reasonably travel in a day from ten miles to eighty, it also expanded the scope for romance. Instead of having to make do with the small, inbred selection of potential mates from the nearby village, the new cyclist could now go further, faster and for longer – in all senses.

But perhaps the biggest claim on the bicycle's behalf was made by the American suffragette Susan B. Anthony. 'Let me tell you what I think of bicycling. I think it has done more for the emancipation of women than anything else in the world,' she said in 1896. It was a surprising claim. No one in the 1860s seeing a woman in full crinolines next to an Ordinary bicycle would have predicted that the relationship between the two would remain anything other than distant. The difficulties involved in getting even the most enterprising woman atop a moving penny farthing in full skirts were insuperable. It couldn't be done, or if it could be done then it certainly couldn't be done with elegance.

For a while, tricycles seemed to offer a decorous alternative for women, particularly after their fortunes were given a royal boost in the 1870s. While out in her carriage one day at Osborne, Queen Victoria spotted a lady on a trike at a distance. Intrigued, she ordered her driver to speed up. The trike rider looked round, realised who her pursuer was, panicked and took off. Sadly, the Queen did not succumb to the temptation to give chase. Instead, she asked to meet the trike's designer, James Starley, inventor of the famous Ariel frame. In a letter home to his wife, he related the details of the meeting. 'I was quite overcome and bowed so low that I nearly toppled over as I said I am very honoured Ma'am. Then the gentleman led me away and I was surprised and pleased when the Prince [Leopold, then aged twenty-seven] came along and asked me to explain the workings of the tricycle to him ... We found a nice level drive where I got on and was soon rolling around in fine style. He seemed very pleased with it and thanked me very kindly.' The Queen, continuing her late husband Albert's passion for engineering and innovation, was pleased enough with the trike to order two. Even so, trike fever never really caught on. Not because there was anything inherently wrong with them, but because the bicycle was better.

Even so, it took the invention of the Safety to make a real difference to the numbers of women cycling. Unlike Ordinaries, Safety bicycles could be ridden with ease and didn't require a course in gymnastics. They were widely available, needed little maintenance and carried with them the pleasing sense of participating in something perfectly modern. And during the few golden years before cars became ubiquitous, women could take their time learning to ride in places where the greatest hazard to road safety was a shying horse. As an American cycling magazine called *The Bearings* put it in 1894, 'The safety bicycle fills a much-needed want for women in any station of life. It knows no class distinction, is within reach of all, and rich and poor alike have the opportunity of enjoying this popular and healthful exercise.' Up to a point; in both Britain and America, the average bicycle still cost between £10 and £20 – roughly the same amount as a carthorse and several times the price of a mule. Fanny Erskine, columnist for the *CTC Gazette*, considered that 'The initial cost of a machine is certainly almost as high as that of a pony – but, then, the pony requires its own entourage, to say nothing of a large amount of thought to keep it in good working order. Then to a pony must be added a cart – another £25, harness £7, shoeing, feeding, and a groom; whereas the cycle does not require more than a careful fifteen minutes' cleaning, and fair handling.'

Even so, the notion of women riding bicycles certainly attracted controversy. What might cycling do to a lady's dignity? What effect would so much strenuous exercise have on a body pinched by corsets and weighted by skirts? How would it affect her health? The sticking point, it soon emerged, was not so much the risk of showing an ankle; it was the sheer fact of sitting astride something. At this stage in the late nineteenth century, nicely brought-up young ladies were discouraged even as children from sitting on see-saws or riding on hobby horses, and no one over the age of fourteen would do anything to prove they actually had legs. Since women had successfully ridden horses side-saddle for centuries, it seemed reasonable that they could do the same thing with bicycles. Besides, the results of sitting astride a machine and then leaning forward were too horrible to contemplate. The constant friction of the saddle on the genitalia must inevitably lead to masturbation, and masturbation must lead to a new race of pop-eyed nymphomaniacs riding round Britain in a state of frenzied arousal. Cycling would ruin the 'feminine organs of matrimonial necessity', according to one French expert. Medical journals of the time discussed the 'problem' in coy but lingering detail. By telling young girls of the risks, they fretted, they would also be educating them, but not telling them meant a whole generation of women all debauched by their own bicycles.

The marketplace responded predictably. For a time, framemakers either offered side-saddle options (complex, ugly and unstable) or looked for ways to make the rider vanish. The Cherry's Screen was a device shaped like a large pair of wings which was designed to block the sight of a lady's ankles from prurient view. For those women who continued to insist on outraging public decency by sitting astride, a new range of products appeared which were designed to eliminate 'harmful pressure', including saddles with so many holes in them they were almost unrideable. In 1889, the Starley brothers introduced the 'Psycho Ladies' Bicycle', which offered a proper step-through frame and which tackled the modesty problem by forcing the cyclist to sit bolt upright, even while going uphill. At the same time, companies were set up to provide respectable chaperones for ladies at three shillings and sixpence an hour. This was a bit of a giveaway, since it rapidly became evident that much of the alarm stemmed not from cycling's effects on the female body – either real or imaginary – but from the bicycle's potential as an independent form of transport.

One taste of a sedate parish ride, and the foundations of Western civilisation would be rocked to the core.

And so, hard on the wheels of all the new cyclists came the consultants, writers of both sexes who rushed to advise the diffident or indecisive. As they made clear, cycling was not a matter of sitting on a saddle, pointing straight ahead and maintaining momentum; it was much, much more complicated than that. The novice rider needed someone to tell her where to ride, how to behave and, most importantly, how to dress. Fanny Erskine in *Lady Cycling*: 'Some wise people say that corsets should be discarded for cycling. This is not correct. There should be no approach to tight-lacing, but a pair of woollen-cased corsets afford great support; they keep the figure from going all abroad, and protect the vital parts from chills.' The insistence that women should continue to wear corsets while cycling seems almost cruel now. In the 1890s, the average middle-class woman would be expected to wear an outfit that fully covered every inch of flesh from neck to toe. Skirts were full and gathered, and cyclists often attached lead weights to their hems. The sheer weight of all that fabric was restricting enough; women's underclothing alone often weighed up to 14lb. Even on a step-through frame, the effect was roughly the same as attaching a mainsail to the handlebars. Unless fitted with guards, the fabric would get tangled in the back wheel or the chain or it would billow out, making movement almost impossible.

Far more serious were the long-term consequences of binding the body. The hourglass figure demanded of the respectable woman came at a price, since the fainting and vapours associated with whey-faced Victorian damsels were in fact often symptoms of chlorosis, a syndrome connected with disruption in blood flow which sometimes stopped women's periods and in some cases led on to uterine prolapse, in which the womb itself was pushed outwards and downwards by the force of tight lacing. The condition was often endured in agonised silence, since women were reluctant to seek help for gynaecological ailments and were accustomed to wearing corsets even while heavily pregnant. One doctor who did treat the afflicted reported that 'uterine derangement had increased fifty per cent within the last fifteen years as a result of tight clothing, corsets and high heels'. Not all doctors managed to trace the cause back to its true origin, and in many cases all they did was create an equal industry for supports and pessaries as violently restricting in their way as chastity belts. For those who had worn corsets for many years, there were also cases in which the ribcage had been so severely constricted that the ribs began to overlap or to press inwards on the lungs.

The Rational Dress Society, founded in 1881, tried to deal with both the cycling problem and the corsetry issue at once. 'What,' asked the Society's President Lady Harberton rhetorically, 'can be the true state of intelligence of a creature which deliberately loads itself with quantities of useless material round its legs … and then, in order to correct the ugliness of such a dress, squeezes in its body until the vital functions can only be carried on imperfectly?' The Society's solution – the introduction of looser, lighter clothing or 'Bloomers' (huge pantaloons tied at the

Ladies in Rational Dress.

ankle) – produced mixed results. Unfortunately, the sheer quantity of fabric in the new bloomers made them almost as impractical as corsets, and rational dress (a shortened skirt over voluminous trousers) did nothing much, either, for the wearer or for the cause. The authors of the *Badminton Cycling Guide*, published in 1887, recommended that no female cyclist should ever leave home without first donning a pair of sturdy woollen combinations, thick merino stockings, loose cotton knickerbockers with a pair of worsted trousers on top, a plain gathered skirt in 'a happy grey medium', a jacket, a hat and a pair of doeskin gloves. A 'shorter' dress (fitted to the ankle) made some difference, as did divided skirts which disguised knickerbockers underneath or skirts which could draw up with strings into knickerbockers. In an early attempt to corner the cycle-friendly clothing market, Hoares of

London began offering the Patent Rational Omnidress. It failed to catch on. 'With all due respect for rational clothing,' noted a reporter at one of the Society's meetings in 1887, 'the wide Turkish trousers, although they are of richest black satin, and the cutaway coat, although it be of softest velvet trimmed with laces and beads, could not be numbered with the "things of beauty".' Swiftsure, columnist for the *Clarion*, thought the whole idea a joke. 'It requires no small amount of resolution to ride out in knickers,' he wrote, 'but I feel sure that in time the custom will be almost universal.'

Inevitably, the opponents of rational dress turned to religion to strengthen their cause. In 1893 in Binghampton, New York, a Methodist widow who bought a bicycle was denounced from the pulpit as unladylike, unchristian and a disgrace to the Church, and a year later *Cycling* magazine began its attack on rational dress by quoting from the Bible: 'The woman shall not wear that which pertaineth unto a man, neither shall a man put on a woman's garment, for all that do so are abomination unto the Lord thy God' (Deuteronomy 22: 5). In Palm Beach, Florida, a female cyclist in rational dress was threatened by a pistol-wielding man who declared that no modest woman would appear in such clothing, though he was later forced to retract and apologise. 'There is no use,' said the *Chicago Tribune*, 'in waiting for the Coming Woman. She has already come.'

Unfortunately, not everyone had got the message. In 1899 the Rational champion Lady Harberton marched into the lounge of the Hautboy Hotel in Ockham, Surrey, after a hard ride and ordered a drink. Since she was wearing bloomers, the landlady, Mrs Marta Sprague, refused to serve her in the lounge area and showed her into the bar. Sprague had previously complained about women nearby cycling in tights. Harberton examined the bar. Since there were already several men drinking there, and since for a lady to be found drinking at a bar in the company of working men was akin to announcing you had gone on the game, she was forced to find refreshment elsewhere. Harberton subsequently sued. As the *New York Times* reported on 6 April, 'Lady Harberton, who is treasurer of the National [sic] Dress League, said on the witness stand that she had travelled four thousand miles in bloomers, including the West End of London.' Sprague, unrepentant, 'claimed her business would be ruined if she was obliged to serve some women attired in bloomers'. The jury found in favour of Sprague.

Even so, others were delighted at the prospect of change. Hoopdriver, the 'counter-jumper' hero of H. G. Wells' 1897 novel *The Wheels of Chance*, is out for a ride on his day off when he meets a young lady cycling along 'wearing a patent costume with button-up skirts, and mounted on a diamond-frame safety with Dunlops, and a loofah-covered saddle'. He is so awestruck by her that he falls off his Ordinary. 'Rational dress,' he discovers, 'didn't look a bit unwomanly … How fine she had looked, flushed with the exertion of riding, breathing a little fast, but elastic and active! Talk about your ladylike, homekeeping girls with complexions like cold veal!' Some years later, Rose Macaulay explained what it felt like when cycling really took hold. 'We're all doing it now,' she wrote in *Told by an*

Idiot. 'It's glorious; the nearest approach to wings permitted to man and woman here below. And it's transforming clothes. Short jackets and cloth caps are coming in. Bustles are no more. And my dear – *bloomers* are to be seen in the land! … We're all getting most thrillingly fin-de-siècle!'

Frances Willard was equally entranced by the bicycle's potential. A powerful campaigner in both the temperance and women's rights movements of the 1890s, she considered the bicycle crucial to both campaigns. Willard was American by birth but British by adoption. Though a late-comer to cycling, she was delighted by her new discovery – so delighted that she later wrote a book called *A Wheel Within a Wheel.* 'From the day when, at sixteen years of age, I was enwrapped in the long skirts that impeded every footstep, I have detested walking,' she announced. She had watched her younger nieces master the tricycle, and, 'Even as the war horse snuffeth the battle from afar, I longed to go and do likewise.' A couple of willing teachers, a large English castle and a bicycle she called Gladys provided the opportunity. It took her, she calculated, about three months to learn to ride, practising for fifteen minutes daily in order to master pedalling, turning, and – most difficult of all – mounting. Unsurprisingly, Willard was also an ardent supporter of the Rational Dress Movement. Sensible clothing for cyclists was, she considered, just a precursor of much more substantial changes. 'We saw that the physical development of humanity's mother-half would be wonderfully advanced by that universal introduction of the bicycle sure to come about within the next few years.' She herself did not wear bloomers, favouring instead a loose ensemble including, 'a skirt and blouse of tweed, with belt, rolling collar, and loose cravat, the skirt three inches from the ground; a round straw hat, and walking shoes with gaiters'.

But if recreational cycling for women gradually earned acceptance, racing did not. The UCI began admitting female riders from 1893 onwards, though women's races were often presented as a novelty interlude between music-hall or freak-show acts. Thus the brief boom in women's track racing during the mid 1890s petered out quickly – not because of low audience figures or too few competitors, but because it was not tolerated by public opinion. When Tessie Reynolds cycled the return journey between London and Brighton in 1893 in eight and a half hours, she was criticised by *Cycling* magazine for causing 'real pain, not unmixed with disgust'. Fanny Erskine was, as usual, unequivocal: 'Women ought not to race, if they have the slightest regard for their own health; and if they do, it is a suicidal policy, which is bound to end in disaster.' Her alternative was the bicycle gymkhana. Participants were expected to get round a course filled with different challenges: picking up and putting down dummies, letter posting, riding while leading another bike, a musical ride, an egg and spoon race, a vegetable race. The gymkhana phase was short-lived, though it would be good to think that one day the Tour de France might include a vegetable stage.

Nor did things necessarily improve with time. Even in the late 1950s, the Dutch were still refusing to let women race in their World Championships. When the great British champion Beryl Burton went to see her doctor in 1954 when she was eighteen and had just started racing, he was 'aghast at my cycling. He told me to take it easy, and always walk up hills as he was sure the others would wait!' Burton continued racing while pregnant with her daughter, merely raising the handlebars a little 'to accommodate her'. She later attributed much of her success to a training regime devised by a rhubarb-growing farmer who was also a keen amateur racer. During the day, she would work on his farm, 'Carrying, lifting, bending, digging, all day long in all weathers until my back ached, my arms ached, my shoulders ached, my legs ached … Then at the end of the working day, most nights were spent out training … It was not only crops I was planting but the seed of my future success.' Her approach to diet and nutrition was as prosaic as her training. With diets and food fads one should 'Stay clear of them all,' she wrote. 'Eat what you want. Obviously you should not load your stomach in the hours before a race, but if you fancy a large slab of cream-cake the day before, then go for it! … The way to get fit for cycling is on the bike. Miles – plenty of 'em!' As for doping, she took a similarly no-frills approach. 'If any so-called doctor ever suggested mucking about with my blood … he would feel my toe-end up his backside! … I have the personal satisfaction of knowing that my successes have been achieved by means of training, strength of will and solid, Yorkshire grub.'

Many years later in 1967, having won virtually every event worth winning, she was competing in the British Best All-Rounder twelve-hour event against Mike MacNamara, who was himself chasing the national record. As she recounts in her autobiography, *Personal Best*, the two pursued each other minute by minute and hour by hour. One by one, Burton passed all other competitors. Finally, eleven hours down, she glimpsed MacNamara on the road ahead of her. 'Goose pimples broke out all over me, and for some seconds I just stared at his heaving shoulders, the sweat-stained racing jersey … "I'll have to pass him," I thought. "Poor Mac, it doesn't seem fair" … Mac raised his head slightly and looked at me. Goodness knows what was going on in his mind, but I thought some gesture was required on my part. I was carrying a bag of Liquorice Allsorts in the pocket of my jersey and on impulse I groped into the bag and pulled one out. I can still remember that it was one of those swiss-roll shaped ones, white with a coating of black liquorice.

'"Liquorice Allsort, Mac?" I shouted, and held it towards him.

'He gave a wan smile. "Ta, love," he said, popping the sweet into his mouth.

'I put my head down and drew away.'

Burton became the only woman to beat the record, riding more than 277 miles in twelve hours, and holding it for a further two years. Her example, and the achievements of those who came after her – Jeannie Longo in France, and now Nicole Cook, Victoria Pendleton and the other British Olympic champions – proved inspirational not just to succeeding generations of female pro racers, but to all cyclists. Women-only road racing still gets nothing like the exposure that men's races do ('like watching paint dry,' say male pros dismissively), but with the increasing coverage of track, BMX and mountain biking events, women's events are beginning to get the same kind of attention that men have long taken for granted. Even so, there will probably never be parity between the two. Watch from a waypoint at an audax or a sportif, and probably about one in five of the competitors riding past will be female. Or try Richmond Park where London's cyclists come to spin circuits round the deer and the parakeets. There are girls, but in nothing like equal numbers. It seems that at present there are just more men who like racing bikes.

歬 歬 歬

SIX

The Worst Journey in the World

*'Not everything that counts can be counted,
and not everything that can be counted counts.'*

EINSTEIN

The feeling you have when you first get the hang of riding
a bicycle never really goes. It doesn't terribly matter how
you learned – with your parents shouting encourage-
ments out on the street, or by crashing your elder broth-
er's bike into the shrubbery, or privately, secretly,
somewhere where no one could see you fall. However
you learn, it always feels as if you've mastered the
universe. You're there, perfectly in control of your own
motion, sliding through the landscape faster than you've
ever gone before. Astride this perfectly balanced assembly of lines and curves, the world seems suddenly a place
of infinite potential. There's something about the rightness of bikes that your body always recognises whatever
age you are. It recognises something that your mind may
not: that bikes are really just about two things – simplicity and joy.

And so, in one of those splendid perversions of which human nature is so often capable, someone went and invented racing. Racing has absolutely nothing at all to do with simplicity or joy. Racing, according to its followers and practitioners, is mainly about suffering. Suffering and, if you're lucky, death, thereby leading to immortality. Racing is about heroism in the face of appalling odds. It's about man or woman locked in mortal combat with the laws of physics. It's about flinging down a challenge to the mountains and the earth, conquering gravity, transcending environment. It's about nanoseconds and geometry, conversion rates and lactic acid thresholds. It's about knowing how far you can flog your physique to the nearest decimal milli-point. It's about pain and humiliation, complexity and endurance, violence and self-punishment. If it's fun, you're doing it wrong.

The basic principles of racing have been established for at least a century or so. You take a bike. Then you break it down and rebuild it in a variety of lightweight materials so it's very light, very expensive and very unstable. Then you go out and find the most difficult roads in the world. You find places with cobbles, or 25 per cent gradients, or twenty-one hairpin bends – or, if you're really ingenious, cobbles, gradients *and* hairpin bends – and then you wait. You wait until the seasons turn and the rain or the sleet or the snow appears, or until it is so hot the asphalt melts beneath your tyres, or until you can't see the road at all for the mud in your eyes. Then, when everything's in place, you get on your very light bike and you ride. You ride until you're so cold you have to piss on your fingers to feel the brake levers. You spend your life climbing vertically up a north-east wind or a Flanders field or an Alpine moon-scape. If you're lucky and turn pro, you do so as a domestique (the literal translation of which, according to one French dictionary, is 'household waste'), shielding your team's star riders against 80mph winds or violent rivals, then moving aside just as the finish line comes into view. You fall off. You break or bruise or snap or graze or fracture. You leave important bits of yourself scattered over the tarmac of Europe. You arrive at the finish line late and unnoticed, trailing blood-soaked gauze. You live like a monk and dope like a fiend. You tinker with the things that make you male or stuff yourself with more steroids than a village fête vegetable. You pretend you're living at 30,000ft or inject the hormones produced by pregnant women. You eat things with ingredients listed as numbers, not words. You take things that make you feel invincible or things that make you feel nothing at all. You submit to the indignities of the doping control officers who arrive demanding samples in the middle of the night, while your wife is in labour, or at your own child's funeral. You get used to the fact that the media and thus the public assume that if you didn't win you're rubbish, and if you did you're drugged. Even without additives, you pay a heavy physical price for your profession. Drilling your spine into your socks while doing 50kph on icy Flemish cobbles is an excellent recipe for gastro-enteritis. If you make it to the line, in other words, you might well do so smeared in your own shit. You starve yourself. And then, having made it through unscathed to the point of retirement, you have so profoundly altered your own metabolism that you switch from supermodel to sumo in half a season. You spend your working life in eye-popping Lycra, performing as a human sandwich board for German milk processors or French agricultural tubing. When you're not actually racing, you're recovering, training or travelling. Your behaviour and form are scrutinised and critiqued on a million fansites and geekblogs by the kind of people who would probably have trouble keeping up with you in a car. Truly, pro racing is the day job of masochists.

At the root of it all is the never-ending quest to find the world's best and fastest bicycle rider. That quest gets played out almost every day of every year all over the world. But most particularly, it gets played out in Europe. Because one of the crucial things to understand about bicycle racing is that it is European – European to the bone. It isn't British, and despite being effectively possessed by a Texan for seven years, it isn't American either. There are several good reasons for this continental bias. Europeans invented bicycles, so Europeans got a head start in racing them. Europe has the perfect climate and the perfect conditions; generally temperate, full of highs and not-too-lows, well stocked with good-quality asphalted roads. And Europe has the ideal geography. Which is not to say that there is no culture of racing in Colombia or New Zealand or South Africa, or that there are no great races in other parts of the world. But, vital though they are, races elsewhere are sideshows and dress rehearsals. They provide warm-ups, indications of form for the coming season, chances to test out the politics of a team. They tend to place themselves very early or very late in the year, partly because in somewhere like Qatar or Australia it makes more sense climatically, but also to avoid coinciding with any of the main events.

And the main events all, without exception, take place in the heart of the Old World – France, Spain, Belgium, Holland, Italy or Germany. All of these countries have venerable racing histories and a passionate audience. It's sometimes difficult for a Briton, raised on the concept that bicycles are a mild and marginal part of the sporting scene, to understand the centrality of racing to audiences in Europe. The best way to express it is probably in audience figures. In its homeland, the 2009 Tour de France gathered an average of 4.2 million viewers every day – the penultimate stage on Mont Ventoux was watched by 5.2 million people on TV. France has almost exactly the same size population as Britain, but even when the Tour came to London for the day in 2007, the most we managed was half a million. In 2007, when the Danish rider Michael Rasmussen won the eighth stage of the Tour de France, four-fifths of his countrymen watched him do so. In Belgium and Holland, there may be ten or fifteen races a day during the summer months, most of them broadcast on national TV. In other words, cycling has the same level of popularity in most European countries as football has here.

Sitting on the sofa and yelling at the TV might give one indication of a sport's following, but actually turning up to watch a race is different. The Tour de France has always been scheduled to run in July, when the whole of France is on holiday and therefore in theory has plenty of opportunities to turn up and pour beer and spittle all over their favourite riders. But watching a race in person is not like watching football. It can be a curiously unsatisfying process: you turn up, you stand around and then a lot of very fast cyclists pass you at speed. That's it. Unless you want to pursue them by car down the road in order to watch them do exactly the same thing again, it's probably better to wait for the edited highlights at home. The difference with cycling, and the reason for the huge audience figures, is that anyone can do it. Watching a group of riders flash past you in the rain feels very different if you yourself came whirling down that selfsame road in a bunch sprint just two days earlier. You know exactly how those cobbles feel or how steep that incline is or how cruelly the wind hits on the bends. And, as the organisers of bike races have realised, many cyclists are prepared to go a whole lot further – in every sense – than ordinary tourists. Other sporting fans might turn up for a weekend, watch a game, have a fight and disappear back home again, but cyclists want to be involved. Fans of football don't get to turn up at the Santiago Bernabéu the day before a vital Real Madrid game for a thousand-strong kickabout, and nobody suggests co-opting Murrayfield for a dry run of the Six Nations. But 30,000 assorted Europeans can and do ride part of the route of the Tour of Flanders the day before the real race, and 8,500 compete every year for a place on the Étape, a day-long race for amateurs through a mountain stage of the Tour de France held just before the real race passes through.

When the Étape was established in 1993, participant numbers were set at around 8,500. About a quarter of those are always tourists, and in the past few years an average of about 1,500 of them have been British. The Étapes have now achieved a kind of cult standing among riders. Anyone can enter, but to stand a chance of finishing the course you have to do the preparation beforehand. You need exactly the right equipment and back-up, and you should be prepared for a monumentally uncomfortable day.

Kate Gallafent is a London-based barrister who has ridden two Étapes and knows exactly what they're like. 'The organisers close the road for you, so it's exactly as the Tour itself would be. You start at 7 a.m. and you have a broom wagon that sweeps up behind you all day [the van which picks up straggling riders or those who have abandoned a race], and you have a certain minimum speed that you have to maintain. I think it's based on double the peloton time for the professional riders, so you have to do a minimum 19kph. I know that sounds really slow, but this is incredibly steep – 3,000m climbs and things like that. And it's over 190km so you start at 7 a.m. and you basically just pedal all day – twelve hours on a bike, or thereabouts.'

Entrants' focus on the race is so total that a certain ruthlessness develops. 'The first year I did it, I came down a climb and someone had fallen off really badly at the bottom and there was blood everywhere – this man had obviously really seriously injured his head – and you just carry on cycling past. Everyone just cycles on past. It is an extraordinary event for that. And because you're racing with 8,500 other riders, you're so close, people get jostled in the pack, it can be quite scary. And the sheer exhaustion of it – the last year I did it, it finished with Alpe d'Huez, a famous climb, twenty-four hairpin bends. I think Lance Armstrong did it in forty minutes. I did it in two hours and felt extremely proud of myself. But I went up it in 40° heat, and it was unbelievable. The guttering by the side of the road was just full of men lying there trying to cool down. People suffering the most terrible heat exhaustion, people having collapsed – you'd literally be riding behind someone and watch them wobble and fall to the side of the road. It was extraordinary – it was like a death march.'

So does she think that Étapes attract a certain type of cyclist? 'Definitely. Men. Out of 8,500 people, there are two hundred women every year, roughly. Which tells you a lot about the nature of those who want to do it. I think it attracts a lot of overachieving professionals – lots of bankers, lots of lawyers, lots of people who think they need to compress their leisure time into achievement. They like to be able to say, I've done this and I've done that, and the Étape is very good for that. It's not like running a marathon where you don't need any kit apart from shoes. With an Étape you can have enormously lengthy conversations about your bicycle, your shoes, your cleats, whether you should have a certain alloy or a certain double-butted or treble-butted frame – the most minute detail of your bike's set-up is of interest to other people, and frankly of almost no interest to me whatsoever. And you can spend a huge amount of money, that's the other advantage.'

Not just on the bike, either. A racer's Mecca like Alpe d'Huez is considered such a trophy that an average of a thousand cyclo-tourists climb the hill every day during the summer season. And however cheaply they fly or drive or eat, they'll still need the occasional roadside espresso or spare inner tube. They'll still need to refuel or camp or get from here to there. They'll still celebrate or commiserate in local bars, pay for entry and persuade themselves into a souvenir capo. It's all money coming into the local economy and it's still an excellent reason for the organisers to keep holding races, year after year. That, and the fact that they've been holding them for years anyway. The infrastructure is there, the police are primed, the public expectant and the races just a short bus ride away. While Britain struggles to get beyond the basics – irate motorists and hostile Health & Safety – Europe somehow manages to organise, administer and marshal several different road races almost every single day of the year.

Aside from World Championships, there are two main cornerstones of the racing calendar. The Spring Classics are day races held in Western Europe during March and April often on partly cobbled roads. And then in midsummer there are the Grand Tours, the main three-week stage races: the Giro (Tour of Italy), the Vuelta (Tour of Spain) and the Tour de France. Each of those races has a distinct and particular character of its own – a reputation for being unusually gruelling, or for being a real purists' race, or for being ideal for sprinters. But behind all of them, even (you could say) the Northern European Classics, lurks the shadow of one man, a Frenchman who put his stamp so indelibly on racing that it still bears his initials even now.

Henri Desgrange was born in 1865, and after a successful career as an amateur cyclist took up first the law and then a post as editor of the new daily sports paper, *L'Auto*. It was a surprising appointment – Desgrange's sole qualifications for the job were an ability to ride a bicycle and the fact that, in the eyes of the proprietor Adolphe Clément, he was on the right side in the controversial Dreyfus case. It rapidly became evident that Desgrange knew little about the print media. Faced with plummeting circulation, a vigorous rival and nothing with which to fill the paper, in January 1903 Desgrange called an emergency editorial meeting at which a junior reporter called Géo Lefèvre diffidently suggested the idea of a six-day bicycle race around

Henri Desgrange.

France. Initially, Desgrange was not convinced by the idea and it was only once the paper's backers had given their enthusiastic support that he consented. The initial terms he set for the race were so harsh that only fifteen riders entered. Having then amended them to include a daily living allowance for each rider and 20,000 francs in prize money, Desgrange left all the organisation and practicalities to Lefèvre, failing even to come to the original start. The first race was deemed an unequivocal success, with thousands of paying spectators at the race finish and rocketing circulation for *L'Auto*. Desgrange took most of the credit for himself.

The Tour had caught the public imagination – and to an alarming extent. The following year's race was marred by so many instances of violence, cheating and skullduggery that it very nearly killed off both itself and half the racers there and then. As the race passed through the different *départements* of France, spectators showed their support for local riders by assaulting their opponents with cudgels and sticks as they rode, firing revolvers at each other, or strewing tacks all over the roads to ensure that half the peloton punctured. Nor were the riders themselves above corruption. Some simplified things enormously by taking the train between stages. A couple of riders took a tow from one of the race cars by attaching a wire to the back of the car and placing the cork at the other end between their teeth. Others brawled with spectators, bribed the organisers to give them illegal feeds or disputed the final results. Some were reputed to be armed; after a fight between spectators and riders at St Étienne, Géo Lefèvre stepped in brandishing his own smoking revolver. Desgrange threatened to cancel the 1905 race but then relented, knowing perfectly well that nothing would improve his audience figures like a week-long rolling riot.

Over the next few years, the organisation and logistics of the race changed repeatedly. Individual stages were shortened, but the overall length of the race was increased. Night rides were eliminated (thus making it more difficult to catch trains), mountain stages were introduced, as were brief excursions across the border into France's neighbouring countries. The broom wagon was introduced. 'We have already explained that the new itinerary will be harder and longer than before,' said Desgrange in 1905, 'in order to create new obstacles and allow the riders the chance to banish new difficulties.' In 1910, the race claimed its first fatality, though not in particularly legendary fashion; a rider called Adolphe Hélière died after being stung by a jellyfish during the rest day. Sabotage continued to be a problem – in 1913, a bed of nails forced twenty-nine riders to abandon, and many others grew so wary that they locked both themselves and their cycles into their hotel rooms at night.

The Tour began the slow process of accumulating its own legend, helped along with enthusiasm by Desgrange. When, in 1910, the ride to the top of the Aubisque in driving snow proved so unpleasant that the first rider to get to the top was incapable of speech and the second, appearing out of the snow on foot using his bike as support, merely hissed '*Assassins!*' at the stupefied organisers, Desgrange recognised a myth in the making. The following year, he announced, he was going to introduce lots more mountain stages. And make the stages longer; ideally, things should be made so difficult that only one rider could possibly finish. By the time the First World War broke out, the Tour was up to 5,000km. By giving them more and more miles and less and less help, Desgrange was breeding his own race of superheroes.

The geographical rules of the race remain roughly the same even now. The mystifying trajectory of the race – clockwise then anti-clockwise, one minute up and the next minute down, sometimes north-east but often south-west – is based partly on the requirement for drama and variety, but also on the demands of individual stage towns. For a town to be included as a start or finish point, they must apply to the Tour organisers (now the Amaury Sport Organisation, or ASO) for inclusion. On payment of a hefty lump sum, their application proceeds very, very slowly through the annual lists. When the requisite number of years (or decades) has passed and the money has been spent, the organisers do a long chin-stroking reconnaissance. A year after that, the Tour passes through; there for an evening, gone the next day. Though the price is high, the kickback in tourism is worth it. It's not just the teams that have to be fed and watered. It's the flocks of followers, the caravan and the media, too. And the afterglow lingers for months after the peloton has passed on, banners still waving above shops, posters still nailed to the plane trees. That glow – and the money it brings in – is a lure strong enough to attract towns far beyond the French border. At some point during the Tour's one-hundred-year history, it has passed through parts of the world which stretch the definition of 'de France' to its extremities: Amsterdam, London, Barcelona, Brighton, Geneva, Rotterdam, Plymouth, Stuttgart, Turin, Zurich.

Meanwhile, the riders were responding to Desgrange's slow clean-up and streamlining of the race with appropriate élan. He had decreed that all riders must start and finish on the same bike, and were responsible for all their own maintenance throughout the race. Riders therefore had to carry spares with them, and, since all tyres were then tubular, if they punctured riders had to sit by the roadside and sew their own repairs – often onto a wooden wheel rim. Because of the ban on receiving any help, when Eugène Christophe's bike cracked under him at the top of the Col du Tourmalet during the 1913 race, he ran 14km down the hill with it, found a local blacksmith, spent three hours repairing the frame, got back on, climbed two further Alps and arrived at the stage finish at midnight. Since a small child had pumped the bellows of the forge, Christophe was deemed to have accepted help and was accordingly docked three minutes.

For the first three years, riders used only fixed-gear bikes (one gear, no freewheel), which made both climbing and descending the mountains exceptionally difficult. Desgrange liked this; there was something satisfactorily minimal about these sparse men on their sparse bikes. The Tour de France, he felt, should be all about purity of soul and honour (if not of body), and messy, complicated things like gears only got in the way of that. Riders were permitted to change gears only by dismounting and swapping the chain over from one sprocket to another – one for the mountains and one for the plains. Derailleurs were banned. 'I still feel,' Desgrange said, 'that variable gears are only for people over forty-five.' It wasn't until he finally retired in 1937, handing over control of the race to Jacques Goddet, that gears were officially permitted in the Tour. In fact, Desgrange disapproved of almost any innovation which made a bike lighter, faster or more comfortable to ride. Part of his early dislike of framemakers sponsoring the race was because they competed with each other to introduce improvements. Like Lance Armstrong a century later, Desgrange felt that the Tour was 'not about the bike', so much so that in the 1908 race he did away with all variation and simply issued his own.

But the obsessive focus on heroism was coupled with an equally pragmatic alliance with commercialism. It was Desgrange who put the race leader in yellow (the same colour as *L'Auto*), introduced the publicity caravan and upped the prize money to the point where working-class riders would hazard almost anything – health, sanity, life – in pursuit of that prize. Many of the riders in the early days were farm labourers, chimney sweeps, butchers and dockers who simply wanted to change their fortunes, and were desperate enough to ride almost an eighth of the way around the world in the attempt.

In the early years, riders raced as individuals, then as national teams, and finally as teams sponsored by companies. Business sponsorship seemed the ideal solution; in theory, it meant fewer internal disputes between riders and it meant local councils no longer had to fork out for maintaining a team. In practice, it means that bicycle racing is and always has been the most commercial sport in the world; without the combination of TV money and corporate support it would virtually cease to exist. The relationship is symbiotic – the Tour still sends *L'Auto*'s descendant *L'Equipe*'s circulation through the roof every July. That strange alliance between commercialism and courage still informs the Tour and most other major bike races today. In Desgrange's absence the caravan has flourished, along with the sponsors and the media.

The curious result of this is that the Tour now feels less like the ultimate expression of skill on a bicycle than a vast national celebration of the internal combustion engine. Appropriately enough for a race started by *L'Auto* magazine, it now takes three weeks for 2,400 vehicles and 14,000 gendarmes to get 170 of the world's best bicycle riders the 3,445km between Monaco and Paris. During the 2009 Tour, 4,500 full-time assorted team personnel, organisers, media, sponsorship partners, advertisers, technical staff and mechanics followed those riders up the Alps and down the Pyrenees in buses and coaches and custom-built mobile homes. The caravan alone – the blaring parade of customised cars and vans which precedes the arrival of the riders – has around 160 vehicles; somewhere in France, twenty-three people spend a significant proportion of their working lives making polystyrene figurines of soda bottles or giant sweets or blow-up kangaroos which will bounce their way across the country for most of July. And following the Tour are all the thousands upon thousands of fans who have travelled from near or far to cheer on

Framebuilder Dave Yates working on a bespoke order at his workshop in Lincolnshire.

Dave Yates with the newly brazed lug joining the head tube to the down tube.

The completed frame in Richmond Park, fitted up and ready to fly.

[left] Alex Brown, head of the Scottish Vintage Cycle Club, with some of his historic bikes now on display at Drumlanrig in the Scottish Borders.

[opposite bottom] Jan Rijkeboer, founder and head of Azor bicycle factory in the Netherlands.

[below] Station bike park in the Netherlands.

[above] A cargo trishaw under the Howrah Bridge in Calcutta.

[opposite top] One of Calcutta's hand-pulled rickshaws. The West Bengal government's attempts to outlaw the rickshaws have so far had only limited success.

[right] Noor Hussein and his rented tricycle rickshaw – one of India's most stylish transport experiences.

Vinod Punmiya, the man who raced the Deccan Queen.

Standard-issue Indian roadster. Now considered the cheapest and most unsatisfactory of options, the old roadsters were almost all single-speed and designed to last several lifetimes.

Riders on the Ronde van Vlaanderen (or Tour of
Flanders) sportive cleaning their bikes after the finish.

Sportive rider after the Ronde van Vlaanderen.

[opposite] The 2009 Tour of Flanders along one of the cobbled sections of the course.

[below] Traditionally the last few kilometres of the Tour de France involve a seven-lap circuit around the Champs-Élysée in Paris.

See no evil, speak no evil… Andy Schleck, Alberto Contador and Lance Armstrong on the podium at the end of the 2009 Tour de France.

Charly Wegelius at the end of his sixth Tour de France.

Graeme Obree. 'I was sacked from racing.
It just took me twelve years to realise it.'

Eva Ballin and Jim Young
at work in Edinburgh.

Cyclo-cross near Glentress in the Scottish Borders.

The Athertons: Dan, Rachel and Gee.
Reigning champions of the mountain biking world.

Pulling stunts on track bikes at a bike show.

Danny MacAskill, YouTube phenomenon.

Nik Ford: 'so enthusiastic about something that killed him'.

Love and Souplesse.

their favourites, wave flags, paint slogans or pick up the goodies hurled from the caravan – the majority of whom, of course, will have got there by car.

The only thing which has changed quite markedly is the backgrounds of the riders. Racing no longer draws so many working-class men hoping to win the physical lottery; riders now come from all over the world and from every sector of society. They all share a desire to race and, when young, the capacity to buy a one-way ticket to France or Belgium or Italy or Spain. Once there, they serve a standard apprenticeship testing themselves on the amateur circuits, racing against similar amateurs from Luxembourg or Poland, Scotland or Portugal. If they've got a knack for it, by the time they've reached twenty-one they'll probably have more European languages than Strasbourg under their belt. Most of the races the young riders enter are small amateur events, criteriums or kermesses often planned to coincide with local town festivals. Criteriums are usually a kilometre or a kilometre-and-a-half lap around a town centre, repeated eighty to ninety times. A kermesse is twelve times round an eight- or nine-kilometre circuit. During each town's festival week, there will be endless individual kermesses – for women, for juniors, for amateurs in different categories. And since there is money, and since, in some corner of Belgium, there's always a kermesse going on, the races also function as an excellent way of staying on form. Racing, in other words, is the best possible way of training for racing. For amateurs, the small races perform several useful functions. Firstly, they give them a place to test themselves against their international peers and find out where they stand in the pecking order. They sort the good from the bad, the physically sturdy from the emotionally uncommitted. They allow the managers of both pro and amateur teams to find and isolate emerging talent. And they effectively pay the wages of anyone wanting to make it as a racer.

Amateurs can spend most of the summer travelling from kermesse to criterium day after day, earning bread and butter prize money as they go. The sums won't be huge, but since there will usually be prizes for all placed riders in each of the different categories, it's a good incentive to turn up. In many cases, a certain amount of 'result engineering' is rumoured to take place, with towns or sponsors paying handsomely to ensure that their boys or girls come in ahead of the pack. Which doesn't necessarily mean that the whole thing is fixed; riders have still got to be good enough to get themselves to the front of the pack.

And, unusually, there is no short-circuiting the system. There are certainly riders who are sufficiently gifted and disciplined to rise to the top faster than others, but all of them must have done their time in the training camps. They must have taken their place at the back of the peloton and pedalled their way through races where their only function was to provide a windbreak for the pack leader. They must have worked out whether they have the desire and intelligence to read the unwritten rules of each race, and have understood exactly when it's acceptable to shaft a team-mate and when it is not. They must have impressed the right people in the right places at the right times and they must have demonstrated at least a little bit of what it takes to hit the big time. And they have to have the physique for it. Meeting pro riders in the flesh can sometimes be a strange reversal of those moments when you see someone famous on the street and think, 'But they're so much smaller than on TV.' Pro riders are often twice as tall and twice as skinny in real life. The grimpeurs (climbers) of the mountainous stage races like the Tour de France are no more than long thin gristly strings of muscle and bone topped off with a pair of faraway eyes and a tarmac tan. The sprinters – those who, like Mark Cavendish, win stages but not Tours – are bigger, more solid and muscular, primed for great explosive bursts of energy a few yards from the finish line. And those who excel in the flatlands of Belgium or the Netherlands, the rouleurs and baroudeurs, can manage both endurance and exceptional acceleration, albeit over shorter periods.

Tim Harris is an ex-pro rider who now sells furniture all over the Continent. When he retired, he settled in Belgium with his girlfriend Jos Ryan but kept his links with racing. They soon found that young British riders were turning up on their doorstep asking for bed and board, so they now run three separate houses in different parts of the Belgian countryside where young riders can stay. The houses have the same feel as student accommodation always does. Young riders come and go, make themselves coffee, squabble mildly about the biscuits, get themselves ready for a training session. Three people from the New Zealand national squad, over in Belgium on a reconnaissance mission, have been camping in the front room and emerge blinking, looking for laptop connections and a lift to the airport. On a sideboard, a row of trophies is framed by a bright plasticky backdrop of artificial flowers. 'Bradley Wiggins', says a lavish arrangement of roses and foliage. 'Mark Cavendish', reads the label on a bunch of granny-pink Michaelmas daisies. Cavendish was one of those who passed through here on his way to fame and a pro contract. 'If you're young and British and you want to race, you still come to Belgium,' says Tim. 'You haven't got much choice. There's only really two ways – you're either very, very good and you get picked up by British Cycling and they send you to Italy on their fast-track system. What we do is to pick up all the kids who are not quite good enough to be on that scheme, so they come to Belgium.'

His star pupil at the moment is Adam Blythe, winner of two golds at the European Track Championships, Olympic hopeful and recent signatory to a Belgian pro team. For a while, Adam and his girlfriend Lizzie Armitstead – a member of Britain's Olympic cycling team and one of the winning pursuiters in the 2009 track world championships – stayed with Tim and Jos, training and racing with a local amateur team. The regime here is less highly pressured than British Cycling's academy. For most riders, this is their first time away from home, so the experience is just as much about dealing with homesickness and washing their own kit as it is about getting a contract. As Tim says, 'The average rider who turns up – very, very few are really going to make it, to be honest, even though they're full-time cyclists. A lot of them come over here, try it out, and if it doesn't work out, by the age of twenty-one, twenty-two they have to go back home again. You either get to a standard where someone's going to pay you to race, or you have to stop – there's not a lot in between.'

The Tour of Flanders (or Ronde van Vlaanderen) is the summit of the Belgian racing year. It is run over a cold weekend in early April with a sportive over a section of the course on the Saturday and the real thing on the Sunday. In theory, anyone can enter the sportive. You have a start time and a finish time, and the fastest rider round the course is the winner. But the point of riding a sportive is as much a test of your own personal speed and fitness as it is a chance to spend a day stuffing mud up your orifices just like the pros. Thirty thousand people entered the 2009 sportive; thousands more lined the race route on the Sunday. As Tim says, 'The only way you could describe it is like Wimbledon, the FA Cup and the Grand National all on the same day.' For sheer numbers alone, the Ronde van Vlaanderen is extraordinary. Even in wet or frozen years the whole of Flanders turns out for it, and on a sunny day it feels like most of Belgium is on the road. Not that good weather is necessarily a bonus. For the purist, things only get really exciting when conditions are foul. Riding into a brick-wall headwind on soaking cobbles requires a degree of skill and tenacity which usually wipes out a good percentage of the field – only the real experts have a chance of completing the race.

At the race start in Bruges, thousands are already lining the route long before the riders sign on. Team buses roll into the market square and the usual ruthless hierarchy develops: Quickstep (Belgian team, lots of stars) is instantly surrounded; Barloworld's remains deserted. It's here, if anywhere, that you can really smell the money involved in cycling. The Katusha bus appears a little behind the others, a mighty thing with darkened windows and the magnificently sinister inscription *Russian Global Cycling Project* down its side. Only the Russians could make bicycle racing sound like a front for world domination. As if on cue, ex-pro team manager Andrei Tchmil steps out, immaculately suave, the spitting image of Daniel Craig. 'Our future,' he declares on the Katusha website, 'will be in great victories which will bring glory to our native land. The economic crisis storms in the world, it will not be reflected onto Katusha.'

That's a bonus, since keeping this lot on the road in such style must be villainously expensive. Leaving aside the costs of staff, race entries, tour buses, kit, food, specialist medical equipment, IT, media and communications equipment, the bikes alone make for some fairly spectacular mathematics. Perry, a mechanic for Columbia, had explained earlier that every rider in a pro team would expect to have a minimum of three bikes per race. The best riders will have five or six, each of which will be custom-made for the individual physique of the rider and the different types of terrain; mountains, flat stage, time trial etc. The bikes must conform to certain criteria imposed by the UCI – none can weigh less than 6.8kg, disc wheels should only be used for time trials and, following Graeme Obree's controversial modifications to his track bike, there must be no funny business with handlebar positions. But within those restrictions, each team is perfectly at liberty to spend as much money as it likes. All the bikes strapped to the tops of the team cars are built of carbon fibre – light, but rigid. 'After the Classics season from March until the end of April,' says Perry, 'all the races like Paris–Roubaix, Tour of Flanders, Amstel Gold, the bike is totally destroyed. I mean, you could use it, I could use it, but it's not for professional use any more. They've lost all their stiffness, the paint has gone, there have been crashes. You do the races on them and … that's it. Also the paint starts to chip. Look at this one.' He points to a bike with a small chip out of the Columbia logo. 'The sponsor doesn't want that. They send them back to the factory, they repaint them and they give them to the junior teams or whatever – they don't want them used. There is a waste of bikes. We have one of the biggest budgets in the peloton, and we use like between three hundred and four hundred framesets a year, because we change frames every three or four months.'

Anyway, what with the bikes and the bespoke team buses, suddenly the square in Bruges starts to look less like a sport and more like an industry. The Serious Men have arrived. They walk between the buses with their hands behind their back, pacing like Prince Charles as they scowl over groupsets or talk in low, urgent voices about yesterday's results. Sometimes there are two or even three generations, fathers using their toddlers as cover for their own shamefaced urges to own a Cervélo pen or pose by an Astana bike. Each holds a compact digital camera and uses it either to take pictures of vital details – a bidon (water bottle), a brake system, the retreating backside of a Garmin rider – or to pose, too cool to smile, beside their favoured bet.

Before the race, the men outnumber the women by a factor of four to one. But out on the road, along the race route, the demographic changes. Here, it's babies and housewives, families and workers. Ten-year-old girls in full team Lycra stand beside grannies in windproof gabardine, and half a primary school sits in a hay trailer, waiting respectfully for the race to appear. The bits that people really want to see are the hilly sections along ancient, high-sided narrow lanes full of blind corners and unexpected shocks. Near one infamously tricky cobbled section of the race, a whole motorway has stopped, parked up and scrambled through the muddy fields to watch. The lane is a deep old canyon with a grassy bank on one side and steep scrubby undergrowth on the other. Half an hour before the riders arrive, a single woman in late middle age is sitting on the edge of a bath currently in use as a cattle trough. Five minutes later, a family arrives – a girl and a boy of about eight and ten, parents in respectable city coats and shoes. A few minutes after them, another family appears. The children are younger and the parents play games running down the bank with them. A man walks up the lane, handing out flags to the gathering audience.

If this were the Tour de France, the flags would be branded – the name of a sponsor or a marketing partner. Here, every single one of the flags just shows the Black Lion of Flanders. It is everywhere. It is there in miniature being fluttered by children, it is there as a cloak draped around shoulders or used as an impromptu travel rug. It is on the side of a couple of the team buses, on the newspapers reporting the race, on the side of houses, on cars, on products, on people. Today is just as much about national pride as it is about cycling; in this place, the two have become indivisible. It is a reminder that somewhere below every bike race, buried under a surprisingly shallow layer of brand values and high-tech componentry, is a very great deal of history. Somewhere beneath these roads are two thousand years of religious dissent, the scars of two world wars and half an eternity of international rivalry. And for a century or more, bike races have been both a method of expressing that history and an attempt to escape it. The Ronde van Vlaanderen was originally established in 1913 as an explicit attempt to restore Flemish pride and self-respect after generations of oppression by the French-speaking Walloons to the south. Its fellow classic, Paris–Roubaix, the second half of which was nicknamed l'Enfer du Nord (the Hell of the North) not as a catchy macho title for a bike race on cobbled roads, but because the post-war organisers could find no more appropriate name for the butchered fields of Flanders. Even Eddy Merckx, still considered by many to be the greatest racer of all time, was drawn in. He was born in Meenzel Kiezegem in Flanders but moved to Woluwe-Saint-Pierre near Brussels (a French-speaking enclave within the generally Flemish north) just after his first birthday, and grew up bilingual. When he started winning big, Merckx was claimed as a national hero by both the Walloons and the Flemings. He resisted siding with either, but when he married in 1967 the service was conducted in French, a choice which sparked national debate.

Meanwhile, the field below is beginning to fill up. Groups of people start appearing through the undergrowth, children swinging excitedly from the saplings, parents readying their cameras. A couple of spectators who had been sitting down sharing a thermos of coffee stand up and drape their flags along the top of the fence. Very faintly, the TV helicopter becomes audible in the distance. A couple of organisers' cars race up the narrow lane, their tyres ripping along the cobbles. Here, there is no caravan, only the slow build-up of expectation. The helicopter moves nearer, obscuring the disparate voices of the audience. More cars, then motorbikes, a couple of neutral service vehicles. The people on this side of the bank can just about see the riders now. They're three or four fields away, snaking their way through the lanes. At this distance, no one appears as an individual but as part of a multicoloured mass continually moving and reshaping itself, their progress marked as much by the raised and fluttering flags as by the slightly surreal shape of the team cars, each with a dozen or more spare bikes strapped to their roof, wobbling emptily over the paving.

The noise gets louder, the chatter increases and before anyone has really worked out what's happening, the leaders have been and gone. People yell out the names of their favourites, of people they recognise, of past heroes. The peloton appears, flashing across the fields as bright in their colours as advertising. In an unlikely burst of sprightliness, some of the men start running after them, shouting encouragement or insults. The riders keep going, pushing their way up the road and vanishing round the bend. Behind them, the luckless stragglers get the worst of it: a crowd of excited spectators, all yelling and shouting, some of them running behind and shoving. The audience pause for a moment or two and then begin to walk back over the early April fields to reclaim their cars. Within minutes, all that's left in the lane is a couple of abandoned flags and a single word painted onto the cobblestones and repeated three times with feeling: BIER.

Beer is essential to this race. Outside the tent at the sportive, a man is offloading a vanful of fresh kegs ready for this afternoon. The Belgians can be exceptionally fussy about their beer, he says. It's no good offering them something blonde; it has to be heavy, and it should preferably be made by Trappist monks. In the next few hours, the main beer tent here will get through 14,000 litres, drunk by all those people who have sustained themselves round the route by thinking of the golden liquid to be found at the end of it. Beer, nationalism and bicycles – inseparable. In fact, the only people not drinking beer are those it's meant to celebrate – the riders and staff themselves. By the time most of Flanders has settled down to the serious business of getting drunk, the teams are over the border and away. To the next race, to the next assignation, to the next date in a perpetual and unceasing calendar.

To maintain this extraordinary rolling circus takes a truly awesome level of back-up. Whether they've been around for many years or only received UCI pro-tour accreditation a few months ago, each team must be prepared to hold together a staff of between eighty and a hundred individuals, including managers (or DSs – directeurs sportifs), physios, soigneurs, doctors, nutritionists, mechanics, drivers and psychologists. Potentially, it's an

ever-expanding group. Several teams now include quali-
fied doctors and psychotherapists, and almost all now
separate out the roles of physio from soigneur. Of all those
roles, it is the soigneurs who have been around for longest.
In the past, they blended the roles of doctor, driver, valet
and masseur. They still sort out the cars, prepare the
musettes (the feed bags thrust into the outstretched hands
of the riders at intervals during the race), make up the
water bottles, sort things out at the hotel, prepare the
rooms and the massage tables, do the laundry and drive
the riders to and from airports if so required. Half the
soigneurs on a team will cover the race, and half will
remain back at the hotel.

Most of the team staff themselves either have some
family connection to racing or they were once pros or
amateurs themselves. Toby Watson is an Australian physio
for Garmin-Slipstream who doubles as a soigneur when
numbers are low. He's open and welcoming with none of
the air of separateness that team staff can occasionally
project – perhaps because he doesn't come from a cycling
background himself. 'Never ridden a road bike in my life,'
he says cheerfully. Before he came here, he worked as a
physio for the Australian track and field team. When the
team director Matt White asked him to join Garmin, Toby
thought, what the hell. He had no ties, no wife and nothing
to lose. 'It's not uncommon to start work at 7 a.m. and
finish work at 10, 11 p.m. depending on how far the transfers are. And, yes, on a three-week stage race, you're just
shagged by the end of it. You have a really great time, really
hyped up for the finish, and then when it's over you just

collapse – three-day coma. You have a really good time with your mates on the race at the time, and then you're just like ... No one wants to talk to anyone. It's never 100 per cent serenity all the time, people blow up, stuff goes wrong. Usually, the big races, we try and pick the people who are the coolest under pressure. It might be personality, it might be an experience thing, but whatever it is, we try and make sure it's that way. Because for the riders to perform their best they don't need loads of tension and stress within the staff itself, you want everyone to be pretty chilled out. So we try and keep it under control, but every now and then, something goes wrong.'

A team in a three-week stage race consists of, say, nine riders, most of whom will be there in a purely supportive role. They will not be expected to win a stage in their own right – though obviously it's great if they do – but to increase the chances of the star riders. They can help by leading a sprinter out (riding in front of them for long periods, thus sheltering them from the wind and allowing them to conserve their energy for the final few kilometres), by leading breakaways to help wear down the opposition, or by helping to push the star riders up the general classi-fication. The GC is the daily tally of the riders who have completed the course so far in the shortest amount of time. So, after a couple of weeks hurtling round the French countryside, a team's best-known rider may not have won any stages at all, but could still be top of the GC. And if they want to stay top of the GC, then they need a group of people around them who will take their turn at the front blocking the wind or pushing out new breakaways, or making sure they've got enough food and water to maintain a decent speed.

So which are the most difficult races? 'Notoriously, the Tour has the worst food and the worst hotels, and the Giro has the best food and the best hotels. French food is the worst, though all the teams now take their own chefs so at least you can take that out of the equation. But other than that, the Tour is so well organised it's not a hard race. They tell everyone exactly where they're meant to be and exactly how to get there, all the roads are cleared for hours beforehand, so it's not difficult. With other smaller races, you kind of have to make it up as you go along a little bit, and that's not as accurate. So usually the smaller races are harder to do logistically.' Collectively, he and the rest of the Garmin staff are responsible for between twenty-five and thirty-five riders, each of whom could be competing in one of three separate destinations. In the summer months when the racing season is at its height, there might be one group riding a stage race in Spain, another riding a criterium in Belgium and a women's team competing in Poland. Inevitably, team structure is tribal, just like cycling itself. 'Oh, yes. All the soigneurs hang out together, all the bus drivers hang out together and they all bitch and moan about all the other staff types. It's very funny. You get the mechanics all going, "Fucking soigneurs!" And then the soigneurs all going, "Fucking mechanics!" And then everyone complains about the bus drivers not helping out enough. It's just tradition – you can instantly tell who's who – we all live up to our stereotypes.'

In theory, the choices over who races what are made in winter before the race season starts by the management team. The aim is to have a group of riders at any of the important races who are best equipped to cope with the local conditions. Thus, for a three-week stage race with flat, mountain and time-trial sections, it's necessary to have a group which includes climbers, sprinters, rouleurs, domestiques and all-rounders.

In practice, nothing can be set in stone – riders fall, or fall ill, or it's impossible to get the right combination of people, or life (child's illness, crisis, team meltdown) intervenes. As everyone knows, riders have foibles, tantrums, enmities and friendships. They are human, in other words, and no matter how sensible it might be to send your best domestiques, your best lead-out men and your best sprinter all to the same race, if they can't stand the sight of each other, then you have a problem. And, since racing is a sport in which intelligence and foresight are at least as important as a good pair of legs, you also need riders who have the expertise to read a race right. Bicycle racing, it is said, is chess on wheels; it doesn't matter if you're the fastest man on earth, if you can't learn how to use the terrain, your team-mates and the weaknesses of your rivals to best advantage, then you will get beaten. Similarly, real tactical cunning can sometimes take the place of physical skill, so it's always worth mixing older, more experienced riders with younger, fresher ones.

Tim Harris moved between eight different teams during the eighties and nineties, becoming the British road-racing champion in 1989. Twenty years ago, the set-up was different, not because there was less money involved, but because there was less of an infrastructure. Then, teams might have twenty or thirty riders, but only one soigneur and a single directeur sportif. Now, the staff almost outnumber the cyclists. Describing his schedule during one summer halfway through his career, it takes Harris five minutes to list all the different events he was entered for. He was living in Spain, and in a two-month period he raced almost every single day, whether it was three-week stage races, six-day races or criteriums. 'After that,' he says now, 'I was never the same – I was just absolutely dead. I'd just left home with enough clothing for a weekend and I was away for three months. It was unbelievable. And if you take a day off, or if you sit out a race, then you don't get paid and that's that. It's absolutely and utterly a brutal sport, and you're basically just pawns in the big game.'

Why was it – why is it – so extreme? 'It's big business, isn't it? At the end of the day, the sponsors are putting in millions of euros, the team manager wants to cream off a load of it, and you're just sat in cars because they want to save money on air fares on driving you from Portugal or Spain. So if you're told to race, you race. We had a lad on our team and his wife had a baby during one of the races. He wasn't even allowed home for that.' Just the same as with any desirable job, pros always know that if they drop out or complain, there'll be plenty of others more than willing to take their place in the peloton, so the pressure is on to ride until you drop. Would it be the same as that now? 'Probably not – the teams are definitely better organised. What would happen then was that they'd just basically get riders, pay them as a billboard, and then when they're worn out, get new ones. So you're just a disposable item, really. But you don't realize that when you're doing it.' So why, when it left him so disillusioned, has he remained so connected to it? 'After a while it gets into your blood – I spent years criss-crossing Europe, and now I still do the same, but with chairs. You get used to it – hotel, race, drive, hotel, race, drive.' The majority of riders are those who, like Tim, ride because it's a job, it's what they do. And it's what they're really good at. Anyone on a pro team, even the most humble and inconspicuous domestique, still has the skill to beat the padded shorts off even the most passionate of club cyclists. And then, in a tiny minority, there are those of a whole different order of being. Like Lance Armstrong.

The image that we the public get of the Tour de France is very far removed from the world that Harris has just described. Certainly the image has heroism and hard graft, but it isn't the quiet heroism of the average pros. Instead, it's the big, gothic, self-mythologising stuff that Henri Desgrange spent so long trying to foster. The 2009 Tour had been about the contest of two vast egos, both of them on the same team. One was the Spanish rider Alberto Contador, who eventually won. And the other was Armstrong.

Talk to anyone in cycling about Armstrong and they always preface their remarks with, 'But he's an exception/a freak/an extreme/a one-off.' He's not representative, he is not a useful comparison, he is not *normal*. Of course he's not normal. Normal people don't win the Tour de France.

Lance Armstrong.

Armstrong just happens to be unusually not-normal. Opinions differ as to what it is that makes the difference. Entire books have been written about Armstrong's physical peculiarities – his stratospheric VO2 max, his slow-twitch muscles, his pre- and post-cancer physique, his resting heart rate. But there are also whole books (including his autobiographies) which concentrate on his mental and emotional strengths. Armstrong has an exceptional will to win, a capacity to close down everything extraneous (pain, discomfort, doping allegations, personal connections) for the time that it takes to achieve victory. Famously, it was he who pulled the notion of a team from being a group of similarly clothed individuals to being a single military-style unit prepared to sacrifice individualism for victory and Lance Armstrong. It was a notion which worked triumphantly until he found himself older, and on a team with another equally gifted rider.

Either way, everything in racing always seems to come back to Armstrong. He fascinates and he polarises. The French hate him ('We don't hate him,' the French protest when you ask, 'but he's always so … (insert long list of insults)'), the racing community seem to admire him without liking him, and even his fellow countrymen find his ultra-ultra-alpha need to beat absolutely everything a bit puzzling. Things shifted a bit when he came third in the 2009 Tour, but in the past the main charges against him have been that he is arrogant, that he is not an all-rounder and that he broke cycling's unwritten rules: that there should be a minimum standard of discomfort for everyone, that amateurishness is something to be cherished and that it's not just the British who can do exceptional heroism in the face of pointless adversity. Here, after all, is a man who thinks losing and dying are the same thing. Worst of all is that he is not only not French, not even European, but – boo, hiss – a Texan, and proud of it.

It was bad enough that Armstrong beat the pants off even Eddy Merckx's Tour record, but that he should do so without having paid due obeisance to the gods of history made it far worse. Certainly, it was his misfortune that his dominance of the Tour coincided with the Iraq war, the (Texan) Bush presidency and the lowest period in Franco-American relations for decades. It did not help that Armstrong could not be dismissed as a mindless jock. If racing is chess, then Armstrong was a Grandmaster. He represents the best and the worst of America all wrapped up in one highly articulate package, and through his story you can trace every itch of friction between Old Europe and New World.

In practice, the main battleground for France *v.* Armstrong is over doping. The acres of published print on his skills and achievements are equalled by an often virulent series of allegations that at various stages of his career he took performance-enhancing drugs. Armstrong has always denied the allegations – the only drugs he's ever confessed to taking were the various anti-cancer medications and cortisone for saddle-sores – but it hasn't made the accusers go away. Given the foam-flecked nature of some of the allegations, it may seem strange to say they aren't necessarily personal. Though they target him as the biggest of the beasts they'd like to bring down, much of the argument is not with Armstrong himself but with the era he was racing in. As his accusers see it, in the late nineties and early noughties, doping was as obligatory in racing as Lycra or mountains; if you didn't dope, you didn't ride. EPO's early technical hitches (life-threatening blood clots, sudden deaths of otherwise prime athletes) had been if not corrected then at least improved, and it still remains awkward to detect.

The riders themselves confirm this. Those who have confessed to doping say that the external pressure to do so was almost irresistible. Riders were faced with a choice: either they rode clean, in which case they would probably come in a virtuous last, or they rode doped, in which case they faced not only the disgrace of detection but the potentially disastrous long-term consequences of steroid, hormone or tranquilliser use. At some point during racing's history, everything that could possibly have either speeded riders up or made the pain of riding more manageable has been tried: cocaine, heroin, opium, ether, chloroform, strychnine, amphetamines, benzedrine, Ritalin, cortisone, painkillers, diuretics, uppers or downers, blood transfusions, even allegations of genetic modification. Each has its own known or unknown side effects and each involves a significant physical gamble on the part of the racer.

In 1998 a Festina team soigneur called Willy Voet was stopped by police on the Franco-Belgian border while carrying 234 doses of EPO, 80 flasks of human-growth hormone, 160 capsules of testosterone, 10 saline drips and 60 pills of Asaflow to make blood less viscous. *Breaking the Chain*, the book he wrote following his arrest and imprisonment, detailed in sometimes comic and sometimes excruciating detail the lengths to which some riders used to go to dope. Since doping controls became more stringent during the 1990s and urine testing became a matter of course, much thought and ingenuity went into substituting clean urine in place of contaminated. Condoms full of clean urine under arm bandages on the arm, condoms up the anus, a syringe up the urethra to extract clean urine before doping, caffeine and amphetamine suppositories … All of it unpleasant and undignified, but all of it somehow lending riders the vital sense that they had a secret, an edge that no one else had.

And yet to expect an otherwise sane individual to spend three weeks riding through storms, heatwaves and deranged spectators is peculiar enough. To expect him to do it without palliatives is even weirder. Jacques Anquetil, the great French rider (who led a strike in 1966 for the right to take drugs), complained in 1969: 'It is not possible for a man … to ride every day without recourse to stimulants. It would be naive or hypocritical to spread the idea that a Tour de France, a Bordeaux–Paris, a Dauphiné Libéré can be negotiated simply on mineral water … All the riders take something.' When asked to turn up for a urine test after Liège–Bastogne–Liège in 1966, he responded testily, 'I'm a human being, not a fountain.' He was not alone in this belief. Henri Desgrange did not believe in supplying the teams with drugs; he told them to bring their own. The great Italian rider Fausto Coppi was famously asked in a 1950s TV interview if he doped. 'Yes,' said Coppi. 'Whenever it was necessary.' When was it necessary? 'Almost all the time.' When Tom Simpson died on Mont Ventoux in 1967 in 55° heat, having taken a cocktail of amphetamines and alcohol, Anquetil wrote a piece suggesting that his death might have been connected to anti-doping measures, since, in order to climb in such conditions, 'it was absolutely necessary to take something simply in order to breathe'. Anquetil's frankness about the need for drug use was considered both controversial and anachronistic by many fans of racing even at the time. Not all, though. When Anquetil was proposed for the Légion d'honneur and someone queried his stance on doping, French President Charles de Gaulle's response was 'So what?'

🚲 🚲 🚲

At the end of the last day of the 2009 Tour, after the eight-lap sprint round the Champs-Élysées, the podium presentations and the victory lap, the Hôtel Méridien Étoile is seething. Hundreds of team personnel, fans, media, guests and menacing men in black polo shirts are all milling around outside and around the foyer. Outside, fans with paparazzi lenses are waiting for their prey. Occasionally, one of the riders arrives or leaves and an instant scrum congregates around them. In a corner, a large group surrounds Yukiya Arashiro, one of two Japanese riders in the Tour, cameras popping with excitement. At about 8.15 p.m., Bradley Wiggins appears with his wife and a small, terrified-looking object in a pram. Wiggins prances through the gawpers, shouting at the top of his voice, clearly having celebrated the end of the Tour-long ban on performance-enhancing substances with a few commemorative drinks. David Millar follows a little more quietly, and the two spend about ten minutes trying to call a lift while grandstanding for the audience. Mark Cavendish is nowhere to be seen. A quarter of an hour later the fourth British rider appears.

Charly Wegelius's entrance was so quiet I didn't even see him walk past until he stopped to talk to the rest of the Silence-Lotto team. He's a long, thin, pale man with a riven face and the deep-set expression of someone whose thoughts hurt him. He looked far older than thirty-one and his voice was flat. Wegelius is known as a super-domestique – a pro who rides only in the service of his team's star riders, and is very, very good at it. The word domestique was originally used as an insult, but then passed into general racing terminology and became universal, though nowadays riders like Wegelius are just as often called helpers or gregarios ('one of the team').

Born in Finland but brought up in Yorkshire, he spent most of his career riding for Italian teams before moving to Silence-Lotto earlier in the year to help Cadel Evans. Having made it to Paris for the fourth time, does he feel appropriately heroic? 'Yes. Especially for me because my role is as a helper rider. But the problem with that is that the way my work is judged is directly in proportion to the result that the person I help gets. And this is a specific example – Cadel's race didn't go as he hoped it would, and …' – there is a diplomatic pause – 'people might think that I did a less good job. But I actually did a better job and I worked harder than I would have done if he had been more successful. So there's a lot of people who worked really hard in the race for very little reward.' Do you find that demoralising? 'When you're in a very big team in a very stable environment, it doesn't really matter because you know that that's going to be acknowledged within the team that you ride for.' Another pause. 'But if you have doubts about where that team is going to end up … A ride like I did isn't going to improve my value in the market because nobody knows what I did, nobody really noticed.'

But doesn't it get frustrating riding for others? Don't you want to win? 'It's a question I get asked over and over again, about the role that I play and whether it bothers me not being allowed to win. But if I was allowed to ride for myself, I would ride a really anonymous race and finish twentieth or twenty-fifth or something. And that's not productive – it's not productive for me and it's not something that allows me to have a place in the food chain, you know? So either you win things and guarantee that you win things, or you make yourself useful. People often mistake what riders like me do as just being bad riders – as finishing hundredth or eightieth, but the ones who win couldn't win without the people like me. You've got to know what you're doing. I think I'm quite good at what I do, but it's an incredibly difficult thing for people who haven't ridden bikes at a certain speed to understand. And I think it's also about a lack of pressure on myself which allows me to perform better anyway. Because when my end result is going to be judged, I put a lot of pressure on myself and I don't … it's like I don't breathe properly, you know? If you asked me to ride for somebody else, it's like I can do it a lot easier. I'm not a Good Samaritan, it's just … easier.'

The previous day's stage had been on Mont Ventoux. Goaded onwards by the half-million people who came to watch, the riders pounded across the plains of Provence to the great bald moonscape of a mountain. Through the heat and the shouting, it was possible to see the tops of the trees on the lower slopes almost bent over with the strength of the wind. Watching this small, ragged, brightly coloured group of men turning and turning into a gale that seemed intent on shoving them right back down to the stage start, I thought – no one could do that without either being very scared, very well paid or besotted with the sport to the point of blindness. Wegelius nods. 'I've wondered before if you could put an untrained person under the pain that we feel, how long they would last before they said stop. I think that for a lot of people who aren't trained physically, it's almost as if they can't hurt themselves in that way as we can. You can't be normal and do this job. Because even the money doesn't get you through it when you're really …' He stops.

So what is it that's so abnormal? Another pause. 'I don't know. When I have bad moments, I ask myself why I'm doing it too, because it really seems like a stupid idea sometimes. If you look at it in terms of a day, it's just like a dull suffering that goes on and on. But in the course of a race, there's all these emotional highs and lows. You get these moments when you're almost hysterical with enthusiasm, and then you're really down.' He rubs his forehead. 'I think the hardest thing about cycling is just that, if you want to, you can stop it whenever you want. The pain. It's really easy; you just stop. And if I tell my directeur that I can't go on any more, he's never going to have proof that I could have done. Or if I tell him that I can't go a little bit faster, then nobody will ever know. But you know. And you have your own truth. And when you ride one-day races, for example, you go round and round, and every time you go past the shower, you want to stop.' He smiles. 'And all you want is to stop, but when you do, you really hate yourself.' Is that what stops you from stopping? 'When it's really bad, you just can't do it – you don't allow yourself to.' It sounds like the famous Armstrong quote reproduced on a thousand posters and a thousand motivational websites: 'Pain is temporary. It may last a minute, or an hour, or a day, or a year, but eventually it will subside and something else will take its place. If I quit, however, it lasts forever.' What about the rest of the team? 'That's a big part of things. Because everybody has their ups and downs, and if you're in a good team, you'll always find someone to lean on who will give you a hand. It can be a bottle of water, or just a little word sometimes when you're really having a crisis that can get you through.' It sounds very emotionally punishing. 'Yes,' says Charly in an utterly heartfelt voice, 'it is.'

But is the Tour de France more extreme than other races? 'No. I was more tired after the Giro [the Tour of Italy, held in May each year]. But the Tour's just a monster. It's like a huge gigantic monster that can beat you up if you don't pay attention. If I don't do my job properly in a normal race, hardly anyone notices. A few fanatics might notice, or people who look at the internet, or specialist journalists, but if I don't do my job properly here, there's thirty or forty journalists asking where I was at the end of the day, and I'm not used to that. It's huge, it's like a massive pressure cooker, and it really gets to you. Well, it does to me, anyway. You go to the start of a stage and you get off the bus and there's just noise everywhere – the speaker at the start of the race, the radio in your ear, people shouting at the side of the road – and you've got to go and do this and you've got to go and do that, and you go back to the cars to get water and there's forms and people and it's just like … it's … ridiculous. Sometimes your ears ring at the end of the day.' Do you dread it? 'Yes,' he says, 'I hate it.' A wry smile. So which are the races you enjoy? 'I don't know if I could say I enjoy any. Maybe you're talking to the wrong person, because I've been doing it for quite a long time and maybe I'm getting a bit cynical about it now. This is my tenth season as a professional, but I left home when I was seventeen to see if I could become a pro.' And if you go right back to basics, if you step out of all this and you look at a bicycle just as a bicycle, does it still give you pleasure? 'Yes,' he says with a kind of relief. 'I enjoy training more than I used to. If I could find someone to pay me what I get paid now just to train, I'd be the happiest person in the world. I used to hate training when I was younger, but I like it now. It's just like a discovery of your own body, and you can progress and plan things and ... I like that.'

So how did you end up doing this? 'I did all sports when I was young, I did everything. My dad was a showjumper with horses, and I was always around horses. And I didn't like it at all because it was just like ... nausea, you know, I had nausea. It was just horses and horses and horses and horses. And I started pottering around on my bike with my friends in the village. I was really good at all sports but I didn't really find the one that I liked. And I started the cycling almost as a tourist really, to go on trips with my friends. We used to do 200km when I was twelve, thirteen, out all day on our bikes. And then I started racing, and then I just kept going. I had to decide when I was eighteen whether I was going to do a university degree or going to try and be a bike rider. I gave myself until I was twenty-three, and then I just kept going. And now I'm an old man.' Again, that wry laugh. So what do you want to do now? 'Where do I want to go?' he says wonderingly. 'Professionally I don't think I can go any further. Because I'm quite good at what I do and to turn myself into a winner isn't going to happen because I don't have the head for it.' Can you make a decent living out of this? 'Yes. I'm not getting rich but I'm making a secure future for ourselves.' The following Friday, he's getting married in Finland to his long-term girlfriend Camilla. 'So at the moment I hope that I'll have enough money when I stop to be able to be picky about what I do to make up for the fact that I don't have a degree. So that maybe I can do something a bit more fun instead of just …' He fades out, sounding painfully raw. The rest of the team are about to go into dinner. I thank him, take a few photographs, and we both go on our way. The following year, Wegelius pulls out of the Tour after the tenth stage, citing ill-health.

Back outside the hotel, there are a few fans still waiting for signatures. The last of the groupies are dispersing and there's nothing much left but a few team cars and the men in black. The teams have distributed themselves over the restaurants and bars of Paris, and the whole immense Tour circus with all its smoke and mirrors and special effects is already beginning to break up. I round the corner, and it's gone – no trace of flags or barriers, no Armstrong wincing and grimacing on the podium, no life-or-death struggle. Just an ordinary Paris street on an ordinary summer night.

To an outsider, it's almost impossible to tie up all the contradictions within racing. As with any major sport, so much money and angst is expended on something so small and fragile. In the end, it's just a bunch of middle-aged men in cars chasing a bunch of young men on bicycles. Those who line the route of Paris–Roubaix in the freezing rain, or pack up their *poffertjes* and camper vans and make their way from Amsterdam to Alpe d'Huez, or pay thousands to take a VIP tour of the Giro course, or sit on the Champs-Élysées on their beds of flags, do care about the state of the racers. But far beyond that, and most of all, they care that in amidst the whole ludicrous spectacle of a bicycle race, with its ugly commercialism, its sponsorship deals, its rows, its infighting, its TVs and radios and helicopters and mile upon mile of trailing wires, its wives and girlfriends, its indignities and jokes, its beer and Lycra, its feuds and legends and compromises – that all of it is still there, every year, without fail. They care that the race is still run, and that someone, somewhere, still keeps the faith. And they do know – because some of them have had a taste of it themselves – that, no matter how lowly, demoralised or insignificant, anyone who can keep racing down all the roads of Europe and through all that a professional career can throw at them is still a proper, copper-bottomed, bona fide hero. Exactly as Henri Desgrange intended.

ڴڴڴ   ڴڴڴ   ڴڴڴ

SEVEN

The Silent Black Line

What people gain or lose from cycling has been studied and will continue to be studied for years to come. As its popularity increases in the UK, more time and effort and resources will go into looking at cycling's effects on every part of the body. Which makes examining those physical effects a tricky exercise, since the science of sport is now moving so far and so fast, and is prone to such violent switches in ideological fashion, that anything written about it tends to be out of date by the time it's published. The only areas of consensus are, one, that cycling places a genuinely exceptional level of demand on the whole body, and, two, that the art of riding a bicycle is all in the mind. More than any other competitive sport, cycling requires its practitioners to be clever. Clever, tactical, experienced, with a good head for both physics and psychology, and with a relish for the darker arts. Which can be a tough call at 80kph.

Dr Damian Coleman runs the Sports Science Laboratories at Canterbury University. He's been a competitive cyclist since the age of sixteen, and has been at Canterbury as student, tutor and now as Principal Lecturer.

Before we talk, he shows me around the faculty – two rooms, one full of training bikes wired up as part of an experiment on group data collection, and another larger room, which contains a huge treadmill designed to give pinpoint-accurate measurements, a lot of computers, a lot of monitoring equipment, a bike with a Union Jack saddle and something called a Bod-Pod, which to me looks suspiciously similar to the Orgasmatron in Woody Allen's *Sleeper*. Coleman himself is efficient, helpful and reasonably expansive, but does not offer to demonstrate the Bod-Pod for me. Instead, we go up to his office at the faculty, a sparse and impersonal space apart from one photograph of a newborn baby and a lot of books about cycling.

We talk tactics and psychology, and I ask what you need to be a cyclist these days. 'It's a sport which, to be very average, you've probably got to put in ten to twelve hours a week training. To be very good, you've probably got to put in fifteen to twenty hours, and that's in this country. If you were in Belgium, where the standard is a significant notch up, probably at eighteen you've got to be doing twenty to twenty-five hours training a week. Now, most Premiership footballers don't spend that sort of time training. To enjoy your sport, to play Sunday League football in this country, you might train once a week and play once a week. You might have a total commitment of two to three hours. But to do the same with cycling, you've probably got to put in about ten hours a week.' So the level of fitness required to get to competitive level is much higher? 'Yes, it's probably 90 per cent fitness. In football, you can be quite significantly overweight but very, very skilful and still hold your place in the team. If you're a very, very skilful bike rider but don't have the underpinning fitness, you'd be straight out the back immediately.'

So first you put the hours in, then you start getting obsessed with weight. There are plenty of fat cyclists out there consoling themselves with the notion that neither Chris Hoy nor Mark Cavendish look short of a beefburger or two. But there are also plenty of cyclists who realise the laws of phsics dictate that, if they really want to compete, they can never have seconds again. 'Cycling's one of those sports where weight plays a massive role, and there's lots of people who get very obsessive about their body weight and their bicycle weight, and then it becomes more like a job than enjoyment of sport, really. At the top end, you can understand if you're two or three kilos lighter and you might then earn £50,000 a year more, but there are lots of people at a very, very low amateur level who still do those kinds of things.'

The sheer level of dedication necessary to compete even at club level requires sacrifices – big ones. And if you want to ride on the Continent, then you must get out there and race as much as you can, because racing is training. And in order to race at peak efficiency, you have to ensure that you're correctly prepared beforehand – that you've eaten and drunk the right things, that you've had enough carbo-hydrates, that you've tapered your training and gone to bed without any fun at 9 p.m. 'So single male, living on your own, totally not an issue. Not engaging in family life, not engaging with friends. But you then take that to some of the guys on the Olympic development plan who are probably seventeen, eighteen. All their mates are going out and enjoying life, and they can't do that. You're missing family and friends for a huge part of the year, or you see them and have a rotten time because you've got to go to bed early and you find a race close to where you're staying but it just doesn't fit together that well. So you end up being quite selfish. And I'm still talking here about an amateur level – people who place a lot of burdens on family life for cycling. There's some fantastic juniors that just haven't been able to stick with it because it is such a sterile life. They want to do the things that they enjoy.'

Coleman admits that sports science has itself been partly responsible for this killjoy rationale. With every year that passes, the amount of data available on every aspect of cycling is increasing. But the more numbers there are, the more the experts insist that the really committed cyclist has to behave in a certain way in order to prove that commitment. The danger then is that cycling becomes a numbers game, an exercise in punching in time and effort and extracting results: the body as machine and the landscape as treadmill. If you want to improve your time around the track or take part in an Iron Man or simply speed up your hill repeats, then you become a number cruncher, a data analyser, an IT expert. A bore. Sports science has made a vast difference to Britain's chances in any competition, but it's also created a need for a counterbalancing field of sports psychologists to deal with all the mental and emotional effects of too much information. As Coleman admits of his own racing career, 'It's quite difficult for me, because obviously I'd be sat there on the start line thinking, oh well, haven't done this right, haven't done that right. And you end up talking yourself out of why you're not going to win, because I know exactly what I should have been doing.'

Famously, Britain's 2008 Olympics were won on percentages – minute incremental improvements which together added up to a gold. Or, rather, to several golds. 'I teach a nutrition module here on the programme. If you look at winning margins from the Olympics on track and field, the small differences between even the guy that won the 100m, he looked like he won by a mile, and it was about two point something per cent. And you look at the effect of taking caffeine or a high-carb diet – it swamps that change. So if you're not doing that, you're going to finish way behind. He's probably doing everything legal to get to that stage, so you've got to do the same to even get close. So if you haven't done the training, if you haven't done what you should have done and you're maybe 2 per cent lower than you should be, you're gone, you're absolutely nowhere.' Because the pool of cyclists has got larger in the past few years, the standard has gone up. And because the standard has gone up, so has the quality. There are a lot more cyclists out there taking their cycling a lot more seriously. Coleman's faculty now provides a consultation service for people – ordinary punters, weekend cyclists – who want to improve, and will pay to do it the academic way.

Broadly speaking, Cyclefit does for amateurs what Dr Coleman does for pros: it tries to optimise a cyclist's performance by examining his behaviour and positioning on the bike, and doing what it can to improve it. In Cyclefit's case, this also involves bespoke fitting, either of a new frame or of a lot of superfluous but ridiculously enjoyable accessories – new custom footbeds with horrible 'ladieswear' shoes to match, new pedals, new gloves, new saddlepacks. Cyclefit doesn't really advertise itself. It's tucked down a narrow side street in London's Covent Garden with a plainish façade, discreet signage, a bit of frosted glass. But once inside, there's a strong sense of having stumbled across a private shrine to the gods of the road. Obviously there are bikes – bikes out on the floor, bikes on racks, bikes halfway to the ceiling – but it's more than that. One wall is painted black and has a gradient map of next year's Tour de France Étape inscribed over it in white. On the TV, a recording of last spring's Amstel Gold race replays endlessly. And behind the counter are a couple of doors through which the sound of rapid pedalling can be heard.

Warrick Spence is a Cyclefit fitter. He's very tall and very lanky with a narrow, watchful face with spiky hair and glasses – an athletic nerd, or a nerdy athlete. The first time we meet, I speak to him in the upstairs office, surrounded by Colnago and Serotta framesets. The second time we meet, I go for a fitting. On both occasions he's generous with his time but unwaveringly self-contained – happy to talk about cycling but not happy to talk about anything personal. He has the demeanour of someone who was once very shy or solitary, but now has a quiet, rather competitive sense of authority. There's no doubt, he says, that they've hit the right formula at the right moment. 'Cyclefit has profited from the increasing interest in cycling. We get a mixed bag. We get people who have been riding forever and now can't ride because something physically has forced them to stop – their knee or their back – and they've put two and two together and realised it might be something to do with their position or lack of flexibility. The old school don't think like that. They think a bit of pain is just something to be dealt with. That's the old mentality: if it doesn't hurt, you're not getting anywhere. And we get a lot of City people, cash-rich, time-short. They've probably got the nice watches and cars and stuff, but at the same time they want to be directed to a group of people who can look after them.'

Spence is aware of the pitfalls of overdoing things. In his late twenties, he was busy trying to get a pro licence when he contracted glandular fever. Five years later, and as part of his recovery, he chose to lighten up. 'My training is just commuting, six miles each way from East Dulwich. I don't do too much. In the past, when I was young, I used to do lots of miles, just constantly riding and riding, just a couple of months off. But it's easy to overtrain if you've got too much time on your hands.' Does he still enjoy riding a bicycle? 'Yes, I really enjoy it. If I was still racing, if I hadn't had to stop for five years, I probably would have raced myself flat.' He's thirty-five now, and has gone back to racing. How long can anyone keep going on a bike? 'Indefinitely. You could go on until you're seventy. At the World Masters in August in Austria, there's a seventy-five-plus age category. That's the thing – as long as everything's looked after, there's no physical or health reason why you can't keep going.'

The absence of any deadline on cycling is one of the many reasons people adopt it with such ferocity. As many people have discovered, it's the ideal form of exercise for a mid-life crisis. For the born-again thirty- or forty-something, there are huge benefits to be gained from buying a bicycle. From that one simple purchase, they will get back a world of speed and risk and competition. They will receive proof that, though their ambition in the workplace may long ago have dwindled away to just turning up, their senses are still as sharp, their reflexes just as keen and their will to win just as dominant as it was when they were twenty. They will get a hit from endorphins as good as any they used to get from those fun young-people drugs as well as evidence that they can still do something about the state of their physique. They'll have confirmation that their capacity to derive intense satisfaction from other people's misfortune is still alive and well. And, best of all, they'll have the perfect escape vehicle from all the things – home, family, money – which most persistently remind them that they are, after all, no longer young. Which is partly why, at many races, you can watch the entrants' fully-grown children waiting by the sidelines and yelling, 'Go, Dad!' as something with white hair and saggy knees hurtles past, heading for Spain. And also why, if you turn up at something billed as a sportive or an audax – very relaxed, not really competitive, just a fun day out in the summer countryside – you'll find the start line swarming with Serious Men of a certain age all trying to beat seven kinds of living hell out of each other. For them, this isn't about proving something. It's about proving *everything*.

But what are the long-term consequences of sitting on a bike hour after hour, week after week? With pro racers, says Spence, 'I think it probably does shorten their lives a little bit, because of the intensity, but a lot of them keep riding. The guys that keep going to old age don't stop riding. They shift it from racing to recreational, so they're still keeping fit. It's the people who stop who are at risk. Their bodies are still burning energy, and they get to the point where they're still eating the same amount, but they're starting to clog up their arteries. Also, if they're very, very fit, it's easy for the heart rate to recover too much, to get too lazy, because it's so slow anyway. It's why you get a lot of ex-pros dying of heart attacks in their forties and fifties, but that tends to be the cyclists who were pretty drugged-up as well. But you're still getting young guys in Europe who are dying in their sleep even now. Because they are that fit. Modern training methods, the support, the coaching – they are paid to ride their bikes, and that's all they're doing. There are no outside stresses as such, so they are fully relaxed and recovered, and their heart rate is getting down into the twenties. And when it's like that, sometimes it just forgets to beat at all. You know, it's just gone, boom … boom … boom …' – he starts whistling unconcernedly – '… There isn't another beat to keep it going, and it just stops. My heart rate can get down to thirty-four.' He puts his hand on his chest. 'Sometimes … *I can't feel* … oh, there we go! Probably the hardest thing for an athlete like that is to have a nasty crash, where they're forced to stop riding. The body and the muscles, because all the strain and the stress have been taken off, the body overcompensates – there's all this energy, and it can't burn it.'

Coleman has seen the same thing. 'Anecdotally there are lots of cyclists who die in their fifties, they would have been cycling twenty, thirty years ago when steroid and hormone abuse, and blood doping might have been used more heavily – not EPO but transfusions of your own material. Back at the '84 Olympics, the American cycling team actually admitted doing this because it wasn't a banned process. If we took a pint of blood out of you, within six weeks that would be totally replenished by your own mechanisms. If we spun the blood down, got rid of all the water and just put the red blood cells back, you'd have a greater oxygen-carrying capacity. Now, the problem with that in the eighties was that a lot of guys killed themselves doing it. Because they made their blood too thick, so it put too much stress on the heart. Our blood, normal blood, has a viscosity almost like water. OK, it's got some solids in it so it's a bit thicker than water, but still. But if you put more red cells into that, it becomes more viscous, in which case the heart has to work much harder in order to move it.' And, as with other drugs, long-term use leads to dependence. 'In [pro legend Marco] Pantani's case, he was one day away from winning the Tour of Italy and he failed a drugs test for having too high a red cell count in his blood. He served his ban and came back, came back two or three times, but was never the same rider – he won Tour de France stages and things, but he was never the same. He had a massive crash in a race – hit a car coming down the mountain that wasn't supposed to be there, broke both his legs, got taken to hospital, and bearing in mind your resting red cell count should be about forty, his was way up in the fifties but then went down to ten, because obviously in hospital he wasn't getting help from exogenous EPO. The doping thing is difficult because people don't admit to it and therefore it's difficult to know what the implications are – if you're caught, you have to repay all your prize money and you're stripped of your titles etc., so people tend to suffer in silence.'

There's another controversial downside to racing. A 1997 study by Irwin Goldstein MD, an American urologist at Boston University, suggested that around 100,000 men were trading the chance to win for the ability to breed. They had lost the ability to get or maintain an erection because of their obsession with cycling. 'Men should never ride bicycles,' said Goldstein. 'Riding should be banned and outlawed. It's the most irrational form of exercise I could ever bring to discussion.' The problem is the same as it was a century ago – the angle at which the rider balances on the saddle. When you sit upright on a chair the weight of your upper body is taken by the bones of the pelvis. But when you're on a saddle that weight is supported not by bone, but by the perineum, the area which in men protects the nerves, musculature and blood supply of the penis. 'When a man sits on a bicycle seat he's putting his entire body weight on the artery that supplies the penis,' said Goldstein. 'It's a nightmarish situation.' His vision – a race of men all with thousand-yard stares, thighs of steel and sperm like corkscrews – caught the public imagination and the study became notorious. The only trouble was that Goldstein's original terms were themselves flawed and the findings suspect.

He did, however, have a point. More recent studies have consistently found a link between saddle shape and impotence in men, and urological complaints in women. A Norwegian study also in 1997 appeared to back up his claims. After a 560km bike race with 260 male entrants, 13 per cent of the group were still reporting numbness in the penis; ten riders were still impotent a week after the race. And a further study in 2001 at the University of Cologne in Germany discovered that when a group of forty men between the ages of twenty-five and thirty-five were tested on laboratory exercise bikes, a full 70 per cent experienced a significant decrease in blood supply to the penis and 61 per cent reported genital numbness. 19 per cent of the study group, all of whom cycled regularly, also complained of impotence. Nor is it much use swapping disciplines; bashing yourself about on a mountain bike is only slightly less damaging to fertility than actually fracturing your pelvis.

Counterbalancing this terrible news is another University of Cologne study which found that the solution to the issue was not so much the amount of padding in the saddle, but its shape and width. In other words, any design that did not compress the perineal arteries left the rider as virile at the end of the journey as he had been at the start. And the huge potential benefits to be gained from cycling – a healthier heart, improved circulation, better muscle tone etc., etc. – generally outweigh the drawbacks. Besides, there's usually compelling evidence from the podium at the end of every Tour de France that the world's most elite racing cyclists are devoting plenty of time and attention to the issue of reproduction.

🚲 🚲 🚲

Dr Rob Child works as the nutritionist for the pro-tour Cervélo Test Team. This in itself is unusual – he was only hired earlier in the year, and the appointment of a dedicated nutritionist started a little ripple of curiosity and alarm round the other team buses. We meet backstage at the 2009 Tour of Britain, while the racers are off doing their thing and the team staff are housekeeping in Admiralty Walk. Most are either closeted in the buses gossiping with the curtains shut or – in the case of Katusha – out on the pavement keeping the team washing machines under overt surveillance. Child is tall, early thirties and on his mettle; when I mistakenly refer to him as a soigneur, he is genuinely offended.

In matters of food, he's in agreement with Coleman; at the top level, you're trading in fractions. How, I ask him, do you mess around with the diets of people who only have 4 or 5 per cent body fat? 'It's almost like directing the course of a river. If the river is flowing quickly and you dam it off and change the direction, i.e. you lose or increase body weight, it's a lot easier to do it with people who are doing a lot of exercise than if they're sedentary. In something like the Tour, there's huge physiological and thermal stress on the body. They won't call the Tour de France or the Giro off just because the temperature reaches 40° and it's a mountain stage – they just have to get on with it. Which means that some of the guys are sweating around 10 litres a day. That's a lot of sweat – about 15 per cent of some of these guys' body weight. And if you're on a bike for five or six hours and you've ridden for 120, 140 miles, the energy intake to meet that is around 10,000 kilocalories depending on what you've done in the race. And to eat 10,000kcal. and drink 10 litres of fluid while you're on a bike is quite a challenge. And then if you include the muscle damage from all that pedalling – it's not like a marathon where you do the muscle damage and that's it, with racing you still have to get up and ride your bike again the next day, and the day after that.

'So you get this accumulation of muscle damage, dehydration, injuries from crashes, healing – there's a huge number of physical stresses on the road in addition to the psychological stresses. You've got to race against your competitor who's looking fresher than you, who didn't crash, you've got the mountain stages coming up and you know you've got to deliver there … there's a huge number of pressures on the riders. The sprinters will be revelling in the first week and the last few days of the race where it's flat, the mountain climbers are being crucified by the high pace in the early part of the race and hoping that when they get to the mountain stages they can do something before being crucified again at the end, so the riders are continually imposing pain on each other in one form or another.'

At least the majority of stage races are on flat roads. The core of the Spring Classics is Paris–Roubaix, a portion of which is over cobbles. As Warrick Spence says, 'A lot of racers don't like it – they get told they have to do it, and they go, I just don't want to do it, it's too dangerous. There's other riders who want to do it because they know it takes tactics. They just cruise on the flat bits and they actually go faster and harder over the cobbled bits to really nail it home to the guys who are struggling. That's why you get such a difference. On the flat, if you want to go faster, you put more effort in and you will actually see your speed go up. On cobbles, you can change gear up or down and it doesn't really have any effect because you can't feel your legs. You go numb, and you're just having to deal with so much information to try to keep the bike straight. But you see people who flew through one smooth section hit the cobbles again and just go right back because they haven't realised how much effort they put into the other section and they haven't got anything left. That's what makes a race. It just gets rid of one aspect – you don't have to worry about attacking the field because you know that a certain amount of them are mentally done for anyway – they just don't like it. It's the same with racing in the rain.' According to Rob Child, 'You probably get more muscle damage from that kind of race than you would do from a normal road stage.' What type of riders would it suit best? 'They need a lot of power. So they're guys who can probably knock out five hundred watts or so for an hour. Your one-bar electric fire is one kilowatt, so imagine a person who could light your one-bar electric fire for half an hour. That's a fair bit of power.'

There's a strong streak of masochism in racing, isn't there? 'Yes,' says Child. 'Absolutely. Definitely. If you push yourself to the limit, then you're going to the boundaries where you think, something's going to break here, or how much pain can you take? It's a really interesting concept. You've got to go at absolutely full gas to break away from a group, and then you have to keep on burying yourself maybe for the next ninety miles to try and stay away. And if you don't stay at that pace – say you're at the back and you think, I don't want to go 30kph up this hill, it's too difficult, you have to think, well, what are the consequences if I drop off the back? If I drop too far off the back, I'll never catch them up. And that's it – not only is your race for the day over, but maybe the whole race is over.'

Coleman agrees. If half of racing is about masochism, then the other half is about sadism – inflicting pain on yourself, then doling it out to others. Either way, it would appear that competitive cycling doesn't exactly spotlight the warm, fluffy side of human nature. 'I think people who get into cycling are probably a little bit sadistic.' He smiles. 'That's probably the wrong way to look at it, but if you're a runner and you're in a race and you break the person who's trying to stay with you, they sort of drift backwards from you very slowly. If you're cycling and you do that to someone, it's like a parachute opens, because they can use the slipstream and as soon as they lose that, they're gone. And it's a very, very nice feeling if you have the capacity to do that to people. It is a very, very nice feeling. Every cyclist will experience it the other way – trying to hang on to someone and when you go, you go. And it's a great form of sport for that, because if you can do that to people, you're much stronger than them. And it's that game of trying to get rid of people out of your slipstream and trying to win races. And that is a huge part of the enjoyment that I think a lot of people get from the sport – it's very dramatic when things happen compared to running. It's so dramatic when you're stronger than them – it's a very, very nice scenario if you are the strongest in a race and you manage to do that to people.'

Which goes back to the other aspect of cycling, the unquantifiable bit, the bit that matters almost as much as a functioning pair of legs. Some of cycling may be about sitting on the bike and putting the hours in, but the other part is about needing to be there in the first place. Again and again during the research for this book, I kept bumping up against the same thing – that bicycles are just a form of self-medication for the obsessed. Anecdotally, too, there's plenty of evidence that cycling is ideal for the sore of spirit. It's solitary, it requires very little preparation, and people find a kind of sustenance from locking into the physical rhythm of turning the pedals. They call it being 'in the zone', and sometimes being in the zone means that, for a few precious minutes or hours, they don't have to think. All they have to do is pedal, and breathe.

Many of the couriers I'd spoken to had mentioned the same thing – that riding a bike all day had lifted them out of a bout of depression, and that couriering itself had a strong element of the lost and found about it. There was no data to support this theory, and – apart from the School of Stating the Bleedin' Obvious stuff on how regular cycling made you healthier – no studies done on any possible correlation between mental health and cycling. Still, it always seemed interesting to me that all the experts talked about it as much in psychological terms as in physical ones, and that those who became most obsessed with cycling always seemed to be those most in need of healing.

🚲 🚲 🚲

EIGHT

The Burning Man

And so, since I wanted to know about death and obsession in cycling, I went to Saltcoats.

Saltcoats is over on the west coast of Scotland below Glasgow, though it's definitely not the same bit of the west that they show on the tourist posters. This is the low-down dirty bit, the post-industrial place by the sea. This and nearby Lanarkshire is the part of Scotland where all the raw materials came from – the coal and the trees and the iron ore that they took in order to build the ships which long ago floated away down the rivers of Britain. During two world wars this is also where the men and women labouring in the steel works gathered the old rusting tractors and ploughshares and turned them into swords. All of that history is still completely visible in the landscape. There are hills and holes in this place that shouldn't really be there – the strangely symmetrical heaps are great big black mounds of slag from the opencast mines in the area, and the holes are the result of digging down so hard that everything on top falls in. There are still kids round here being called scabs because their fathers broke the miners' strike back in the 1980s.

It's the week between Christmas and New Year, that tricky moment when everyone's indoors watching telly or pacing the streets filling the gap between hangovers. Pensioners scurry down the path by the bowling green on their way to the social club and teenagers gather in flocks by the station, waiting for something to happen. In the High Street, built side-on to the sea, there are groups of kids ostentatiously calling or texting each other on the mobiles they just got as presents. And everywhere – in the shops, in the old kirk now turned into a temporary market – is the proof that Saltcoats is both tied and divided by one thing and one thing alone: sport. Saltcoats loves sport, is passionate about it, dreams of it, identifies with it, stakes its faith on it. The only trouble is, that sport isn't cycling. It's football.

Here, if you so wish, you could live in an entirely green or blue universe. You could sleep on Rangers sheets below a Rangers duvet cover in a room with Rangers wallpaper before drying yourself on a Rangers towel and eating your breakfast off a Rangers plate. Or, if you play for the other team, you can wear your Celtic shirt with your Celtic necklace over your Celtic pyjama bottoms and under your Celtic robe, light your first fag of the day with a Celtic lighter and time yourself to work with a Celtic watch. If you search for long enough in Saltcoats, you could probably furnish an entire household in football-related products. The rest of Scotland might be closed for the holidays, but the Old Firm is definitely open for business as usual.

While I'm standing at the local jeweller's window contemplating the purchase of a miniature Celtic team bus, a figure in an old baggy tracksuit detaches itself from one of the doorways. Watching him come towards me, there doesn't seem anything particularly unusual about this man. He looks like any other Saltcoats local: an old razor-faced guy in a bobble hat. It's only upstairs in his flat that he becomes Graeme Obree instead.

Graeme Obree is a cycling legend. He's a legend because he broke the hour record twice over and he's a legend because, in doing so, he changed everyone's sense of what a bike should look like and how it should be ridden. Obree was and is living proof that it's usually the outsiders who prove to be the real revolutionaries in life. The first time he broke the record was in Hamar, Norway, in '93, just a week before Chris Boardman broke it back. The second time, a year later, he kept it. He was a genius for turning disadvantages – lack of money or support, coming from a place where they've barely heard of bicycles – into advantages. He knew about framebuilding because he'd once run a bike shop, so he built the frames he then used to compete on. The first of them, Old Faithful (which famously included the bearings from a washing machine), proved so successful that the UCI banned his design. He couldn't afford the kind of scientific back-up that Boardman used, so he made his own science instead. *The Flying Scotsman*, the book he wrote describing his own rise and fall, was made into a film which gave him some of the recognition he had long deserved. 'I was sacked from racing,' he said later. 'It just took me twelve years to realise it.'

Now Obree is here in Saltcoats. He's just moved in a month ago, having split up with Anne, his wife of fifteen-odd years. The flat is still unfinished and he asks me not to describe it – except for one thing. On one wall of his front room is a large oval of slatted wood which at first I take to be a piece of driftwoodish art. The lower third of the oval is painted blue and the top is a cross – a vertical red line bisecting a horizontal black line. It's only later when I look at it closely and pick out the writing on the wood that I realize what it is. 'Where It All Started', says one signature, 'Well Done Graeme'. It's the piece of the Hamar velodrome track where he first took the hour record in 1993. The black line marks the point at which he passed into the history books.

Obree fixes tea and sits down. It hasn't been straightforward finding him – he's surrounded by a group of friends and allies who do their best to protect him from timewasters – and when I did make contact, he was very clear on his terms of engagement. He's not interested in publicity or in maintaining his status as a cycling icon. Quite the opposite; he recently turned down a couple of honorary doctorates, 'so I don't have my face in the newspaper'. Why? 'Why? Because I was going through a phase of insularity. I mean, for example, there were a couple of occasions when' – he points accusingly at himself – '"*that* is the Flying Scotsman!" I was looking behind me, going, "Are you talking to the lamppost?" I was like third person singular. I don't want to be third person bloody singular. Right? I want to be me, the person.' Sitting on the sofa now with the low winter sun slanting through the blinds, he's got a face like a Jesuit – lean, furrowed, narrow, with those thousand-mile eyes and a weird burning kind of beauty. The only incongruous note is his big, slabby hands. He manages to look both incredibly healthy and incredibly scarred at the same time. He radiates a contained kind of energy, an almost flammable intensity. There are moments when you can see how that intensity could become illness, and when it's genius. When he's uncomfortable, he speaks so rapidly it's almost impossible to hear what he says.

All of Obree's achievements are coloured by the state he made them in. He has a history of depression and of mental illness, and has attempted suicide on three separate occasions. Perhaps ironically given his profession, he has what many of the psychology textbooks now call 'rapid-cycling depression' – bipolar disorder which moves swiftly from mania to suicidal low. And perhaps there's something about being on such close speaking terms with death that makes him twice as alive as most people. He began writing his autobiography while in Crosshouse Hospital recovering from his third suicide attempt. Once it was adapted into a film it became another story entirely, but the original is eye-watering in all senses – for its honesty, for its extraordinary delineation of the highs and lows of Obree's life and for its account of the darkest parts of the human psyche. 'I started writing it as a therapeutic exercise, and then it came to the point where I thought, oh, that's a bit heavy. And at that point, I had to say, if I'm actually going to do this as a book, then it can be a real poppy, picture diary-type book, which is totally inconsequential – I won this and I won that and this is the bike I used, and this is the size of gear – a really, really anorak-type book, fluffy nothing. Or I'm just going to say it all as it is. So I wrote it as I wrote it, with impunity. There was days I wrote six thousand words. Longhand. Most of it just came flowing out. It was as if it wasn't even me.'

I say I don't think I'd ever read anything quite that extreme. 'I wanted ordinary people to try and get a feel of what it's like. It's terrible to say because a lot of my friends understand, but unless they've actually suffered from depression they're a bit like, why can't you just pull yourself together? Like that. Like a pair of curtains. Just pull yourself together.' And after the book had been published, did your friends understand better? 'Aye. I think they did to an extent. I think people are afraid of it because it's almost like it could be catching. But you know what was strange about that book? Once I'd published it, there were people who you would not imagine come up to me and say confidentially, I totally relate to that book. People who have won major events, major championships, major people, major riders, saying, I totally got your book, and I just suffered in silence. All that British stiff upper lip.'

In the past, he would drink when he was low, and the drink would make him lower. It was Anne, his wife, who finally got him to go and see a therapist. 'It becomes its own spiral, and it gets worse and worse and worse, until it's completely out of control. But deep down – well, I've been in the mental wards like seven times, interred for months. So I've had a lot of hands-on experience of people, and people talk to each other much more than they talk to psychiatrists. People imagine that in a mental institution people are going to join hands and do group therapy. No! You spend ten minutes a week talking to someone – ten minutes! And the rest is just hanging about, smoking.' He laughs. 'So we talk to each other. It's almost like group therapy of our own – disorganised, unorganised, uniniti-ated group therapy. But you get to see and hear an awful lot. And my impression is that most people have a funda-mental deep-down cause.'

What did cycling do for him? 'Well,' says Obree, 'I can't speak for everybody, but I think within most human beings there must be a spectrum of depression or propensity to be depressed. And going off and doing loads and loads of exer-cise and being obsessive about something is a great way of avoiding self-analysis. And actually cycling's a great obses-sion because you can just do it for ages and ages, until you reach a point of collapse. It's also an equipment-based obsession, so you can be obsessed about that part of a bike that's going to be three grams lighter or is it a faster wheel or a slightly more aero helmet. You can set your bike up any way you want, or change things, or drill holes in things, or squash things. I'm always drilling holes and squashing things – "Oh, it might take a gram off that." My friends wouldn't leave their bikes in my house – "I'll just make that a bit more aero, a bit lighter, a bit cheaper."' He laughs. 'So you've got the duality of physical and mechanical obsession.' When they filmed *The Flying Scotsman*, Obree was played by Johnny Lee Miller, though many of the scenes on the track were filmed using Obree himself as a stand-in. He took to the prop copy of Old Faithful with a brazing torch, believing that its mono-fork construction might prove too weak.

'What unites an awful lot of people with mental illness or the symptoms of mental illness is that they don't fit into mainstream society. They don't fit into a group – they don't know why, but they just don't seem to fit. So they go off and do something on their own, and a bicycle is a great thing for that. I can't think of any other thing which is a pastime, a sport and also a vehicle of transport, all at different times and all at the same time. There's no team-mates, there's no bonding, there's no interaction you need with anybody else – you just go and do it. And your bike won't reject you. It won't question anything. It's a great thing. If you go back and you ride your bike and think, OK, imagine this is the first time I done this. If you're a child the first time you get a bike and you ride it, you go, wow! I can just bowl through the atmosphere at my own pace, I can cover four times the distance that I can on foot, I can go flying down hills and round corners and things. I mean, could it be that most cyclists are Peter Pans or Tinkerbells or something like that? They just haven't yet grown on to cars and bigger things.'

But Obree took it to a place beyond, a place where most people never go. His truly exceptional quality was the ability to suffer and the capacity to break through all the accepted barriers of pain or performance. As Steve Peters, now psychologist to Britain's Olympic cycle team, notes in *Full Circle*, a documentary made during the nineties recording the rivalry between Chris Boardman and Obree, there was something very damaged and damaging about the way Obree achieved what he did. And something very Scottish. With the first of the hour records in 1993, Obree was persuaded at the last minute to ride an unfamiliar bike. In front of the world's press and the UCI bigwigs, he broke the world sea-level record, but not the one that mattered – Francesco Moser's hour. 'At that moment,' he says in the book, 'I saw Old Faithful sitting sidelined and lonely at the side of the track, and something just snapped inside me. I stated that I was going again – on Old Faithful.' Most people would have needed at least four day's worth of recovery time. Obree spent the following night ensuring that his muscles didn't stiffen up by drinking enough water to force himself into waking up every couple of hours to pee. This time, when he arrived at the velodrome, there were only nine people watching. Just before the hour was up, the organisers fired a pistol; he had broken Moser's record. 'I felt like I had survived a near-catastrophic event, rather than performed one of the greatest turnarounds in sporting history.'

To do what he did, to have averaged a speed of more than 52kph for an hour twice in less than twenty-four hours, took something from 'a different physical level. I thought this in the past – I actually was willing to die rather than walk away without it. It was metronomic – I *will* pedal at this rate, and to hell with the consequences. Because the consequences of not breaking that record will be so much worse than …' – he hesitates – 'dying.' He laughs. 'Sounds awful! But within minutes of getting off that track the first day that I went for the record, the first day I didn't get it, even though I'd broken the world sea-level record, that immense blackness of failure was so *unbearable* it was, like, I've got to go again no matter what. And I *will* pedal at that rate, and I will break it, because this is *unbearable*. It wasn't livable with for a couple of minutes until I said I'm going again, and once I'd said I was going again, I wasn't a failure because I'm going to do it tomorrow so the failure was put back in the box, see? So it was only really a couple of minutes of it, but that couple of minutes was awful. So I thought, no – I'm going again. That sense of failure – *no*.'

Does he see what he did as extraordinary? 'Aye. But that's not normal, I don't represent a cross-section of cyclists. The question is, why did I choose cycling above any other sport?' OK, why? 'It's basically because it was accessible. And because you can do it without the influence of anybody else. You can do it in whatever way you want to and you can do as much of it as you want to. It's not like a football match – you want to play for another couple of hours but you can't just fetch everybody back out. And you can't football to the supermarket.'

Obree was lucky, he thinks now, to have had one outstanding rival, a contemporary who could match him race for race and win for win all the way to the finish line. Chris Boardman's methodology may have been – and still is – very different, but in terms of raw talent there was almost nothing to choose between them. As Boardman admitted in the *Full Cycle* documentary, 'I think Graeme and I are very, very different people, but the basic philosophy behind what we do is the same. We don't take things for granted, we don't accept the norm, we're very questioning people, we always want to know why – have we always done it that way, why should we do it that way? How we've decided to go about implementing that philosophy is very different.' So it was a healthy rivalry the two of them had? 'It *was* healthy,' says Obree now. 'Just being singly dominant in a sport and with no real rival at hand isn't healthy. So you need at least one person certainly to run you to your limit. And I would like to think that was good for Chris Boardman, to really, really have to run to his limit. Chris and I would ride a time trial, and one of us would win and one of us would be second, and there wouldn't be much between us. And the third rider would be minutes behind. So either of us could have turned up without the other one there, and not to diminish the quality of the other riders, but we could have put a good hard effort in and still have a big winning margin. Whereas if Chris was there, I'd have to run myself to my absolute limit to try and beat him. And I'd like to think that he was thinking, oh my goodness, Graeme's there, I've really got to give it full-on, head-to-head. And the other riders weren't even in the race – that's kind of how it was in the nineties. That's how it was, and it was good to have that rivalry. Because otherwise, who's going to push you to your limit?' There's a lovely moment in the documentary when Boardman, freshly beaten at the World Championships, gazes over towards Obree and says ruefully, 'The man just doesn't know what he's capable of.'

Predictably, Obree has a maverick take on training. 'Basically, training is so overrated, so overcomplicated in terms of what it is, because it's got to be complicated in order to sell books. But it's actually very simple; basically, destroy yourself, run yourself to the edge of your ability so that you're really run down, then get a good sleep and eat well. And then do it again. It's as simple as that. You could write it in one chapter, one paragraph even.' More than that, 'Training's actually bad for you.' How? 'Well, when you come back in the door after you've been training, you're less able to do what you did before you left the house. Because you're tired and you've used up a whole pile of energy, your blood sugar's probably diminished, you've probably strained or damaged your muscles to some degree. So you're less able to cycle than before you left the house. So it's bad for you. The only way it's good for you is when you over-recover from it, like you eat more good food, and you sleep well and you recover from that physical damage of training. You don't flog yourself to bits on the bike every day – that's why people fail.' What about Damian Coleman's estimate that fifteen hours a week would be a minimum commitment even for a club cyclist? 'It's excessive. It's not even accurate. You've got to train for what you do. There's no point in training for tennis if you're going to play snooker, is there? So if you're going to cycle up to a hundred miles a day, and then you want to win time trials at, like, twenty-five miles, very intense, and you've never actually trained at that level, then doing a hundred miles a day is not going to be any use. You'd be better doing twenty-five miles' hard training for the event you're doing.'

As for nutrition, 'If you look at the type of food I was eating – for example, my marmalade sandwiches. Now, what you've got is a mix of long-chain and short-chain carbohydrates. Whereas now people get these carbo-mix things' – he grimaces – 'ooeech, I would never countenance such things. These carbo-mix drink things they have are trying to imitate that, but you don't make money out of telling people to have a jam sandwich, do you?' An old racing friend of Obree's from the 1990s recalls watching him at breakfast in a hotel just before a race, picking up one of the small cornflakes packets and crushing the contents to a fine powder. All the racers at the other tables watched him surreptitiously and then started doing the same. Obree laughs and points out that his influence as a guru doesn't extend that far; he started wearing really loud jackets and shades at about the same time, and no one followed those.

So is he still experimenting with the way he rides? 'Oh, absolutely – I never stop questioning things. Even the simple things – the things we always accept. I just know that if I want to test something, I'll go out on the roads and up the hills, and I'll think, that feels right. And what feels right usually is right.' And does he get asked to train other people? 'Occasionally I have done. The problem being that I don't think other people are obsessional enough.' He smiles. So would people need to be devoted to cycling and nothing else? 'No, not at all. I think just being obsessed about cycling is actually a bad thing. I think people spend too long thinking about it. You should only really think about it and obsess about it when you're actually doing it. But I know people who think all week about a race – "Oh, that race, I really need to train, I really need to work, really going to give it large, really going to go for this ..." They're really, really on edge. They get to the start line, and they're, right, here we are, let's do it, and they're so drained from all that thinking that all this pith, all this magic energy, has just gone.'

He made another attempt at the hour record a few years ago, but it didn't work out. In an echo of his first attempt in 1993, the bike the sponsor wanted him to ride didn't feel right and the pressures on him seemed to be coming from the wrong direction. 'If I did it again,' he says now, 'I wouldn't do all that. I would do it my way.' Do you think you might try again? There's a long pause. Then he smiles. 'There's a distinct possibility.' Another, longer, pause. 'Do you want to see my record machine?' Yes! I say, absolutely! 'You do? Right, I'll bring it through to you. Wait here.' He gets up and goes out. A moment later, he wheels in a bike. The frame is a conventional diamond shape, round tubes, painted light powder blue with narrow drop handlebars, eighteen spokes to each wheel and the largest chain ring I have ever seen. Compared to Old Faithful or the World Championship bike, it looks astonishingly retro, the bike to end all bikes; sheer pared-down essence of bike. 'There!' says Obree, standing in front of it. 'Now you see what I'm saying! *That* is a beautiful machine. Built with my own hands. And you saw it first. Totally UCI legal, down to the absolute minimum of what the rules and regulations say this bike can be, sitting there nicely. So ...' And presumably this one doesn't include any bits of washing machines? 'That's right, it doesn't. It's completely 100 per cent kosher. And it's the first bicycle of all the bikes, Old Faithful and everything, it's the only bike I've got on to and it truly felt like an extension of my body.'

But, I say, you're forty-five. Obree sits down again. 'There's a whole age thing going on in cycling, and in sport. People think, oh, you're thirty-five or forty, you've really got to stop because you're on a downhill run, when in fact, I would never have been able to use that gear [67:13] in my twenties. No way. So I'm thinking, hold on, this is nonsense! There's no science to justify that you can't do your best at forty-something. And there's a forty-three-year-old man won the gold at the Olympics. If you're twenty-five and you're suffering from a bit of knee problem, you think, oh, what's happening with this knee, I better get it seen to and it will come good again. Whereas if you're thirty-five, you're then thinking, ohhh, I'm getting too old for it. So there's a different psychology. And I've heard of so many cases of people coming back and actually feeling stronger than ever. Guys in their forties thinking, "Why?"'

Just before I leave that day, I ask him if he'll let me know when he tries for the hour record. 'I'm not going to try for the record,' he says. I look confused. But surely ... 'Try – *try* for the record. That's such a Scottish way of looking at it. I'm going to *do* the hour record. I'm going to bring it back. Aren't I?' In the event, neither happens. Firstly, Obree discovers that the UCI now require six month's notice before any new attempt can be made. Then he's knocked back by a bad bout of flu. And then, having trained on the blue bike for months and publicly announced his intentions to take back the record, he finally tries the bike on the velodrome track. It doesn't work. As he says, 'That bike went so not good on the track and the riding style that was so good on the road was no good on the track.' A year later, I get an email. 'I'm doing ok but I must say it was a long dark winter.' He has signed up to read bio-medical science at university, riding to stay fit, working with another author on a new edition of *The Flying Scotsman*, and thinking about producing a training manual for novices. It sounds, I think, a healthy schedule.

What was it about the hour record, I'd asked him. Was it about beating Moser's time, or was it about something else? He replies without hesitation. 'It was the absolute purity of singular personal endeavour. It was the pure absolute cleanliness of it. It was the fact that you prepare the best you can mentally and physically to do this and there's no hiding place – it's like you and the track. There's no traffic, there's no other riders, there's just the whole world watching you going round that track on your own, seeing how fast you can push your body to break the record. It's like black or white – you either broke the record, or you didn't. Did, didn't. Just you and the silent black line. That is the ultimate test of fortitude. I mean, I was never that interested in doing the Tour de France or anything like that – it was always the hour record, the ultimate time trial. There's no team tactics, there's no anything. Even on an open road, you might get a tailwind or a headwind, or traffic pulling the air along a bit. None of that. Just nothing, apart from you and a bike and this set standard track. And that's the beauty of it. There's nobody else to blame, and nobody else to share the credit with. That's the beauty of it, and the cruelty of it. Sport is beautiful because it's cruel, it's the ultimate law of the jungle. The law of the jungle and survival of the fittest – literally.'

🚲 🚲 🚲

NINE

Bad Teeth No Bar

If Graeme Obree was fighting one kind of war with a bicycle, then the world's armies found another. Up to the Second World War, the history of military cycle usage was a patchy one, though most Western European countries had begun experimenting with the notion of establishing separate cycle corps by the late 1890s. In Britain the army had been equally quick to recognise the potential in bicycles, if not to fully exploit their advantages. By 1885, three volunteer Cycle Corps had been established, initially serving solely as scouts and messengers. There followed a long and unspectacular interlude while the army experimented with the idea of combining bicycles and artillery. The problems in getting cyclists to haul cannon were ably demonstrated when the 26th Middlesex Cyclist Regiment staged an exercise involving firing a Maxim gun from a cycle carriage. The gun weighed well over half a ton and the 'carriage' was no more than a couple of bikes welded together crossways. The whole apparatus could go no faster than a walking pace, was too heavy to cope with even the gentlest slope and required two further soldiers to pull it along. Later experiments with tricycles were equally

U.S. Cycle Corps in 1897.

demoralising. It was bad enough to invite public ridicule, but even worse when you were going too slow to escape it. Bicycles, it seemed, were ideal for reconnaissance and for moving around infantry troops quickly, but they couldn't be used for heavy weaponry. They weren't even ideal as transport. Soldiers who had ridden huge distances to get to the battlefield would be exhausted before they even began fighting. It was no use expecting them to carry huge loads, or to perform effectively after 100km or more.

So those who opposed the introduction of cycle corps realised that their best line of attack was not to compare bicycles to other machines – tanks, armoured vehicles – but to compare them to animals. A great warhorse, they argued, was an intelligent fighter in its own right, knowing exactly when to move forward and when to hold back, how to shield its rider from attack and where best to position itself. It could sense and hear danger long before a man could. It would work as hard as its rider for no more reward than a bit of forage. It was loyal, disciplined and courageous. It would deliver its rider to the battlefield rested and ready for action. And, most important of all, a horse provided a connection. It could be loved without condition or reserve by its rider for as long as both survived.

Still, those who supported bicycles counter-attacked, there were equally strong grounds for devoting more resources to cycling. Bicycles were cheap, small and cost-effective. They did not need stabling or fodder. They did not whinny or neigh at crucial moments, thereby betraying their riders' position. They did not suffer from exhaustion, illness or shellshock, and they could not be wounded. They had standardised replacement parts. They never got spooked. You could make them by the dozen. And, at the end of the day, they could be slung down anywhere and forgotten.

Unfortunately, as the cavalry lost no time in pointing out, bicycles had another insuperable disadvantage. It is much harder to fire a gun or rifle from a moving bicycle than it is to fire from the back of a horse. For centuries, cavalry officers had been using first swords and later guns as standard parts of their training. Warhorses were expected to ignore not just the sound of gun or cannon fire close by, but a gun being fired by their own rider. But trying to fire a rifle while maintaining a straight trajectory on a bicycle was a different matter. In order to take aim, a soldier needed to be properly balanced with one hand supporting the stock. If that soldier happened to be an extremely skil-ful cyclist on a perfect road surface, he might be able to let go of the handlebars long enough to aim and fire accu-rately, but war tends not to take place on perfectly level surfaces with no obstructions. As the cavalry argued, cyclists were infantry, mere foot soldiers who got around with the aid of these ugly new-fangled machines but who had to stop, get off and position themselves before they could even begin to do any real damage to the enemy. Besides, as Napoleon had long ago realised, a man on horseback – particularly if that man is armed and that horse is galloping towards you – is an altogether more daunting prospect than a man on a folding bicycle.

Which highlights the other main problem for army cyclists. Bicycles are just too nice. They may be no more than bits of steel slung together, but, like horses, people are fond of them. They associate bicycles with the more benign and open-hearted side of human nature, not with bombs and ingenious brutality. So much so, in fact, that those who have tried writing about bicycles in war have occasionally found themselves attacked for maligning them. Bicycles are also comical, and comedy and war don't really mix. A crack troop of cyclists, however brilliantly trained, still lacks the deadly gravitas of, say, a lone sniper or a battle tank. Which may be why, though the Americans brought over 29,000 bicycles for use during the First World War and 60,000 during the Second, none of them was used for front-line action. Instead, they were used to relay messages, reconnoitre positions, transport staff and chase down retreating Germans – occasionally in tandem with the horses they were originally intended to displace. The Second World War is always thought of as a fully mechanised conflict, but the Germans alone used 2.7 million horses between 1939 and 1945, double the number they had used during the Great War. They took or requisitioned over three-quarters of a million horses during the

A recruitment poster for the South Midland Divisional Cyclist Company.

invasion of Russia, many of which they were later forced to eat.

Back at the beginning of the twentieth century, cycles and cavalry were still squaring up to each other. By the outbreak of the First World War, there were almost 3,500 cyclists in volunteer regiments all over the UK – a generous number, particularly considering that they were all expected to supply their own cycles. They were used extensively during the Boer War for scouting, spying, moving troops and dispatch riding (messages or maps being rolled up and hidden in the seat tube), and even more so twelve years later. Despite the fact that trench warfare and two-wheeled transport were fundamentally incompatible, bicycles were used both at home and around the battlefields of Europe for patrols, reconnaissance and medical roles. Having been reluctantly accepted into the regular army, cycle messengers and scouts were now included in almost every unit. There were also between 14,000 and 18,000 men in separate cycle corps.

Frank Turner, a private who served on the Western Front, remembered the government's hunger for men. As a keen cyclist already, he turned up at the recruiting office in Holloway Library and was told by the officer on duty to fake his own birth date in order to appear older. His training in Hounslow was supplemented with 'Night operations on [Hampstead] Heath and going all over the place and all sorts of drills with the bikes and starting to shoot, firing at ranges'. As one of the elite who had mastered the tricky business of shooting and riding at the same time, Turner was picked out along with thirty others as potential snipers and sent to the ranges at Runnymede and Bisley. The train-ing was not an unqualified success; in hilly areas, there were so many falls that 'We left about eight chaps in hospi-tal.' Having landed in France in 1916, Turner and the rest of the Cycle Corps rode down towards the front line. 'They'd amassed hundreds of thousands of cavalry and cyclists over what was to be the Somme Front.' But instead of being pitched immediately into battle, they were forced to wait a couple of weeks, drilling and patrolling while the killing crept closer. Riding on to Loos, he was told to be on parade with the rest of the snipers the following afternoon. 'Out come the skipper, he's almost in tears. He said, I've had orders from the Divisional General to say you must go in line with the Infantry.' Assigned to the 119 Brigade, Turner's role was to cover the line. 'That was our primary object, dislodging enemy snipers.' Having by some miracle remained alive through everything, Turner later recalled the strange double life of war. Once in a while, he and the other surviving members of the corps would climb out and disappear for a few hours. 'I used to play the piano a lot. I only play it by ear, but at nighttime we used to walk back out of the trenches – only us, you know, the cyclists … in a mining town, it's a mining area all round Loos, civilians were living there I would think only about a mile and a half from the front line.' And there Turner would play the piano for a few hours, and by doing so keep his sanity intact.

The First World War's ravening appetite for men, materials and munitions inevitably gobbled up bikes as well. Within months of the outbreak of war, the big framebuilders in Birmingham and Coventry found their factories co-opted for machinery, their labour force conscripted for war work and their raw materials requisitioned for arms. Workers who had spent half a lifetime making handlebars or brake cables suddenly found themselves churning out shells. During the Second World War, J. A. Phillips, one of the largest bike manufacturers in Birmingham, turned their entire production over to munitions. It was later estimated that they had produced eighty-nine million shells as well as aircraft parts, grenades and landmines 'by the million'. As a result, the industry found itself in the peculiar position of taking on thousands more workers to make thousands fewer bikes. By 1918, employment at BSA had almost quadrupled, but their cycle exports had fallen by 80 per cent. Nor did the demand for iron and steel stop at raw materials. By 1940, anything that could be turned into arms – old farm machinery, park railings, kitchen utensils, bicycles – was being gathered up by the Ministry of Supply. For a while, the whole country devoted itself to turning ploughshares into swords. George Bernard Shaw, who remained convinced that the great steel barons of the inter-war period had actively encouraged conflict with Germany to boost demand, put his suspicions on stage in *Major Barbara*. When introducing the film version in 1941 he thanked the Americans – with heavy irony – for their loan of a few aged destroyers in exchange for what remained of Britain's bike frames.

But at the same time as many British bicycles were being melted down, others were finding alternative combat roles. From 1939, the Camouflage section of the Special

Operations Executive was housed at the Thatched Barn in Borehamwood in Hertfordshire. While other parts of SOE concentrated on decoding ciphers or improving armaments, Station XV's mission was disguise and deception. Its job was to concentrate on producing false documents to allow the free movement of Allied agents, and to dream up new methods of camouflaging vital equipment for use in the field. Thus the two most essential qualities for anyone working at Station XV were ingenuity and a complete lack of scruples. It was not for nothing that they later became known as the Dirty Tricks Brigade. Two things made their work easier. Firstly, they were led by Captain J. Elder Wills, who had served briefly in the Royal Flying Corps during the First World War before spending the next twenty years working variously as an actor, a stagehand, a producer and a film director. Twenty years' experience in illusion and make-believe plus a light dusting of military discipline was just what SOE needed. Better still, the Thatched Barn was almost next door to Elstree Film Studios. Wills and his agents found they had the resources of an entire film studio to draw on. When he required help with ideas or supplies, he needed nothing more than to consult his list of contacts and put in a call to the studio. Elstree spent the war years churning out fortifying movies for the home audience, so Wills made full use of their expertise, recruiting propmakers and stage managers from the studios and setting them to work.

Many of the objects used at Station XV to disguise bombs or traps have since become famous – the incendiary rats and the blow-up coal, the primed logs and the booby-trapped food tins. Cigarettes which exploded when lit were a particular speciality; it was later estimated that the Thatched Barn had produced around 43,700. Jack Knock, an NCO who served with SOE in Britain and France, spent time at Borehamwood and was later interviewed about his work. As he explained, he and everyone else at the Station knew the value of what they were doing. 'Great care had to be taken by everybody. You didn't go to work with a headache and think, "Oh Christ, another one of those." You sort of told yourself, "Now, come on, son. Let's really be on the ball. Let's not blow our bloody hands off."' Along with the other agents in the laboratory, his job was to find enterprising new ways of sabotaging German communication lines and transports, and where possible the Germans themselves. Which is why he spent a lot of time studying dung.

As part of general sabotage efforts, Station XV was issued with a horse whose sole contribution to the war effort was to provide Knock and his fellow agents with adequate supplies of manure. Once the horse had done its duty, Knock would then take a plaster cast of the resulting manure and make a mould of it. The mould was then filled with explosive glue and shipped over – at considerable risk – to resistance agents in Occupied France. The agents would cover the fake manure with the real thing, place it in the middle of the road, and wait for a German military vehicle to drive over it. 'Now, after a time, the Germans got to know about this. But you see, that wasn't the end of it, because every time they came across a piece of horse dung, they had to examine it to make sure it wasn't [going to explode] ... But until someone had examined it, every

German vehicle, every vehicle on the road, would have to go off the road, over a ditch, into a field, through the field, back over a ditch and back onto the road and start going along again to see another pile of horse dung further along. So, you see, you held up everybody.'

Having found alternative uses for manure, it didn't take long for the Dirty Tricks Brigade to see the potential in bicycles. Bikes were perfect for camouflage. They were innocuous, everyday objects, the sort of thing that (before the war at least) every household had possessed, and they were stuffed full of gaps and crevices in which things could be concealed. As agents in other countries had also realised, they could also be used to produce an electric charge. An ordinary bicycle fitted with a stand and a small generator was capable of charging up a wireless battery. Even better, it was almost completely silent. In Belgium, the resistance movement designated a team of five hundred cyclists to sabotage German communication lines. They worked at night, using country lanes and pathways off the main roads, and in many places became so effective that the Germans were forced to devote their full attention and resources to counter-attacking. As soon as the Germans mounted their own bicycles and set off down the darkened paths, they would be ambushed by the saboteurs.

SOE found other uses as well. The small cans of lubricant which cyclists often carried with them could be copied and filled with explosive. When the cyclist came to use the oil, the can would detonate. Likewise, French agents would be detailed to steal the pumps off a German bike and dispatch them to Borehamwood where exact imitations would be made. When the fake pumps were sent back to France, the agents would select a bike belonging to a suitable German target and let down one of the tyres. Jack Knock again: 'The German would come along, would take his pump and the first pump he gave, of course, he would blow his hands off. It's an awfully dirty trick, now I come to think of it. So after a time, the Germans wouldn't use their pumps, they went around on tyres that were flat, which did not help one little bit for convenience or anything else. The same applied with the Germans' torches. You would remove the German's torch and put yours back in its place and the poor sod would again lose his hands when he switched it on.' Though Knock enjoyed the challenge of his work and the free rein to come up with new ideas, he was not always comfortable with the potential results. 'Some of the things we did could be termed atrocities. They couldn't be termed warfare – not blowing up people with torches. ... I still remember being in this shed, doing these jobs that I was doing and knowing what was likely to happen as a result and not quite liking it.'

The German response to the damage caused by SOE and other resistance movements was a complex one. Clearly it wasn't going to be possible to ban or to confiscate all the millions of bicycles in circulation since, without them, the whole of Occupied Europe would grind to a halt. The bombing of many towns and cities meant that many roads had either been destroyed or were still so covered in rubble they were impassable to motorised traffic. In many places, the only way to get around was either on foot or by bike. Besides, by 1941, the sheer size of the Third Reich was so vast that keeping control of it with cars and trucks alone was no longer feasible. Hitler's new empire now stretched all the way from the ice fields of Finland to the cypress groves of Italy. Keeping control of the local populations in the flatlands of Belgium or northern France was one thing, but keeping control of the population in the Pyrenees or around the Norwegian fjords was quite another. As always, the simplest forms of transport proved the best. Bikes or horses could get up hills or through forests in a way that cars or tanks could not, and could carry loads that men on foot would struggle with.

On the other hand, the Germans evidently had to do something about the ways in which the bicycle was being used against them. They came up with two solutions. One was to expand the ways in which they themselves used bicycles into new areas. Officers trained to deal with chemical and biological weapons were issued with bicycles in whose frames were concealed entire detection kits. Full protection suits, gas masks and boots were arranged in pouches around the bike. The other solution was, predictably, to restrict the use of bicycles by others. In France, it became impossible to buy a new bicycle without official consent or ride one without a permit. By 1942, it was made illegal to ride a bicycle after dark through much of the country. In Berlin, all Poles were banned from owning or using a bicycle at all. If bicycles were to be used, in other words, they would be used by Germans alone.

Perhaps the starkest example of the Germans' wartime policy could be found in the Netherlands. Even now, if you go to a Holland *v.* Germany football match, you'll hear the

Dutch fans chanting at the opposing side, 'Give us back our bicycles!' It's not the best chant ever devised, but the spirit remains the same – a joke makes both defeat and victory a little bit more bearable. The Netherlands were overrun in five days in May 1940, and spent the remainder of the war under occupation.

Like Belgium, they were far too strategically useful to both sides ever to remain neutral. Having bombed the country into submission, the Germans used it as a giant military supermarket, while the Allies regarded it as a vital stepping stone to the rest of Europe. The winter of 1944 was so harsh and the country's natural resources already so denuded that an estimated 18,000 people died of starvation. And so, between the good guys, the bad guys and God, the Dutch ended the war both broke and broken. Their houses had been flattened or flooded, their contents had been burned and their only means of transport – the bicycle – had been requisitioned by the Germans as a getaway vehicle.

To begin with, the Nazis hadn't thought much of the Dutch passion for cycling. As far as they were concerned, bicycles were cumbersome and got in the way, and using a child's plaything as a form of transport seemed ridiculous. Disdain rapidly gave way to pragmatism. Dutch bicycles might appear to be transport throwbacks, but they were at least faster than walking. So the Germans seized everything they could find. In two weeks during July1942, the demand for bicycles grew ravenous; station parks were summarily emptied and anyone who had left a bike outside their house overnight woke to find it gone. The thefts only exacerbated the divisions between the civilian population and the occupying forces. 'No other German enactment has called up such bitterness in all ranks of society as this one,' reported one senior German serviceman. 'The Dutchman, who is practically born on a bicycle, views the seizing of that bicycle to be nearly the worst thing that can happen to him.' Even when the Dutch did manage to keep their cycles to themselves, many of those cycles had become unrideable. The worldwide demand for rubber after 1941 meant that tyres and inner tubes were rationed items. The alternative, with both tyres and other spare parts, was to improvise. Wooden rims could be substituted for metal ones and rope for pneumatic tyres. Broken pedals were replaced with bits of old timber, snapped frames splinted with broom handles. Meanwhile, anyone who wanted a new bike had to demonstrate not only that they'd completely worn out the previous one, but that they lived at least five kilometres from their place of work and thus found a bicycle essential to their livelihood. The scarcities became even more pronounced when the Germans started requisitioning or destroying the machinery from large-scale framemakers. In many cases, much of the essential manufacturing equipment was dismantled and taken back to Germany. Unsurprisingly, the changes meant that the number of cyclists in the Netherlands halved.

Back in Britain, the army was putting its efforts into developing bicycles which might speed up travelling times. In theory, a portable form of transport was exactly what the Allies needed, since it surely couldn't be that difficult to come up with a folding bicycle which cost little to produce and could be easily carried. In practice, the problems

The Welbike, or Parascooter. Intended for use during
the Normandy Landings, most were abandoned on the
sandy beaches.

proved almost insuperable. The French had been working
on a practicable design since before the First World War,
and by 1914 had perfected a version which could be folded
wheel-to-wheel rapidly and elegantly. The bikes had a
conventional diamond frame and, when combined with an
almost painfully chic uniform – including small pillbox
kepi – allowed their riders to look like an advert for stylish,
no-nonsense cycling. When folded and carried on a
soldier's back along with both kit and rifle, they were less
elegant. The sheer weight of all that steel meant that cycle

troops were often bent double, unable to move fast or to lift more than they were already carrying.

By the Second World War, further thought had gone into developing a smaller, lighter folding cycle. For the British, this resulted in two different solutions. First, there were parascooters, or Welbikes, tiny motorcycles with 125cc two-stroke engines and a maximum speed of 40mph. Design-wise, they were indeed a solution to the problem of getting around quickly. Aesthetically, they were less success-ful. In order to be portable, they had to be tiny and very low-slung, effectively just a child's bicycle with a lawn-mower engine attached. According to Raymond Mitchell, an NCO serving as a dispatch rider with 41 Commando Royal Marines, a parascooter was 'A long low engine with about twelve-inch wheels at either end with a seat which folded down, handlebars which folded down. That was to go in a parachute container, so it was – oh, about four or five foot long and must have weighed more than about 70lb … The intention was on D-Day that we would go ashore carrying one.' They spent a couple of months training – 'we had good fun tootling around Hastings on these little parascooters until they told us to keep them for the day. That stopped us surprising civilians who were quite amazed to see big men tripping around on what looked like chil-dren's motorbikes!' Sure enough, the footage of paratroops in training on the eve of the D-Day landings shows several sturdy looking Paras squelched onto their Welbikes, knees flung out at right angles and elbows jammed to their sides.

On 6 June 1944, the 6th Airborne Division brought with them 12,148 men of all ranks and a total of 6,210 vehicles, including 1,362 folding bicycles. Of the six dispatch riders in Mitchell's brigade, only four were chosen to go ashore with the other troops on D-Day. The reality of the landings was something they could never have prepared for. Once ashore, 'The troop doubled off along the beach, passing tanks and vehicles and shells plopping down. I did my best to follow on, carrying this 75lb of metal. When my arms couldn't take any more, I popped it on the sand and tried to push it, but with the small wheels, it was just gouging a furrow in the sand and the wheels weren't turning. So for, oh, about five minutes or so – it seemed an awful long time – while the others were going out of sight, I alternated between trying to carry the thing and trying to push it.' Eventually, Mitchell accepted the inevitable. He had come

The BSA folding bicycle.

up alongside a crew crouching beside their tank. 'I knew that if I stuck to my bike, I'd lose the troop. So I recall saying to one of these crew, I said, "Here, mate, want a bike?" I just dropped it there and doubled off.' Many of the other Welbikes – and a large number of the BSA folding bicycles – suffered the same fate. No two-wheeled object, however ingenious, has ever coped well with sand. And, given the curious shape of the Welbike, it may, after all, be a mercy that most of the bikes were too cumbersome to serve their purpose. If the Germans had seen the British invading on parascooters, perhaps the outcome of the war would have been very different.

The alternative to the parascooters was the BSA bike, a design with double curving top and down tubes forming an elegant central ellipsis. To store it, the user undid two butterfly bolts and folded it wheel-to-wheel in the centre. All the bikes were single-speed and included a strong front rack for carrying kit; army films of the time show the Paras riding round with collapsible four-man dinghies strapped to the front of the bike, which gives some idea of the volume and weight of materials they were intended to carry. They were also meant to be strapped uncovered to the front of parachutists and used on drops. In theory, sending parachutists straight into battle carrying their own means of transport should have been ideal. In practice, the sharp edges of the folded bike meant that several got fouled in the parachutes during drops and very nearly killed their operators. Even when both bikes and riders could be landed safely, they did not prove popular. William Parker Brown, an NCO serving with the Durham Light Infantry, later explained what happened to many of the folding bikes. Having landed safely in France just before D-Day in June 1944, Brown and the other cyclists in the company were supposed to fall into line with the rest of the infantry. 'They was bloody daft to us, cycling along at a marching pace. So I'll tell you how we got rid of them. When they brought the tanks up, there was a tank driver there … I said, "Do us a favour." He said, "What?" I said, "Run over them bloody bikes with your track!" He says, "Run them over?" "Aye," I says. So he just ran the tank down and drove back over them.'

But it is the Swiss who remain most closely identified with military cycling. For almost two centuries, their policy has been one of armed neutrality, now maintained by part-time conscription for all healthy individuals between the ages of seventeen and thirty-two. After four months of basic training, recruits are sent back to civilian life but expected to keep themselves fit in preparation for the annual refresher courses. 'Switzerland does not have an army,' as one of its own writers put it, 'it *is* an army.' When the first experimental cycle corps was established in 1891, most of its recruits were drawn from local clubs and touring groups, all of which preserved their own amateur ethos. Thus the early Swiss army cyclists were often criticised for being undisciplined, unreliable or prone to desertion. Many recruits failed basic fitness tests or had trouble staying upright at all. Their bikes were badly constructed and often fell apart at crucial moments. When recruits were informed that they were expected to be able to cycle at least 100km a day, several insisted on transfers to the infantry.

Even so, and despite the difficulties in finding recruits fit enough to deal with Switzerland's diagonal landscape, the idea of a cycle corps took hold. The realisation that cyclists could travel four times the distance of either infantry or cavalry proved a major incentive to the army high command. Just as persuasive was a 1904 review in which it was noted that it cost six or seven times more to equip, train and pay a member of the cavalry than it did to maintain a cyclist – 4,838 SFr for a cavalry officer's full period of service compared to 834 SFr for a cyclist. They also proved their worth in combat. During the First World War, the cycle corps were involved in around five hundred or six hundred days of active service. Their role was considered so valuable to the army that by the mid-1920s their numbers had been boosted from 2,500 men to 6,300. Even so, being a Swiss army cyclist was not an easy job – the bikes themselves weighed a minimum 30kg unladen and between 40 and 70kg with their full complement of food, kit and munitions. The bike that was introduced in 1903 remained almost unchanged for nearly a century, and was only reluctantly exchanged for a stunning new lightweight 20kg model with hydraulic brakes and an unprecedented seven gears because they'd run out of spare parts for the old ones.

By the mid-1990s, the Swiss army cycle corps had three infantry regiments of cyclists. All conscripts would be expected to manage a 200km ride in twenty hours before completing their basic training – which, since the weight of a bike went down by a mere 10kg to around 50kg and Switzerland is still as hilly as it ever was, was a significant achievement. Over the years, their role had expanded from the basic scouting and dispatches duties to include security patrols and border control; in the event of war, they would have been used for urban warfare, countering air attacks and in tricky or otherwise inaccessible areas. Stefan Schaerer, who served as an officer in the cycle corps, explained that 'the cyclists were trained just as infantry troops (shooting, mining, tank defence, blasting, guarding etc.). We were known as a fast mobile intervention force without motor vehicles. In addition we were deployed as support units for mechanised forces.' Despite the ferocity of the training regime, the Swiss army cycle regiments were held in high esteem; most regiments had waiting lists, and all benefited from a strong sense of national pride in their achievements. Schaerer was 'Proud to be a cyclist in the Swiss army. The esprit de corps was extraordinary and the cyclists were well known for their team spirit – I really wanted to be part of the troop.' But by the turn of the millennium, the need for the corps was beginning to fade. After one final 200km cross-Alpine yomp for auld lang syne, it, too, finally went the way of the cavalry, the carrier pigeons and the packhorses, and expired completely in 2004.

橞 橞 橞

TEN

Axles of Evil

Michael Barratt: You can break the job into three or four parts: riding, picking up stuff, and dropping …
Adrian Davies: And the arguing in between with motorists.

It's a strange thing that the bicycle messenger as a species seems to be wobbling on the brink of oblivion just at the moment when half the cyclists in Britain start wanting to look like bike messengers. Move around any city in the UK, and it seems the streets are full of people with postbags, caps and fixies moving urgently through the streets on their way to another £3 job. The only telltale signs that these individuals are not in fact the real deal are a couple of significant plusses and minuses: no radio aerial poking up above their shoulder, no crackle of static, about three stone in additional weight and several hundred quid or so on the bike.

There are, of course, bigger differences than that. It isn't that difficult to tell a messenger from a fakenger – someone who's bought the look – because of the way they move. If you spend an average of eight hours a day on a bicycle in all weathers balancing unwieldy weights on a light frame, then over time something begins to happen to your physique. You begin to look like you live on the road, and you begin to ride like it, too.

If you follow a courier for any distance at all down the city streets, you can watch them dance. There's something about the way they balance which makes it look like the lightest, most graceful piece of urban ballet in the world. You can see that the bike has stopped being an assemblage of tubes and wheels and become for a while an extension of someone's skeleton. Watch them, and you realise it's a different sort of movement to racers. The way someone sits on a very light-weight, highly geared road bike is different from the way someone sits on a £10 thing hot from Brick Lane on a high street stuffed with rogue pedestrians. Both may ride a bike for money, both may spend all day in the saddle, and both may or may not be using performance-enhancing drugs, but it's different. There's something about being both completely connected to a place and completely disconnected from its rules which is peculiarly exhilarating. Messengers have a sense of privilege, of having been given the keys to the city and of having found some of its secrets along the way. They belong, but they're not on the payroll. They've got no ties and no obligations; they've only got their bike, their knowledge and themselves. That sense of difference makes them loners, but it also makes them a tightly connected group with a particularly strong identity.

Patrick Field: I've been a bike messenger. It's not much of a job, but it's a very cheap hobby. That was in the days when bicycle messengers actually made money instead of being lifestyle heroes. That was before the invention of email. I think it might even have been before the invention of the fax machine, when there really was lots of work. It's finished now, really. It's interesting that Queen Victoria started wearing tartan on the day the last Highlander was driven out of the Highlands, and this fixation with the bicycle messenger culture and people riding single-speed bikes and wearing courier bags comes just as the bicycle messenger rides off to join the organ-grinder and the cinema projectionist.

Messengers have existed for as long as bikes and cities have existed. The first were used in Paris way back near the beginning in 1874. The banks needed to get messages to the telegraph offices quickly, and a man on a bicycle – or, rather, thirty men on thirty penny farthings – was considered the best way of doing so. In the long-gone days before any form of telephones or electronics, couriers were vital to the communication of information. It was a role the military also rapidly picked up on. Recently released archive material includes the records of one Lance Corporal Adolf Hitler serving as a bike messenger to the Bavarian army during the First World War. His job was to ferry messages from the troops on the battlefield to the command staff.

The sense of pride many couriers felt for their work and their city almost inevitably translated itself into racing. Now, messengers organise alley-cat races – timed sprints round some part of the city, either after hours or in the middle of the day. There are set pick-ups and drop-offs at certain points, or there are tasks, or there's a theme to the ride, even if it's sometimes just wearing fancy dress. It's not sophisticated; one race might involve getting a particular receptionist's signature while another might require a love poem in fifty words or pinning the right dick to the right male porn star. In the beginning they didn't involve that many people, but since films of many alley-cat races have started appearing on YouTube and gaining publicity, larger numbers have started turning up for them, attracted by the visceral thrill of playing high-speed games out there in the traffic.

Messenger races are nothing new, though. In Paris they've been chasing each other round the city since bikes and newspapers were first invented. By the early twentieth century, most of the city's newspaper and delivery needs were served by the fleets of porteurs, each employed by an individual publication and each riding specially adapted bikes capable of taking weights of up to 50kg on the front rack. They had extra-strong wheels, wide tyres and almost bomb-proof construction. Since many of the porteurs were amateur racers, they found the challenge of competition almost irresistible, and the Critérium des Porteurs de Journaux regularly attracted more than 170 entrants. In the early years, it was organised much like an alley cat now, with the 'roule-toujours' expected to navigate themselves and their paper loads through the midday traffic while either picking further cargo up or dropping things off at fixed marker points along the route. Hills, cobbles and hazards were naturally built in, and from the beginning there were separate events for both male and female riders. As in pro racing, newspapers took a keen interest, not just reporting on the Critérium, but spon-

The 1937 Porteurs' Race in Paris. Entrants would be expected to make several laps of the centre whilst carrying up to 15 kgs of newspapers on their front racks.

soring it as well. Competition between different titles – evening papers, weekend editions, local rags – leapt from the newsstands onto the streets. Could Ce Soir *prove quicker with that day's headlines than* Paris-Presse? *Would* L'Intransigeant *beat the lead off* Sport-Complet? *As the race evolved and became a regular autumn fixture, so a route settled and established itself. The riders would start from Montmartre, race down the rue de Clichy past the Arc de Triomphe towards the Tour Eiffel, spin round some of the peripheral roads on the Rive Gauche and then sprint back up the hill towards the old newspaper district.*

The whole thing was watched as keenly as the end of the Tour de France is now. Part of its charm was the race's unofficial nature. 'You have no idea of the tumult and obstruction caused by the huge crowds gathered to watch the innumera-

ble vehicles who follow the truly acrobatic efforts of the riders,' reported Le Miroir des Sports *breathlessly after the 1931 race.* 'On their heavy work bikes burdened with 15kg of newspapers, the cyclo-porteurs zigzag in all directions, slip with incredible agility between the cars and overcome the 27km imposed on them with extraordinary panache.' And the speeds were impressive; from the 1940s onwards, winners regularly achieved average speeds of 40 to 45kph round the 37km route. Naturally, cheating was as prevalent in this race as in any other. One 1936 competitor was discovered to have completely hollowed out his load of newspapers, leaving only a couple of sheets over the top and bottom, while others sliced chunks from the edges of their piles on the pretext of being able to reach the handlebars. Inevitably, it was difficult for the racers to get exactly the right balance between haste and stability, and cornering well while going at 50kph on a hill through traffic carrying the equivalent of a medium-sized library took a genuinely exceptional level of nerve and skill.

The success of the porteurs' race spawned several offshoots, the most notable of which was the annual Triporteurs' Race. Back at the turn of the century, much of Paris's smaller freight went by cargo trike. The riders sat behind their loads while on the axle between the two front wheels a huge metal box shaped like a pocket rocket was suspended. The boxes were usually covered in large-print advertisements and had a habit of lurching from side to side when moving at anything above walking pace. Unsurprisingly, audiences loved watching a bunch of men racing through Paris with something of the size and aerodynamism of a coffin strapped to their frames. The triporteurs too obviously loved the opportunity

The rival Triporteurs' race in 1927 – the same idea as the Porteurs' race except with much heavier loads and less aerodynamism.

to show off, though not all of them stayed the full course. Though there were many entrants, there were often 'many heroic abandonments at the cafés', as one reporter noted in 1928. The race had a riotous character and a passionate following, even if at times it must have looked like a Parisian milk-float caper.

Despite fierce competition from Robert Petit, known as the 'Flying Cyclops' because he had only one eye, Marcel Cognasson won the competition seven times, emerging victorious even when the payload was raised from 65 to 80kg. Over the years, the stakes got higher. By 1936, when Cognasson was finally beaten, the winner completed the 40km course in seventy-five minutes at an average speed of

30kph. Photographs show the Tour Eiffel looming foggily in the background as a flock of tricyclists hurtle up the cobbled streets in white caps and short sleeves, many on two wheels and some on just one. The race continued into the war, though with an altered character. Because of the lack of materials, the big cargo trikes were replaced by normal racing bikes pulling trailers at the back. Many of the rules also went freestyle; when competitors lost part of their sandbag cargos during the 1940 race, they simply used cobblestones from the road.

🚲 🚲 🚲

In front of the windows outside the Duke of York pub on Clerkenwell Road in London there are metal bars painted red like the windowsills. A constant stream of commuters and couriers slide past on their way home while the messengers sit in the doorways down the alleyway, thinking and smoking.

The second time I go, Adrian Davies (tall, pale, lanky, never meets your eye, looks like he needs a good meal and a hug) and Michael Barratt (extrovert, with a ruff of greying hair poking out from under his cap, starts out more combative but then opens out) form a double act for the evening. To begin with, Adrian plays the straight guy, Michael plays the joker. We sit in the pub watching the couriers and the wannabes, and I buy them a drink.

Adrian: I'm thirty-three. I got into it because I was married for seven years, then I split from my wife and moved back to London, and in order for me to carry on seeing my daughter I had to get a job, and the first thing I found was courier work. I've been doing it for ten years now, on and off.

Michael: I fell into it. I've been doing it for about ten years. I'm forty-five. I was working as a traffic enumerator for a while.

Adrian: Counting cars, basically.

Michael: Counting cars, counting pedestrians, counting trains. A clicker.

Why did you start?

Adrian: Money.

Michael: I started because I noticed a courier, and I thought, 'I could do that job.' That's why I took it. It probably paid better than what I was getting at the time. And then I stayed because I bumped into a lot of people I could chat to, made a whole lot of friends – and enemies, I guess – and just increased my social circle.

Adrian: The average pay is between £250 and £350 a week. They take advantage.

Michael: We work hard, but we're rewarded for it in certain ways. We have perks. We don't knock over pedestrians.

Adrian: It is low paid. It's hard to get in with companies now – the work's getting thin. There's hardly any work around any more. People aren't sending it out any more – it's going via the internet. You get CDs, lawyers' stuff, cheques, divorce papers and stuff …

Michael: Sometimes, now, I'm coming to work and doing nothing for two or three hours – just sitting there. But when I first started, that wasn't the case.

Motorbikes are effectively their main competitors because they're faster over the long distances and can carry greater weights. But motorbikes are expensive to run and have no particular advantages over bicycles within short distances. So if you've got an 8kg package for a client, by rights it should go either with a motorcycle courier or a van. In practice, the company would much rather send it out with a cycle courier and pocket the van rate.

How many couriers are there in London?

Adrian: City Sprint has over sixty-five pushbike riders, and that's just one company. Our company only has three.

Michael: I've worked for City Sprint. Directions – Directions have got a few. But they're one of the worst companies.

Adrian: They've got the oldest courier. Pete. He's sixty-eight.

Michael: Bloody hell. I've got plenty of time ahead of me.

Adrian: And he never stops.

Michael: He got knocked off the other day as well. Didn't you see him?

Adrian: Monday?

Michael: No, it wasn't Monday, but he got knocked off – old guy he is, Irish I think. It looked like he'd been drinking or been in a punch-up. His face was black, down here (*he points to his legs*) was black … I said, 'Pete, what's happened to you?' He gone, 'You know Holborn Viaduct?' I said, yeah. He said, 'Me and a taxi were having a race to see who could be first.' He said, 'The taxi won, basically.'

Adrian: That's what happened to Mahelly. He got knocked off – some pedestrian walked in front of him and knocked him off. Hit him in the face, and he had to have a titanium plate put into the side of his face. He had the operation this week, and he's back on circuit.

Michael: Hilarious.

Because couriers are classified as self-employed subcontractors, they have no financial security when they're injured – if they can't work, they don't earn. But no one seems that fussed about the lack of rights; if that was the price of freedom, then that was the price they'd pay. Attempts to organise messengers into unions or campaigning groups usually sputter out; in many cities the messenger communities are very strong, but they're not centred around rights or conditions, they're centred around pubs, races and jokes.

The only official study into the occupational risks of bicycle courier work was conducted in 1992 in Boston by the Harvard School of Public Health. They found that 90 per cent of the 113 couriers surveyed had sustained an injury of some sort, and that 27 per cent of them had at some point been injured badly enough to require hospitalisation.

Would you recommend couriering to someone as a profession?

Adrian: From what I know now, no.
Michael: Yeah, but what you know now is about life, really, isn't it? I'm not sure I'd advocate it as a career move, though. It is dangerous, it is very dangerous. Compared

to most other kinds of work … If you had a loved one or a friend and they told you they were going to start a career in central London or central New York or something, it's like, yeah, brilliant, but after three or four months, you start wondering, hmmm, are they going to come home?

Adrian: They say the life expectancy is three years for a courier. (*He gets out his iPhone and looks up the Moving Target site which has several discussion forums. There are several topics on offer – notices of impending races, information about emergency funding for injured riders, the HGV campaign – plus 'Waterproof Fabrics: Do They Really Exist?', 'What To Do If You Get Run Over' and 'My Spunk Has Blood In It'.*)

Michael: It might have something on the courier who had an accident on Monday.

Adrian: It was called Black Monday, wasn't it, because there was three people had accidents – three guys and a motorcyclist. Just by coincidence, in different parts of the city.

Michael (*he had met up with one of the injured couriers earlier in the day*): We met in the morning, said hello to the people we usually said hello to, round about 10 a.m., I went back to the café because it's a nice warm place and we end up hanging round there. I think Errol might have told me first, Errol or Roger. I go, fuck! They said, he's got knocked off, dragged along by a truck, then all the stories about his legs hanging off and blah blah blah. And then a blue tarpaulin and I thought he was dead because that's what a blue tarpaulin means.

Adrian: You know why they put that up? Cos so much blood was coming out of him, draining into the gutter. People say it was his own fault (*later reports contradicted this, saying that the HGV driver simply hadn't seen him*), he was on the pavement, and he jumped off the pavement onto the road, and a lorry come round a blind spot and he clipped the side of the lorry and apparently he got chucked under the wheel and the wheel was still going round, dragging him. He was banging on the side, the passenger side. Someone else broke his ankle that day, and someone broke his arm and a motorcyclist got killed.

When something like that happens, does it affect you?

Adrian: Not me personally because the way I see it, you've got to die, and you die, do you know what I mean? I kind of block it out and carry on. Some of the guys, they were thinking, oh, I don't want to do this any more, I'm going home. Some of them actually did go home. News gets round very quick. One person knows something, everybody will know it within about an hour. You hear about accidents every day, but not like on Monday.

Michael: It could have been me. Then again, it couldn't have been me because …

Adrian: You're very cautious.

Michael: I'd rather be careful than sorry. It could have been me when I first started, definitely. Quite easily. Because the first thing you want to do when you start is jump on the pavements, do red lights, scare pedestrians, buzz out grannies, blah blah blah. But when you've been in it for a while, you change. I've found out I can do the job, it's quite easy, I can enjoy it, and I can also enjoy life without going through a red light. I think you fit in with the job more.

Both of them have had minor injuries – Michael broke his wrist when he first started after his brakes failed, Adrian hit a pedestrian who'd stepped out into the road to take a photograph. He went down, the pedestrian fell on him, smashing a rib and kneecap. Do most couriers accept injury as part of the job?

Michael: Yes.

Adrian: It's what you expect, really.

Michael: I mean, when you first start, that's what you think. When you get knocked off, you pick yourself up, dust yourself down, hopefully you haven't broken anything and if you have, go to hospital, take the rest of the time off. But I've been told by a reliable source that if we were to be insured, it would be high. We're untouchable, really, when it comes to insurance.

'Buffalo' Bill Chidley is the messengers' messenger. Having been a courier himself for fourteen years, he gave it up at the millennium, took over Moving Target, a website 'zine, and began campaigning on behalf of messengers – specifically, and most successfully, on the HGV issue. We meet in a coffee bar on Charlotte Street; he's wearing a better-laundered version of archetypal messenger kit: baggy rolled-up jeans – which he rolls up further at one point to show the network of scar tissue covering his calves – and a shirt with a flower

print. The look has obviously been worked on. In person, he's wary, not particularly friendly, asks for money halfway through – his eyes stay cold, and he's quick to take offence. We get off to a bad start when I ask him about the alley-cat races; races, he says, are not what messengering is about, and I don't need to know. But on the tape afterwards, he sounds fine – none of the coldness seems to translate. At the end, he gets up mid-sentence and vanishes. A journalist friend says later that Chidley did the same to him – just dropped him halfway through.

Bill Chidley: When I was on the roads first, there was hardly any other cyclists. And it kind of … You know, you were just unusual for being a cyclist, and the idea that you were a cyclist and also making a living was just weird. When I started in '86, there wasn't anything, really, in the media about it. Like now, there's books, and there's a bit of film, and we're now part of urban culture. Back then it was just weird and it did make me feel special. I think that's what the guys don't like about other cyclists, because they don't feel quite as special as they used to. Do you know what I mean? Because anyone can ride a bike. So they've got to make themselves different – you know, we're better at riding a bike than them. Well, maybe – maybe you are, maybe you're not. We know more about bikes than you – well, sometimes you do, but not always. We're cooler than them – well, don't know about cooler, but you definitely smell worse.

A 2004 study at the University of Cardiff found that most British couriers are young, or youngish (average age is twenty-eight) and highly educated – 80 per cent had at least one A level, 35 per cent had a degree and 8 per cent had a Masters or Ph.D. Many chose couriering as their first job after leaving college, but there were also former barristers, journalists, teachers and bankers out on their bikes.

Does being a messenger suit certain types?

Michael: I would characterise them as nomadic.

Adrian: A lot of them are technically homeless, moving from house to house. I'm at my mum's at the moment, looking for somewhere for myself. They're loners – they like working on their own.

Michael: I think a lot of us would find it hard to stick to a job in an office, which is why we're out here.

Adrian: And there's the challenge – seeing how many jobs you can do in a day.

Bill: There's a lot of mental health problems. Mostly depression. I think it just attracts depressive types. It's very, very good for depression, cycling. Very good. But it depends on the kind of cycling you're doing. Like, couriering, you're just going round in circles the whole time, and if you're feeling depressed, it's just the most futile occupation. Because you're just delivering stuff that no one really wants, no one gives a shit about. That's how it can seem sometimes. And you deliver to the same places, see the same people, the same streets, same potholes, same squashed pigeons … So it can be a very, very depressing job. I really liked it, but there were times when it could really, really do your head in.

I ask them if they want another drink. Michael wants a pint, but Adrian asks for fruit juice – he doesn't drink.

Michael: You don't drink? *You don't drink??*

Adrian: No. Teetotal, drug-free.

Michael (*laughing*): I'm sitting next to a virgin, for God's sake!

Adrian: I don't drink. I was an alcoholic when I was at school. Cos I got bullied and I used to smuggle beer and shit into school. I used to sit in the classroom and drink. I got expelled for it.

Michael: I was the opposite, myself. I did bunk off, but it wasn't a regular kind of thing. (*He's still laughing uproariously, entertained by the idea of a teetotaller at the table.*)

Adrian: What did you say?

Michael: I didn't say anything. I said you're a virgin, that's what I said.

Adrian (*also laughing by this point*): I'm not a fuckin' angel. How can you be a virgin if you've got two kids?

Michael: You know what I mean. Why don't you drink or smoke?

Adrian: When I was at school, I used to get bullied. So I started to drink every day at school. And we used to skip school and go up to Leicester Square.

Michael: The only time I bunked school was when punk came out and we used to go down the King's Road. Who bullied you?

Adrian: Loads of people.

Michael: Why?

Adrian: Dunno. Did you get any qualifications at school?

Michael: Yes – I was clever. I got six O levels and one A level in Government & Politics – grade O, so I've got another O level.

Adrian: I'd say, for me, school was just wasted time. But then I went to college, made up for it.

Michael: I went to school, did the same thing, but I had a problem. My family split up quite bad – by the time I went to secondary school, my mum had left the country, went back home to Jamaica and took my two sisters. So it was just me and my stepbrother. And so the only thing I had to look forward to was school. First thing in my mind was to learn to read and write properly, get an education. I got a medal for chess.

Who do you get the most aggravation from?

Adrian: Taxis. Always taxis. They don't stop for you, they cut you up …

Michael: The thing with taxi drivers is, they're saying, 'Fuck you – we were here first.' That's basically it, nothing else, just, 'We were here first. We don't really care and we were here first.' But (*he points to his bike*) WE were here first.

Adrian: They see you in the mirror and then they pull over so you can't pass them.

Michael: I mean, I respect the cabbie because …

Adrian: Because he's got to do the same as us. I did help a taxi once.

Michael: There's no such thing as the average cabbie. They're all different.

234

Adrian: No – if you knock on their window and ask directions, they'll always point you the wrong way …

Another messenger, Chris, stops by the Duke for a chat.

Michael: If we had a decent union, one [rule] would be, listen, if you're rude to people just because you're a courier, I think you should leave the job. I think couriers can be really iffy because of the job – they can use it to their advantage. It's in some people's character to be fucking rude when they don't need to be. I think you learn more if you get on with people.

Chris: Yes, but it's frustration. You're trying to get somewhere for a job, and someone's in your path, and you can't help it. You're not racing, but it is intense.

Bill: What I found was that, with a few exceptions, the only antagonism you got was if you were looking for it. Because when I was on the road, if someone cut me up, when I was younger, I'd have a go. And you have a go at someone so they have a go back, and you can either escalate it or … As I got older, I just realised that the confrontations were costing me a lot of energy. And also, what am I doing? Am I riding from A to B, or am I riding from A to B via random fist fights?

If you could, would you be doing something else?

Adrian: Yes, I would be, yeah. I've got qualifications and stuff. I'm a fully-qualified care assistant, and I used to be a supervisor in a cake factory as well. But I always come back to it. Always. I started talking about it to my friends while I was at the factory, and I'm thinking, sad git. I just do it for the money now. I don't do it for anything else.

Why?

Adrian: It's something – it's like a rush, an energy. When you're on the circuit, and you've got your radio, and you don't know where you're going to be sent next … It's strange – when you're a courier, you don't want to do the courier work, but when you're out of the courier system, you want to come back to it. There's a buzz. And there's the money.

Michael: You get to enjoy it – there are parts of it that are really cool. You meet lots of interesting people. And … umm … (*pause*). Give me a moment.

Chris: I love cycling around in traffic. I miss traffic – I wouldn't want to cycle around in the country in the early hours of the morning, unless they were going to get drugs. I've been a courier for about two years. I still get a real buzz from cycling in traffic. Pack it in for six months, go and do something else, find yourself strapped for cash, have a load of problems in the meantime, get back on a bike, and ride through traffic. It'd be '*FUCKING HELL! This is fantastic!*' I'm not the quickest or the fittest guy out there, I'm sure there's like loads of yuppies who are really killing it. It's not like ego, but when you do ride to your own limit, it's a good feeling, fucking unbelievable, you know what I mean?

Do you still get pleasure from the job?

Adrian: Depends. Like today, I got pleasure from it, because it's nice and sunny. When it's raining, I just want to call up and say, stick the job.

Chris: There's times when you're not making much money and you're not being consistently fast, and then there's times when you get, like, three jobs and you're knocking them out so quick ... And there's times when you're frustrated and angry and you're absolutely fucking sick of it, and you get some shitty job and you're really not in the mood for it and it's miles away and you just want to go and do something else. But then you think, right, I'm going to attack this now, I'm going to ... *really* ... *fucking* ... *attack* it.

Bill: I fucking *hate* cars, fucking *hate* them. They're just always in the fucking way. That's just what I remember. They're always in the way, and they're slow, and they don't look – they're just prisoners in this little box, and they're kind of like little oversized insects almost. Whereas on really good days when I was riding, you just felt like you owned the road. Not that you owned it, but that you were some kind of demi-god, floating above everything and no matter what happened, you'd evade danger and move faster than anything else in town.

Michael: There's moments when you wish there were certain things you could do on a bike.

Adrian: Yeah, what Mahelly does every day of the bloody week. He's got a fixed-wheel bike with no brakes, he'll come 30, 40mph down Wood Street, up into a wheelie, spin the front wheel, back down again, skid round, wheelie it, back up onto the pavement and stop.

Michael: I've seen him do that, and I'm not jealous. But I am perplexed.

Adrian: There's moments when you think two or three moves ahead, like you do in snooker. I've got to the stage with the lights where I shout, five, four, three, two, one, go! I shout it out aloud. Down all those lights at Bishopsgate, specially.

Chris: There's a woman on a red carbon graphite bike, she rides for Reuters, and me and her had a race a while back. Not even a race, just like a shared thing. Let's both ride fast, take our chances, see who comes out in front, but we weren't actually competing, it was just like enjoying the same moment. It's fantastic when that happens, fantastic. She was fucking unbelievable. And fit as well. I mean, I was struggling.

Adrian: Talking about having races, you know Boris Johnson usually rides out of Lower Thames Street two or three times a week? Well, he's trying to keep up with me. I'm going SW1 and he's right down like this, going … (*he crouches down into a racing position*). He stops and talks to the winos on the other side of the road sometimes.

Do you ever cycle for pleasure?

Michael: No (*decisively*). At weekends, I leave my bike alone and get public transport.

So the bike is only work?

Adrian: For me, I'd say it is.

On a cold smirry evening in mid-November, Eva Ballin slides to a stop by the kerb in Edinburgh's Broughton Street. It's been one of those days which doesn't really count as a day – a cold half-light and a thin rain that never increases but never stops either. It's foul to walk in and it must be foul to cycle in. This is not the sort of day to make you love Edinburgh or bicycles or indeed the concept of being out of doors at all. But

Eva is friendly and cheerful, laughs easily, has the sort of face anyone would trust and is plainly a great deal cleverer than most of the people she delivers for. She's dressed in several layers of clothing and keeps her woolly hat on throughout. Though originally German, she speaks Edinburgh Scots with no trace of an accent.

She takes me quickly through the logistics of the job. What they earn depends entirely on how many jobs they do. She could probably manage fifty drops in a day, a few more if things were exceptional; each would be worth between £2 and £3. When she first started there were twenty-five messengers in Edinburgh, now there are twelve or thirteen. There are five major companies in the city at the moment, but they'll all have a fleet of vans and motorbikes as well. When a delivery comes in, the controller will simply use the fastest and most effective method of delivery for each job. Many of their jobs at the moment are picking up cheques and pay-in books for companies, going to the bank, giving them the money and then taking the books back.

After I've spoken to Eva, she suggests another place, a flat over in Polwarth where apparently there's a whole nest of messengers. It's not hard to find; in the glassed space at the top of the door there's a bike frame outlined stark against the light from the hall. Inside the front door, it's one of those big cold New Town tenements with individual flats leading off a stair with stone treads worn into a bow by all the feet which have been up and down here. The layout, style and ambience are those of a student flat: mattresses on the floor, more Rizlas on the table than food, spaghetti, evocative scent of beer and old towels. There are three housemates, all of whom are either couriers or doing something bike-related. Scattered through every room in the flat are frames in various stages of assemblage and demolition; chain rings and gear sets, disembodied bars, bells, saddles, wheels. After the interview, we do a count and discover the beginnings or ends of thirty-six cycles in the flat. This truly is cyclo-enthusiasm taken to extraordinary lengths – a bike shop with beds attached. We sit in the kitchen and the housemates wander in and out, fixing dinner and smokes while we talk. Jim Young is thirty-four with white dreads, a soft Edinburgh accent and an earnest look to him. Michael Napier is thirty-nine, with a north-eastern accent and a bystander's outlook. He keeps his cap on throughout, removing it briefly to reveal a frill of hair at the sides and a gleaming monk's tonsure on top.

Eva Ballin: It's not a long story, but I've always liked cycling – I've never not cycled, but I've never been a cycle nerd. It was always a means of transport, just something to do – plus it was fun. I'm from Germany and I came over sixteen years ago to go to university, and I got stuck here. I graduated and I got married and everything, and then I started a Ph.D., and I got so bored of it. I was working at uni, I just thought, this is not me, I don't want to do it any more.

What were you doing?

Eva: German cinema. (*She laughs. I laugh too.*) Yeah. See?! The films were great, but to write about it and to get behind all the theory, you just think, God, I wish I'd never started this. I just haven't got the patience to sit down and go to the library and read and research and write it all down – I just didn't want to do it any more. I'd had enough. A friend of mine from Berlin is an architect and she was a bike courier for just the summer months in 2000. She said, this is *brilliant*, you've got to do it! So I said, OK. That was in September 2000, and I thought, well, between now and Christmas I might as well get myself a job as a courier and then see what I want to do when I grow up.

How old are you now?

Eva: Thirty-eight.

Mike Napier: I've been really lucky – I started off with a record shop in Aberdeen. That was like a dream come true, being an obsessive record-collector since the age of eleven. I could bore you to tears with label variations. But I got attacked – I got six inches taken out of my ring-finger tendon by six chaps because I threw one of them out. So the others attacked me. Savagely. Hospitalised me for three or four days round about Christmas, thought I'd lost the use of my hand. And if there's ever going to be a wake-up call to get out of Dodge, that was it. So I came to Edinburgh on a wing and a prayer. Didn't have a job. Had plenty of savings. Gave up the businesses in Aberdeen completely. I tried getting into the old stuff, but it's a closed shop down here, so I thought, right, I'm going to have to get myself a proper job. There was an advert in the paper on the Friday, I phoned up, and they were like, yeah, come in on Monday. I thought, you've not even seen what I'm like yet. But that's what they're like; it's just, 'Can you stand upright? Yeah, you'll do.' No questions.

How many jobs can they manage in a day?

Eva: It depends on how busy it is. There's probably fifty
max – fifty drops – but anything above that you would
have to have lots of tiny little ones. Because it takes a lot
of time going in and out of premises as well – lock up
your bike, speak to the security guard or the mailroom
person, speak to the receptionist, have a wee chat. A few
months ago now someone wrote an article about me as
the only female cycle courier in Edinburgh, and they
phoned me up and asked me all these questions and
things. The usual one is, 'How many miles a day do you
do?' Well, you know, if it's really busy, maximum sixty
miles, even though you can't physically do more than a
hundred miles a day, you can do that on the open road
as long as there aren't traffic lights or having to stop and
start to pick things up, but that in itself takes time – you
can't just rack up the miles. So I said, sixty miles on a
really super-busy day, and then they went and made it
into eighty miles – Eva cycles eighty miles a day. I didn't
say that and I certainly don't do that; no one does that.
We don't cycle solidly for eight hours a day. There's
walking and stairs and lifts and …

Mike: I'd just seen the job and thought, 'Paid to ride a bicycle? Wow!' And from the first minute, I was amazed. I
went to Charlotte Square and saw the way people inter-
acted together, and loved it. I had my own group of
friends, but to meet this bunch of crazy fools …

*Inevitably, each city's courier scene is different – Edinburgh's
might be more mongrel while Glasgow's is coherent, London's
full of nomads with a few long-stay patients.*

Eva: It is the scene, definitely. If that scene wasn't there, and if all the other couriers were just idiots, the job wouldn't be so hot. Because then you just think, what do I do? I just pick up stuff, I take it from A to B all day, every day – how boring is that? How uninspired and uninspiring and stupid. What I find really, really interesting is that when I cycled up to Charlotte Square on my first day and they were all sitting there – in those days, there were ten, fifteen people just sitting there at any one moment, because there were just so many of them then – and I just went, 'Hello, I'm Eva, I'm new, hiya.' And they went, 'Hey, hello, how you doing?' Just instantly really, really nice.

The thing about Edinburgh, of course, is that it's built on hills. Half of it runs up the spine of an extinct volcano, the other half down the sides of what used to be a loch. There are the Pentlands round the periphery and Leith by the sea. The other thing about it – the thing that most tourists know – is that it is very beautiful and thus very precious. Edinburgh is proud of itself, proud of its looks and proud of its fabulous architectural heritage. The New Town, begun in 1767, was built on a grid system which was designed to eliminate the chaos and disorder of the Old Town. What that means in practice for a bike messenger is that you're riding uphill on a cobbled street in Europe's most attractive wind tunnel. 'Apparently,' says Jim Young with Eeyore-ish satisfaction, 'we've got the second-worst roads in the whole of Europe. There's somewhere in Albania that's worse, but not much.'

Mike: I was in pain beyond belief – I hadn't worked that hard since I was a competitive runner in my early days. I was doing about 8.30 a.m. to 5.30 p.m. five days a week. I don't get many jobs, but I do get ridiculous distances – a round trip of fifteen and twenty miles. I'm probably doing about forty to forty-five miles a day, probably more. It's the nature of the cycling as well – it's not out on the open road, get a good cadence going. When I used to do that, I'd go out on a Sunday afternoon and I'd do twenty, thirty miles, and I would feel it at the end of the day, but doing fifty in the city where at points you have to go as hard as you can through everything is hard, especially on a fixed-wheel – it's harsh on your legs.'

Eva: Even now, you think, where's that? Especially in the Old Town, a lot of legal offices are tucked away up the Wynds – it's like they exist in a different dimension. And that in itself I find fantastic. The fact that you can just walk into Parliament Square, the courts and everything, and deliver stuff to the advocates – it's just great. You're almost like a tourist, but you can get in anywhere free because you're delivering stuff – the Castle, you get into the Castle and the security guards guide you through to the highest place where there's a little office in a wee tower at the top, and you just think, this is great. Obviously most of the stuff day-to-day is just mundane A to B and return, but some of it is amazing. And it's still good fun.

Mike: I think more than anything else, the hardest thing is the hills. I'd like to see a hillier British city. It's built on seven hills, and climbing on cobbles is horrible – I hate

Howe Street. These guys who race on cobbles on the European circuit, like Paris–Roubaix, they have it easy – they have a superb-quality bike which is maintained by someone else, they get a massage at the end of the day, sure they're going fast and they have more miles to do, but they're fed, they're watered, they're massaged, they're looked after – all they have to do is get on and ride the damn thing. Whereas we have to do everything.

Why do you ride a fixie?

Mike: Because it won't break. I had a really posh bike when I started, £700, £800, a cyclo-cross bike really well built for the job, and it came apart after a month of getting battered around – the chain would go, the drive would go, and I would spend SO much time with it. I'd get back at night, knackered, up it goes, tinkering around, 'Oh, come on, baby, you can make another couple of days till payday, oh, I've stolen a gear cable off of a dead bike for you …' (*He laughs.*) Whereas the Duchess, as I call her, is just an old late seventies, early eighties good, solid road bike that I've turned into a fixed-wheel. And she's never let me down, even though she's squonking and squeaking just now, but she won't stop. They just don't break. We do a lot of hill climbing here, and a fixie will pull with you.

Jim Young: They'll help you up the hill with the momentum – it's like a flywheel. You can get up the hill with a bigger gear on than you would with a single-speed freewheel.

What about injuries?

Jim: I don't tend to have that many accidents. Two this week, though – one yesterday and one today. It happens. You just get back on the bike and keep going. You have to know how to crash, though.

OK, so what's the best way to crash?

Jim: Don't bang your head. I don't wear a helmet. (*He describes an accident he had on Princes Street.*) Landed on my feet, palms down on the pavement, and the bike hit the taxi – I bailed and the bike kept going. The bike was a write-off. I said to the driver, you can give me some money for my bike or we can get the police. I got £20 out of him, but didn't realise that the frame and fork was bent.

Mike: I think everybody has a side you naturally favour to tumble on. If I'm about to crash, I pull this way (*right*) so I tumble that way (*left*). You probably favour the side you write with – the right-hand side if you're right-handed. I've only properly crashed once since I've been here. I've fallen off plenty, but only crashed once. I did a Starsky and Hutch over the bonnet of a Maserati. It was totally my fault, so I apologised – he was cool about it.

Eva: It really, really does depend on how you ride. You can take as many risks as you want or you can be as defensive and as careful as you want. If you're super-careful then you're not going to get anywhere because you'll just wait in the queue with everyone else, so it's a calculated risk. Again, because I'm a girl, I feel I don't have to take risks. I've been pretty lucky so far – I've had two crashes with cars, where they just didn't see me or opened their door and I went flying, but that could happen to any commuter cyclist. But obviously with us, statistically something's more likely to happen because we're on the bike and on the road all day. But you almost get a sense for it – you can predict what cars are going to do to a certain extent. If you're going round a roundabout, you can see, 'You're not going to signal, you're not going to stop, oh no, you haven't stopped or seen me, have you?'

Iain Withers is twenty-nine and now runs a company based in the Scottish Borders which offers skills courses, events and mountain-bike guiding round the area. Before setting up the company with a colleague, he was an Edinburgh bike messenger.

Iain Withers: That was one of the main reasons I stopped. I noticed, I don't know, it seemed to be from the mid-nineties on for about ten years after that, you knew that for a start you were the only person going through red lights. But then, it got to, you knew if the light went red, for about half a second there might be a car going through, and it just seemed to grind down to the point where you couldn't go through a red light and not check for cars. It got to the point where cars were starting to really push it and do stuff that was a bit sketchy – go through green mans and red lights and stuff, which was just born out of frustration. And you could tell you were pissing off the car drivers by not abiding by the same laws as them. It got to the point where cars were trying to take you out because you'd skipped a red or something and they felt they needed to teach you a lesson. They were actively trying to take you off the road, and it got to the point where I was like, this is a bit odd. This didn't used to happen.

Do you get a lot of hostility from drivers?

Eva: Quite a lot, yes. Regularly. And because I'm a girl, I can get away with being not aggressive and just smile at them and usually it just works that way. But you do get a lot of stupid, stupid, stupid aggro. Certainly the traffic has got worse since I've been cycling, people have just become more impatient and therefore more aggressive – there's just more road rage. Everybody's losing patience, doing silly manoeuvres. I can see how, if you have to use a car, you can get really, really frustrated. It's almost … it's not fun any more. Or not as much. But I'm still not quite at the point where I think, right, I've had enough. I haven't really had a bad enough accident yet to kind of make me think, this is silly – don't risk your life or your health for a stupid job delivering letters. You have to do other stuff, though – I do German lessons, private lessons, and I do translations, and I teach companies and stuff, and I'm a sports massage therapist as well. I do these things in the evening.

Can you make it work financially?

Eva: Not any more. We used to pick up a lot of deeds and keys for houses, and that's completely disappeared now.

So you've got the numbers of couriers declining and the numbers of people wanting to look like couriers going through the roof?

Mike: It's one of the strongest-looking subcultures. Culture-wise, there's not that many things that have had strong, distinctive looks. And a lot of people pick up on the idea of a 'courier chic'.

Jim: There seem to be more fakengers in Edinburgh than people who are still actually working. We look the way we do out of necessity – it's not a well-paid job. It's about practicality.

Mike: Or finding the thing that smells the least. Which is harder than it looks.

Does being a bike messenger suit certain characters?

Mike: The ones who last, everybody's got something in common – they're not necessarily that well equipped for the real world. They haven't got that much of a love for it, so this is a great place for them to be. This is a great way for them to earn their keep, and avoid that big scary thing out there.

Iain: Does it suit certain characters? I think so. Like, your stereotype kind of hippy into artistic stuff loves drugs, booze, everything to the maximum. But Edinburgh wasn't really like that. There was a few who were like that, and there's a lot more folk who are like that now, that have almost kind of watched a video on New York bike messengers and thought, that's for me, I need to get that kind of bike and I need to get those kind of clothes and I need to take those kind of drugs. It's like they've bought a book on being a proper kind of messenger, and done everything by the book.

Eva: I would never even consider driving in a car or a van. Because I think, I can do better than that – I don't have to do that. Most people don't have to do this job – it's almost like a lifestyle choice rather than a necessity. If you've got a bike, you can ride the bike so you can be a courier. Well, a) it's not as easy as that, and b) OK, but a lot of people who came into couriering had well-paid, good jobs, but they didn't want that any more.

Jim: Sometimes when the weather's really bad, you think, oh, I can't be bothered with this, but then it always changes. On a good day, it's the best show in the world. Just riding around on a beautiful summer's day, stop in a park, have a beer for lunch, it's great.

Mike: I had proper jobs before, but they were always just living. So I had a chance to put some heart into something, and I ran with it as far as I could. Then when I came here, I looked around for something, couldn't find anything that I really wanted and thought, oh no, here comes the nine-to-five grind. And then I found this. It's given me so much heart again. I mean, I don't do it for the money. Anything pays better than this, for the hours that you do, *anything*.

Eva: You get one really, really nice winter's day, and you come down North Bridge towards Princes Street, ideally when there's the Christmas Market and all the lights are up as it's getting dark, the sun's setting and there's a red sky, you come down North Bridge and look out over Waverley and Princes Street Gardens, and it's just the most beautiful city on the planet. I just love it. And you just take everything else as part of it. But if it's a nice summer's day and you go to the Meadows or to the Park, it's just fantastic. It just is such a stunning place that you just put up with it.

Mike: It brings out the child in you. That's the thing I like best about it. They give me a job and tell me, get from there to there in that amount of time, and I'm like, 'Am I a whippet with a jet-pack on?' I'm just a man on a bike, but you do such foolish, foolish things to get it done. And for nothing! In the cold light of day, it's just like, grow up! OK, you've got a big bagful of stuff, but this is so much more fun. You get free riding, you get the most beautiful city in the whole wide world (*he laughs, slightly embarrassed*) and, yes, it's given me heart again. Absolutely. There's not been a day even in the height of winter when it's horizontal and cutting you in two when I've thought, Jesus, I wish I had a proper job. Never once.

🚲 🚲 🚲

ELEVEN

Knobbled

The trouble with writing about mountain biking is that it does exactly what it says on the can. You go out to the country and find a hill, you get on a bike and ride either slowly up that hill or fast down it. You curve round trees and swerve past roots, you meet obstacles and rocks and things designed to flip you into a shrub. You have a nice time. You have a lovely time, in fact. You're so busy thinking about how to take the next bend that you don't worry about rent or promotion or roadworks on the bypass. You get hot and sweaty and covered in mud. You see the landscape in a totally new way. You do a bit more riding and jumping and whizzing past trees. You get to the bottom of the hill, consume six giant flapjacks and go home with the avowed intention not just of coming back and doing it again, but of bringing all your mates next time. That's it; it's that straightforward.

Mountain biking is probably the most inclusive of all cycling disciplines. Because it's comparatively young, it doesn't have racing's Masonic peculiarities. And because it's rural, it's generally relaxed. If you want to take it seriously you can, but if you'd prefer not to push yourself to the point of breakdown, then that's fine, too. The real essence of it is to get you to the top of a mountain and leave you there, almost tearful with amazement that someone, somewhere, sometime, had the idea of taking a bicycle to places where bicycles normally shouldn't go.

And, strangely enough, it hasn't been around for very long. Mountain biking was developed in the 1970s by a group of kids in Marin County, California, who saw the great empty stretches of fire road up in the hills and thought they looked like fun to ride. The bikes they had at the time were either ordinary road bikes or big, heavy 'clunkers' – cruising bikes good for street posing, but heavy and slow. So they swapped the road tyres for fatter, knobblier off-road tyres and took their bikes climbing. Having had a great time but having also decided that shocking the skin off their bones was not really part of the deal, they set about making the ride a little smoother. To the existing strong frame they added stronger front forks, then straight bars, then a longer wheelbase, then full front and rear suspension. By plundering BMX for ideas and for parts, they gradually built a bike which didn't automatically disintegrate or explode somewhere between summit and base.

That's the received view, anyway. The alternative view is that mountain biking was invented by the British decades before anyone in Marin County got hold of the idea. According to this view, the seventies fire-track story is a self-serving myth designed to sell bicycles, and mountain biking (or at least cycling up unpaved mountains) had existed since the 1890s. Thus the modern sport was in fact invented by people who didn't know they were inventing anything. Instead, they called it 'rough stuff'. The Captain Oates-style tone of rough-stuffing was set by W. M. Robinson, who wrote a column for *Cycling* magazine for many years under the pen-name of Wayfarer and was a keen advocate of making life as difficult for himself as possible.

His description of a jaunt to Wales's Berwyn Mountains in March 1919 is a good example. Having ridden sixty miles to the starting point, he meets another couple of cyclists who 'reported passing storms of snow and hail, through which they had ridden – a pleasant change from the monotony of sunshine cycling'. They ride on through the Glyn Valley in darkness to a local inn where they are told that their proposed route over the mountains is blocked by blizzards. The previous night, according to the innkeepers, a woman had set off on foot to visit a sick relative in the next valley, got lost in the drifts and only been rescued by chance. Wayfarer absorbs the information and goes up to his bedroom where he notes approvingly that the window has been left wide open and that it is now snowing hard inside as well as out. The following morning, having slept well beneath the bracing winter frosts, Wayfarer takes a look at the weather (blizzard, zero visibility) and concludes that conditions are ideal for recreational cycling. Despite a few false leads and blocked gates, he and his companions get going. Sinking up to their waists, unable to find the path and carrying their bikes for much of the way, the group reach the other side in four hours. 'It is an infinitely more interesting and adventurous trip when done in deep snow,' Wayfarer concludes. That afternoon, he cycled a further fifty miles over another mountain just for fun.

Modern readers may find Wayfarer's relish for discomfort extraordinary, but it struck a chord with readers at the time. Many of those who followed his column were young soldiers returning from the trenches of the First World War for whom pass-storming through March snowdrifts probably did qualify as light relief. He himself had been wounded in the leg as an infantryman. His lectures were always oversubscribed, and when his bicycle was stolen his fans raised enough money to buy him a new one within two days. Wayfarer believed in 'as little bicycle as possible'. Gears were obviously unnecessary, wide tyres pointless and mudguards slightly suspect; he rode a light roadster with North Road bars and a Brooks saddle. Like his readers, he took a no-nonsense approach to repairs. Belt braces could be pressed into use to fix dynamos, bean cans would patch cracked down tubes and postage stamps could mend punctures.

Many of those who followed Wayfarer adopted the same tone of bluff sufferance as he did. 'I took my cycle, a Raleigh weighing over 45 lbs, over Sty Head Pass,' wrote A. J. F. Field in 1928, 'and have nothing but pleasant recollections of the crossing.' Or, as K. E. Walker put it in 1954, 'In several hundreds of miles of diverse surfaces, across fields, bogs, boulders, and the like, my machine has yet to suffer damage of any kind. Admittedly the going can be rough, but the reward far outweighs the effort.' Inevitably, a strong but covert sense of competition developed among Rough Stuff

Fellows, with members suggesting routes of increasing length, complexity and difficulty. The Fellowship still exists and is still active; its website gives a list of popular routes, many involving the high Scottish summits known as Munros. Cape Wrath is a good example of the type of route recommended. To reach the north-westernmost tip of mainland Scotland off-road takes one across a beach, a river, a seven-mile bog and an MoD firing range covered in old and unexploded ordnance.

For those who do wish to update occasionally, the modern mountain bike does have its advantages. Because MTBs are in practice so often ridden on-road, manufacturers soon realised that they needed to produce something which in weight terms could stand comparison to a hybrid or a road bike. And so, in order to produce a bike that was simultaneously light, sturdy, capable of being ridden both on- and off-road, relatively crash-proof *and* commercially viable, they had to borrow technology from other sources. Thus the average modern MTB probably uses similar materials and production techniques to the space shuttle programme. The sophistication in front and rear suspension alone is pretty astonishing. Many bikes now have three or four inches of travel (springiness) in both places plus a lockout option for on-road. Riding down a road on a good-quality bike with the suspension on feels like going for a spin on a featherlight version of your favourite armchair.

The upside of all this development has been to open up the landscape in a completely new way. Generally speaking, if you can walk it, you can now ride it. Steep stony sheep paths right up on the moors, rutted old stone tracks, abandoned drove roads … The kind of places which were once associated solely with walkers bearing Kendal Mint Cake and grudges can now be cycled by anyone capable of paying the bike hire fees. Every year, there are a growing number of sportives and races for those who fancy hurling themselves up and down a Dale or a Cairngorm at speed. The annual Three Peaks cyclo-cross race requires participants to cycle up three of the Yorkshire Dales – 5,000ft of climbing, a total distance of thirty-eight miles, and a fair chunk of it with their bikes slung over their shoulders. The race was started by a local teenager, then aged fourteen, who had watched the annual Three Peaks marathon (walking the three highest mountains in Scotland, England and Wales), and who fancied a local version on wheels. Despite the strong possibility of bad weather and a fair number of dropouts, demand for places is growing every year.

Elsewhere, the majority of mountain bikers are happy to cycle in captivity. About ten years ago, when mountain biking looked as if it was going to remain a niche interest, up in the Scottish Borders a man called Pete Laing worked out that if you put together some of the thousands of miles of hillside currently covered by Forestry Commission sitka spruce plantations, and large numbers of overenergised twenty-somethings you might just be onto a winner. The geography of the Borders was ideal – the hills weren't too steep, there was a pre-existing network of tracks, and above all there were two huge ready-made markets no more than an hour or so away in Edinburgh and Glasgow. The idea of putting government land and recreation together had already been successfully tried in Wales; now the challenge was to apply it to Scotland. Glentress, the largest of the mountain biking centres, is now the top tourist attraction in the Borders. At weekends, the place is heaving with people up from the south or down from the north coaxing their children over the tree roots.

As mountain biking has changed and expanded, so inevitably it has split into further sub-tribes. Broadly speaking, there are now five different groups. First are the cross-country lot. In most ways, they stick closest to the conventional notion of mountain biking, riding the trails, testing themselves against a landscape, traversing an area from A to B. It is also the broadest and most inclusive of the different groups, and probably the side of MTB that new converts will see and try first. Competitively, cross-country is now an Olympic discipline, with races taking in three or four laps of a predetermined course with a mass start – the winner being the first across the line. Second is downhilling. You start at the top of a mountain, you finish at the bottom and the fastest rider wins. Races are conducted on a time-trial basis, with each rider out of the gate at thirty-second intervals, and relatively short courses.

Then there's cyclo-cross, originally devised in France by racers wanting to find a way of keeping fit during the winter months and combining the skills of both racing and MTB. The bikes are lighter and less fussy than normal mountain bikes, more like road bikes with knobbly tyres. They also have more clearance around the wheels to allow for the build-up of mud. Most races last an hour, there's a mass start and the aim is for the riders to complete as many laps of a two- or three-kilometre course as possible within the allotted time. The course will be full of natural obstacles (rocks, trees, track, muddy slopes) and barriers which the competitors can either bunny-hop on the bike, or get off and carry their bike over. In fact, so much of a cyclo-cross race is spent off the bike and hauling it bodily over obstacles that they are often just as much a test of the riders' running skills as of their riding ability. Cyclo-cross has barely begun in Britain, but it's been a big deal in Belgium and other parts of the Continent for a while. Because it's a winter sport, and because there's a certain pleasure in standing in the warm holding a pint of beer and watching a bunch of cyclists running round and round an awesomely muddy field with their bikes on their shoulders, the big races attract huge crowds. Then there's four-cross – four riders lap a short course of man-made obstacles in a knock-out race. It's similar to the BMX version popularised at the 2008 Olympics, although the two are beginning to diverge. The riders lap the course for about three or four hours, and it is as much an endurance event as a test of virtuosity. And last is freeride, which involves standing around in a queue trying to look cool while other people ride over bumps.

Iain Withers teaches MTB skills courses at both Glentress and its downhill neighbour, Innerleithen. He enjoys the variety of different types who hang out at Glentress. Who does he think is the typical mountain biker? 'There isn't one. Not any more. It used to be like some twenty-year-old guy with fuck-all money who'd jump in the back of a van with eight mates and go and rough it, go out there, find routes and get lost and stuff, but now you get guys in convertible Porsches turning up with a five-grand bike they've somehow managed to get a bike rack on. They've just got a chequebook and gone, whack! All the gear, there we go. And then you get battered old Transits turning up with, like, twelve people crammed in the back, cockle-picker style. It's the full range.

'I've learned not to generalise, really. You've got your stereotypes – your downhiller who's like' – he puts on a deep bass voice – 'the "fuck you, you're shit, I'm great" type. That's the right attitude to do something dangerous. You've got to be a bit of a dick, basically, to want to do it fast and better than other people. And then you've got your cross-country lot who want to spend all day in the saddle. They're a bit more open and friendly, and a bit more geeky-looking, clad in Lycra and that. But I don't know – especially with trail centres, it so just doesn't matter what your background is because once you get your clobber on, everyone looks the same. You can't really tell if someone's a lawyer or a scally or a thief or what. It seems to equalise things a bit, apart from when you see the person with the £5,000 bike and £2,000-worth of gear on. That gives you a bit of a hit. We're kind of in the second wave of people getting into mountain biking. There was one in the nineties and now there's one in the noughties. The people who got into it in the nineties, with some people there's a bit of an attitude that there's all these people getting into it now, it's not like it was back in the day … I run quite a simple bike, no fancy suspension, and you do get a bit of satisfaction from catching up and overtaking the guys who are on the £5,000 machines with all the body armour on and that, and you're just dressed like this' – he points to his shorts and T-shirt.

🚲 🚲 🚲

At the moment, the reigning family of mountain biking are the Athertons – all three of them. Dan, Gee and Rachel Atherton grew up in the countryside mucking around on bikes in the normal way. Then they got into BMX and began developing their individual skills a little bit further. And then they transferred to mountain biking and took over the world. Dan is the eldest, a National Champion several times over, a specialist in four-cross and down-hilling. Rachel is next, and – until 2009 when she was temporarily knocked out of the running by a collision with a car while training – had more or less cornered every category in biking, including winning the UCI Downhill World Championships the previous year, and being named the Sunday Times Sportswoman of the Year for 2008. And Gee, as National, European and World Champion, now has more cups, trophies and palmares than he knows what to do with.

At present, their operational HQ is at their parents' house in Wales. Driving west from Oswestry, the landscape becomes progressively lovelier – hills and valleys and hidden clefts and hills that grow with the miles from little hummocks into proper mountains. It's a perfect green place, a landscape built for riding. On the road from the nearest village, I pass a dark-haired man on a road bike pounding out the dips and rises. A little further on, he passes me. I watch him taking the curves with the simplicity of a gymnast, and realise it must be either Dan or Gee. We reach the turning to the house at exactly the same moment. At the bottom of the track, an old Welsh farmhouse has been heavily added to – bike sheds, extra porches, conservatory, outhouses, sheds, a complete dirt track out the front, a gym, extra space for a tour coach, signs of continuing expansion. The Athertons are now an industry, and as an industry they require a sizeable support staff of sponsors, accountants, PRs, managers, mechanics, soigneurs, physios, psychologists and assorted extras. Fitting all of that into a cosy, low-ceilinged family home in the middle of Carmarthenshire leads to an interesting sense of things bursting at the seams. Squelched into the space between the front garden and a field full of sheep is a freeride course built many years ago by the family and still very much in use. Elsewhere, there's a newish gym, a workshop and a team bus. And, inevitably, laid against trees, stacked against bushes, parked or flung, new, old, expensive and cheap, there are a lot of bikes.

In the kitchen, Dan and Rachel chat while Gee goes to get changed. Gee returns after a bit, and so they sit in line – Rachel with her arm in a sling, then Gee, all angles and thrust, and finally Dan, older, softer and more contemplative. There's something friendly and likeable about the three of them. Part of it is about who they are as individuals and how well that slots into place when the three of them are together, but part of it is also their overwhelming passion for mountain biking and their desire to communicate that to the rest of the world. That sense of zest is so strong that I get the feeling that it's all they can do not to demonstrate a point by leaping up, hurling themselves onto one of the bikes outside and taking off into the summer air.

Having grown up with cycling and having access to so many aspects of it, the three of them see cycling's intense tribalism more clearly than most. So why is everything always demarcated? Dan laughs. 'I think everyone is … whatever the cycling equivalent of racist is.' So mountain bikers consider road cyclists ridiculous, road cyclists take the mick out of BMX, BMXers wouldn't be seen dead on a downhill bike, and so on. And what about downhill? Doesn't it just attract complete nutters? This time it's Rachel who laughs. 'That seems to be the thinking, yes. And when you describe downhill to people who don't know it, their automatic reaction is, "You must be crazy, you've got no brakes." But you've got to be so clever about it, otherwise you're just going to crash. If you have no fear about it, no concept of danger, and you just go as fast as you can, you'll crash straight away. You've got to be really quite calculated about the way you're going to play it, which line is the fastest, because races are won and lost on point nothing of a second.' Dan nods. 'In the past it was the opinion of most people that the downhillers were the crazy wild party people, getting drunk before the race and then just hammering down the hills not having to think about it much and the cross-countries were much more training hard and working hard and putting the effort in. But nowadays, anyone who's top ten at a World Cup is very much putting the effort in. In downhill now, it's very professional – there's no way it can be anything else if you want to succeed. The two are not as far apart now as they used to be.'

In their line of work, much of the pressure comes from sponsors. Since there's almost no funding available from government bodies, most riders rely solely on private capital. Unlike racers, who sign with a corporate team, mountain bikers and BMX champions do individual deals with companies. And, because the sponsors pay the piper, they can call whatever tune they want. The most prominent stars like the Athertons will be given huge leeway to develop but lesser-known riders are, it is said, often put under pressure to push themselves harder than they know is reasonable or safe. Sponsors will always want a good return for their money, and merely having a kid on a bike riding round in their logo isn't enough. The brands who are interested in cycling want edginess, risk, the faint underground scent of danger. They want their riders to give them a wolfish kind of glamour, and someone who expects to stay on the right side of risk doesn't really fit into that. As Gee says, 'Downhilling is all about exposing the sponsor to the media, making it look good and putting on a bit of a show, so we spend our whole lives trying to push it and get as much exposure as possible. You know when you're at the start gate that every single one of your sponsors is watching you and that there's companies and businesses relying on you doing good.'

Part of the attraction with them, of course, is that they come as a package – three for the price of one. Three different styles, three different ways of approaching things. Then and now, that proximity had huge advantages. To begin with, the two boys started out with BMX. If one of them mastered a new jump or stunt, then the other would have to follow. As Dan says, 'You knew that if he (Gee) could do it, you could do it, because you knew you'd done everything up until that point that he's done, so there's no, like, possible way that he could have got a little bit extra skill than you' – he laughs – 'so even if in your head, you think, "shit, I can't do that …"'

They use a sports psychologist to help them with their preparation. As Rachel says, 'We train our bodies and he trains our mind.' How much of a difference, I ask, does your state of mind make to your performance on the day? 'Pretty massive,' says Gee decisively. He nods towards Dan. 'We train together all the time, we ride together, we do everything together. Like, last night we did, like, a road race, and I beat him. I'm fitter than him, maybe I'm stronger than him. But when it comes to the track, he's stronger in his head, and he'll beat me every time hands down. It's massive mentally, it's huge. If you watch us, Dan's very much a good rider at picking lines, a very smooth rider, very composed, very controlled, but it won't always be the fastest route. And I'm sometimes not as controlled, getting a bit more ragged, just getting from here to there as fast as possible without paying attention to what's happening in between, which is good some of the time, but a lot of the time causes me trouble as well. And Rach is very much a race-driven style. When she was younger she rode bikes a bit, but it wasn't until we were racing and she was coming along to the races that she started riding. So when she started riding, to her it was very much about the racing, rather than time on the bike. So her style is very much about going as fast as possible – similar in some ways to me, a little ragged and a little loose at times, but also she's got a lot of Dan's skill at picking lines. I've walked the track with her a lot and she'll be very good at spotting lines, spotting fast ways to go. So I imagine she's taken the fast bits from me and the fast bits from Affy and created her own winning style.'

Perhaps realising that if she couldn't beat them she had better join them, Rachel started following her brothers around, 'with my basket and my rabbit on the front, trying to keep up'. As Gee puts it, 'She would be at BMX races – she was really tall when she was young, and she'd be at the start gate with all these young boys, and she just like kicked their asses straight out of the gate. We'd watch her powering down the track, beating all these young boys … We knew from the start she was born to race. She was quite aggressive sometimes.' Rachel grins, delighted. Does she think there's any difference between the way boys and girls ride? She nods. 'We run training camps and we do a race clinic occasionally. All the young lads that come on it, they're all good and fast, but when you talk to them you can see that they just want to go up to the top and go down, wheee! as fast as they can. We talk to them and tell them to slow it down, go as slow as they can, think about what they're doing. They still go up to the top and come screaming down as fast as they can, all over the place. The girls learn so much faster, because they listen and they think and then they just do it, whereas boys just learn by making mistakes.' Gee: 'As soon as you talk to them, you can see them kind of mist up, you can see them thinking, "I'm still going to go as fast as I can!" The girls are always so worried that they're not good enough, whereas the boys always think they're too good.'

And what about the level of injuries? No matter how much body armour people wear (and, should you choose to, you can ride the mountains dressed like a human Hummer), falls and knocks are, very literally, part of the scenery. The Athertons take a philosophical attitude, pointing out that much of their training is directed towards avoiding injury. 'You have to be able to bounce back up,' as Dan says. 'If you're going to break a bone every time you go down then you're not going to get far.' Still, Rachel will have missed the whole of the 2007 and 2009 seasons because of injuries. It is one area, she thinks, where her brothers have an advantage over her. 'The boys rode their bikes all day every day when they were younger and their skills base is just so huge. Their bodies are just built to ride bikes and so it doesn't seem they get injured as much because they're like machines. They've just been riding for so long that they're perfectly formed towards it.' Still, if nothing else, injury time is very good for building motivation since there's nothing as frustrating as watching from the sidelines while your siblings win.

If anything, it's not the physical injuries but the psychological ones which matter more. So how do they deal with defeat? Rachel: 'You try not to let it happen!' Gee: 'I think everyone has to have a reason to train, when it's in the winter and it's hammering rain and you have to get out on your road bike for a few hours … Everyone has a reason at moments like that, something that spurs them on, and for me, it's that feeling of getting beaten, because it really is such a terrible feeling.' Is that what the will to win comes from, or does winning come from a different place? Gee again: 'I'm not sure really, it's hard to say. I wouldn't say you're, like, someone who wants to get rich and famous and have all this glory and have everyone watching you all the time, like a rock star, but winning a race is almost what that brings. You get everyone's attention, everyone's going to be looking at you, like they're telling the world that you're the best. When I started racing, I don't think I'd grown up with that built into me – that want to win, that want to beat people. But because I got into racing and did it for so long, that want developed and grew inside me.' Rachel nods. 'Even when you don't win, even when you come in twenti-eth, you still believe that you're the best and the fastest, and that it just didn't all come together today. I think that's a key if you're going to be the best again and again, then you need to believe that you are always the best, even when it's proven that you weren't.' She laughs. Gee: 'I think we all feel that there's nobody out there that's better than us. Like, on your day, when you race your best, then you are the best.'

Inevitably, that kind of status also means that they have to put the hours in. After a while, all the youthful single-mindedness broadens out into something which is equally ambitious but directed towards different aims. Or, as Dan puts it, 'When that happens, it gives you another angle to race for. You're not only racing because you love it and you want to race, because that's not enough. You're going to events all over the world and pushing yourself and pushing yourself because you know you need to build your career. With that comes money. If you did it just for fun then you probably wouldn't race, because it's not that much fun at the end of the day.' Rachel: 'It does turn into a job.' Even so, it is she who best describes what keeps both World Champions and total mountain novices coming back for more. 'From the point of view of someone who hasn't ridden a bike for a while, I can't wait to ride and race and win and blah blah, but actually I just can't wait to go off up the hill and just be on my bike and get covered in mud and cold and crashing in turns and just … there's nothing that can give you that feeling. If you're on a horse, then the horse is doing half the work; it's got its own mind. And if you're in a car then you're not one to one with the elements. And if you're walking, you're not going fast enough!'

There will almost certainly come a time when the major World Cup downhill races are televised (if only for the peculiarly human satisfaction of watching grown men riding into trees), but until that happens, the easiest thing is to turn up at somewhere like Glentress and try it. It needn't even involve much exertion. Since, as their name implies, both freeriders and downhillers aren't really interested in the 'up' bit of hills, many centres are now either installing ski lifts or are originally out-of-season resorts. The parallels with skiing don't stop there – all the different centres use the same black-red-blue-green classification system for assessing the complexity of runs.

And there's something else – something more subtle. Both skiing and cycling require one to 'read' a mountain.

They require the skier or the rider to assess the terrain, take notice of hazards and obstacles, be mindful of wind and weather. Both of them are about taking a line and following it with faith all the way to the end. Both require that you stay absolutely present and completely aware, intensely involved with the landscape. They demand that you notice the curves and lumps of a course, that you pay proper attention to trees and rocks and tricks of the light. They both show you a little of yourself at speed. And they're both absolutely about going with the flow. Like skiing, mountain biking is a lot harder and more tiring to do wrong – to keep jamming the flow – than it is when you do it right. And, like skiing, there's no pleasure greater than the sensation you get when you've danced your way down to the end.

歲 歲 歲

As the Athertons point out, riding BMX is probably the most obvious nursery schooling for mountain biking. Its ancestry is similar and, though one is associated with the city and the other with the countryside, both are absolutely about making the best out of the available landscape. Which, in BMX's case, was precisely the point. The name BMX is short for bicycle moto-cross, which is what it originally was – a kind of poor kid's alternative to dirt-riding on motorbikes. Like mountain biking, it originated in California in the seventies, but this time among the devotees of engines. Those who were either too young for a moto-cross bike or who couldn't afford one began using their bicycles instead, racing them over dirt jumps and messing around with the frame until they had something which, if you squinted hard from a distance, vaguely resembled a motorbike on a diet. By 1982, the craze was mainstream enough to withstand being featured in limited edition 'Yogic Flyer' form in Steven Spielberg's *ET*.

To non-initiates, the idea of impressing your mates on something that looks like a kid's bike may seem strange. A classic BMX frame has tiny, knobbly 20in. wheels, a low frame, no brakes, single-speed gearing and – if you add 'pegs' to the axles – what looks like recently removed stabilisers. Once in a while, you'll see someone trying to ride them like a proper bike, almost bent double in the attempt. They aren't meant to be ridden like normal bikes, and they're only really designed to be used in short bursts over very limited distances.

Again, inevitably, BMX is split into a further set of subgroups. The version that most people recognise, even if it's just from watching a bunch of kids riding up the walls of the nearest flyover, is freestyle street riding. Then there's vert – riding two ramps, shaped like huge quartered pipes, joined by a flat section at the base. And flatland, where, instead of riding on both wheels in the conventional manner, you go round in circles standing on pegs like a circus unicyclist. And finally, there's BMX racing, which is now an Olympic discipline. Eight riders start round a single-lap man-made dirt track, and the first one through the gate at the end is the winner.

The point of most forms of BMX is not speed. It's about using what's available in the landscape and in the shape of the bike itself to show off. It's about skills and stunts and reaction speeds, and pushing things in front of your peers. And, most particularly, it's about going underground, literally and metaphorically. Like freerunning, the various urban versions of BMX turn the city's uncompromising concrete into a proving ground. They see and use the available street furniture in an entirely different way, and by doing so they help reinvent the city itself. Which is a bonus, since, if you happen to be young, disaffected and capable of getting enough money together to get hold of a bike, then you can make the city your own *and* piss off the establishment at the same time. Ideal. Which may be why, put bluntly, it's difficult to find many great BMX riders who can also string a sentence together.

Nik Ford is an exception. He's been riding freestyle BMX since he was a kid. 'At first it was just fun, it was just something to do at the weekends, and then it just slowly started to take over my life really. It's quite addictive.' In order to give names to all the endless different tricks and stunts, BMX has developed as much bizarre jargon as cultural studies. You start with your bunnyhops and curb endos, perfect your barspins, and move on to the grinds. There are many different kinds of grind, from the feeble to the ice pick. There are tables, tyre grabs and one-foot T-bogs, downsite footplants, driveway doubles and 450 whips. Then there's the squeaker, the fire hydrant, the toothpick hangover and the funky chicken. Nik Ford: 'Take one hand off, then take the other off. Once you've got both off, put them up in the air, which is called an old-skool no-hander. Or you put them out to the side, which is a suicide, or you can throw them down, which is nu skool. Certain tricks often lead to other tricks. If you can take one foot off, then you can take the other foot off. And if you can get two off, you could kick them backwards into a Superman or kick them to the side, which is called a can. Some of the moves that people are doing now are ridiculous. You could go to a competition like, say, four years ago, and do a set of tricks and you would win. Nowadays that set of tricks wouldn't even put you in the top ten.'

But surely, I say, still struggling with the funky chicken, you must grow out of this stuff? BMX is for kids, right? 'You can always ride one down to the shops – I'd like to think I could always jump kerbs and stuff, but in terms of competing, there are guys of forty still competing, but they are world class. You don't tend to break onto the contest circuit at forty, you probably would have been there since you were twenty. You can ride a BMX forever, but because they're so small, you can develop a bad back from being so hunched over. And after a while, because of the knocks you take and stuff, it's going to affect things. I don't pay a mortgage, I just pay rent, so I'm lucky, but sometimes you go to a contest and it's, like, work won't be happy if I fall off and have to have six weeks off in cast. You are aware of it, but at the same time work's secondary to life. Work just puts the money and the petrol in the car to get to these events.'

The Athertons had started with BMX and then moved on, partly for practical reasons and partly because, as Gee said, 'One minute we'd be out in the Alps in some of the most beautiful places in the world riding mountain bikes and then we'd find with the BMX that …' Dan interrupts,

'You'd be on a housing estate in Slough.' Isn't all the aggro from the public a pain? 'Very much so,' says Nik Ford. 'That's why skate parks are cropping up now in towns, just to keep the BMXers and the skateboarders out of the town centres and put them in a controlled environment where they're not going to damage anything. But ultimately, they're always going to go out on the search. It's great to have a skate park, but variety is the spice of life – you could never just stay in the one place. It's more acceptable nowadays. People might even stop and watch you now, just because it's had a bit more media coverage. You often see a lot of kids at skate parks that have taken their front brakes off, taken their back brakes off, taken their pegs off, just to fit in with what's currently in vogue. At the moment, it's cool to have your seat really low down, no brakes, no pegs. And everyone wears skinny, like, their sister's jeans, flat peak caps. You go to a skate park, and it's like a catalogue sometimes. But the guys who stand out as being the greats are those standing there with their baggy jeans and their slightly tattier-looking bike riding the bit in the corner that no one thought was anything. They're the ones that push the sport because what they're doing today might be uncool and daggy but in a couple of month's time, the kids who were there in their sister's jeans will be wearing what he's wearing, doing what he was doing a couple of months back. It really does go in circles.'

Toby Forte's interest in BMX is more straightforward – it runs in the family. Like the Athertons, both of his brothers, Kye and Leo, are champion BMXers, and the family have organised major freestyle dirt-jumping events near their parents' home in Devon. 'At school, everyone else liked football, and I sucked at it, I never liked it. My nan bought us football kits one Christmas, and I felt like such an idiot. And then I started riding BMX. It felt exciting, but it also felt achievable. It was hard, and it was challenging, and that was why we loved it. There was a challenge, but it was a challenge you could feel you could do well at. It was like punk rock.' Now, fifteen years on, it still gives him that thrill. 'I guess it's that challenge. There's still so much to learn. You can worry all day, you can worry during the drive up to the trail, you can worry about life and what you're going to do for a job and how much money you've got and how you're going to get the rent this month and how you're going to afford your car's MOT or whatever, you can worry worry worry, but for that thirty seconds when you drop into that jump, you can't worry about anything because you've got to concentrate 100 per cent – you have to. And you pop out the other side and you feel *so* good. And then the worry starts again! But for that thirty seconds, it's such an amazing feeling. I've spoken to surfers and they describe it in the same way. It's what you make happen.'

It is one of the great paradoxes of the sport that the person who has probably done most to raise the profile of BMX and freestyle riding in general is not a BMX rider at all, but a trials rider. In April 2009, Danny MacAskill and his flatmate Dave Sowerby made a video in Edinburgh. To begin with, the film is mystifying – it shows a guy with his bike eyeing up a stand of park railings. Then it shows him messing around, removing a lamppost, up on a telecoms box. Then, astonishingly, it shows him riding along the tops of the railings all the way to the other side. The rest of the video shows him making equally novel use of the city's street furniture – whirling over the ramped entrance to the Standard Life building, somersaulting round the St James's Centre. At the time of writing, the video had had upwards of 23 million viewings on YouTube. A normal video on the YouTube trials forum could expect to get perhaps 2,500 hits. Within three hours, the MacAskill video was at 15,000. 'And the next day I got a call from the BBC wanting an interview. That same day on the Scottish 6 p.m. news they played about two and a half minutes of the video – I couldn't believe it. And then it was the papers, and as it went to different papers more and more people would see it. On the BBC website for three days it was the top viewed video – it was higher than, like, the Budget for three days. And to this day, it's not really stopped.'

MacAskill and I met in the reception area of his new sponsors in London when he was down doing interviews. He hadn't been riding lately – he'd injured his shoulder on three separate occasions in the past year, the last time while riding with the Athertons in Wales. Trials riding is distinct from both mountain biking and BMX, though it combines elements of both. The bikes look like grown-up BMX bikes with a longer wheelbase, normal-sized wheels and no saddles. Aside from the lack of seating, they do at least look like you could ride them back home if necessary. In trials competitions, the aim is to get round a set number of obstacles on a purpose-built course without ever putting your foot on the ground. The point is to test the rider's handling skills – how long they can maintain a track stand, how far and how high they can jump, how ingenious they can be with the objects at their disposal. For much of the time, they're using the same kind of urban landscape as freestyle BMX.

So how the hell did he manage to ride those railings? 'Altogether, actually being at the spot, we were probably there for about six and a half hours over four days spread over several months. The railings are flat on top, they're not sharpened to a point, but they're maybe the size of your thumb and a few inches apart. The fence is about chest height, so high enough that my toes don't touch the ground, that's for sure.' What gave you the idea? 'I used to cycle past it every day on the way to work and I thought, right, one day I'd like to try riding along the top of it.' He worked at a cycle shop in Morrison Street, and a further clip shows him hurling himself and the bike across the gap between two of the shop fronts. 'I used to get my lunch in the supermarket across the road. Every time I stood on the other side of the road waiting for the traffic to pass, I'd look at that shop and I'd think, look at that gap! And just at the end of filming, one of my friends got a ladder and had a look at the roof because I assumed it would have drainage on top. But he said it was do-able, so I just went ahead and did it on a quiet Sunday morning. I must have done that gap about five or six times. The first time I did it, I crashed – I overshot the second roof and landed on my back on the roof.' One of the loveliest things about the video is seeing the way MacAskill uses the familiar layout of Edinburgh in a completely new way. 'In actual fact, if you compared it to Glasgow or London, Edinburgh isn't very good for what I do. It's all quite old – Edinburgh seems to love its big spaces with nothing in them. Because it's got the Festival, they don't have much modern art, which is what happens to be good for riding.'

What's the usual public reaction? 'Over the years, you do get told to move on. If people come on aggressive it puts your back up a little bit, but if the police tell me to move on, I'll move on, no questions asked. Because if I meet these people again, and it's likely that I will, they're not your enemies. There's like a mutual agreement that if they turn up then I'll go away and come back another time.' Since the video, things have changed a bit. 'The last time I was out riding before I broke my collarbone, I was talking to a homeless guy in Edinburgh. He was like, "Ahh, I've seen you in the papers …" And then this policeman comes up and genuinely he almost got his little book out and got me to sign it for his kid. He was, like, "Ohhh, my kid just loves it!"'

MacAskill comes across as an enterprising soul whose free-range upbringing in Skye had given him exactly the right mixture of strength and groundedness to be able to do what he had done and then to cope with the firestorm of celebrity afterwards. Inevitably, the process is making him a pro at dealing with the media, but he's not yet so far gone that no hint of truth or personality remains. So what was it about bikes? 'For me, I think I'm not a soulful person – I don't really have much philosophy behind what I do. It's just, like, part of me, and I can't really imagine what else I would put my creativity into. I can go out and put my music on, and make all sorts of problems go away, just be like problem solving, playing.' Was he ever attracted by the other sides of mountain biking? 'The competition side of things never appealed to me. Competitions mean stress, and that's not what drives me at all. I just like mucking around. I'm sure in a year's time or something I'll be a total diva with my entourage. But as long as I get to ride my bike at the end of the day, I couldn't be a happier person.'

🚲 🚲 🚲

CONCLUSION

Love and Souplesse

'A bicycle is the long-sought means of transportation for all those of us who have runaway hearts.'
LANCE ARMSTRONG,
EVERY SECOND COUNTS

Flann O'Brien's new atomic theory – that those who spent too long on a bicycle began to meld with their machines – might have sounded surreal at the time he wrote it, but lately it has begun to sound like mere statement of fact. Out there on the A-roads of Britain, ploughing through the rain and the juggernauts' backdraft, are all those who have spent so long on a bicycle that they're incomplete without it. Man and machine, indivisible. That degree of identification is one of cycling's lovely peculiarities, but also one of the things that makes one wonder if most serious cyclists aren't a bit *weird*, frankly.

While researching this book, I spoke to people from every different side of cycling. Some of them had been riding for as long as they'd been walking, and some had only just taken it up. Some could do amazing things with a bike – make it hop, make it fly, make it a source of income or an instrument of torture – and there were those who were just grateful to get from one end of the street to the other. There were people like Dave Yates who knew everything there was to know about the physics of frames and people like Graeme Obree and the Athertons for whom all that mattered was the chemistry. But the most striking of all were the accounts of those who had been injured. These weren't people who had just fallen off and grazed themselves. They were people who had sustained life-threatening injuries, the sort of hurts involving comas and artificial respirators, but one of the first questions that they all asked once they were able to do so was when they could get back on their bike.

The BMX rider Toby Forte had been hanging out in the local skate park with a friend, just warming up. He hadn't put his helmet on because he wasn't doing anything particularly spectacular. When he slipped and fell, he took the full brunt on his face and frontal lobe. His brain swelled, he was placed in a drug-induced coma and hooked up to a ventilator. When he was considered to be out of danger and taken out of the coma, he began the long, slow process of relearning how to live. 'My life changed forever because of it, but the first thing I was thinking was "When can I ride? When can I ride my bike?"' It took him a further year. 'I bought a mountain bike and it just sat there in the conservatory of my parents' house. I'd pass it every day and I'd think, I'm not ready yet, I'm not ready yet, just putting it off because I was so scared. And then one day I woke up ridiculously early, like 6 a.m. on a weekday, and I still wasn't at work, I didn't have any reason to be up at that time. But I just suddenly had the confidence to do it. I walked downstairs, put my helmet on, started riding around. I had tears in my eyes – I couldn't believe it.' What did it feel like? 'Absolutely … normal! It was, like, why haven't I been doing this for the last nine months? It was perfect. It was just like the freedom was back.'

In December 2003 when he was nineteen, Nik Ford had also been riding (with his helmet on) at a local skate park. He fell off a couple of times, but nothing serious – just the usual knocks. That night, he drove home as normal to his parents' house, had something to eat and went to bed. The following day, he passed out. In hospital, they found two large swollen contusions at the front of his brain, both putting pressure on his spinal cord. When they began operating, his heart stopped. 'They asked my mum if they could give my organs away and things. My parents had to ring all my friends and say that I was dead. And then they were giving me my final wash-down before they switched the machine off, and my hand twitched.' The new, resurrected Ford took a long time to heal. 'They said to me after the accident that I'd never ride a bike again, and that really broke my heart. They'd taken my dignity – I felt like that had gone, having people bed-wash you and having accidents in the bed and things, having food through a tube – and when they said that, it was, like, I'd ridden a bike for my whole life, you can't take that from me.'

Unsurprisingly, both Ford and Forte's families were worried by the idea of their sons getting straight back onto their bikes. In both cases, they were wise enough not to stop them. In the end, it was as much cycling as physiotherapy or positive thinking which healed them both. As Toby Forte says, 'I almost feel selfish keeping doing it because I've put my family and my friends and my fiancée through such an ordeal for me. Jess still really worries. If I go riding spontaneously, she says she still gets the same feeling she got on the day of my accident. I hate myself for putting the people I care about through that. But I'm confident that I'm not going out every day to try and push the limits of what's possible, I just want to burn off a bit of steam and come back a happy man.' Along with all those others who had been badly injured, both he and Nik Ford were now a lot less blithe about the risks they took. They were inclined to leave a bigger margin of error and were messianic about helmet use, but they still rode and they still fell off. However serious the injury, every single cyclist I spoke to said they were so delighted to begin again that they were almost always prepared to forgive, if not to forget. That's an astounding thing for two wheels to achieve.

But there's another flip side to all that identification. It would be a fine thing if bicycles could somehow transfer all of cycling's virtues to the rider and if, once astride, people automatically become calmer, more easy-going, more alive to their environment. Unfortunately, it's one ask too far. In the city, the huge upsurge in cycling means that there are now lots of novices out there who love the sense of virility and righteousness that cycling gives them, and have discovered a great new way to get rid of a day's worth of pent-up professional aggression on the commute back home. As Turner Prize-winning potter Grayson Perry (who has been cycling in London for most of his life) recently noted, there's no difference between an alpha male in a sports car and an alpha male on a bike. It doesn't matter if they're trying to break the Dalston–Barnes land-speed record in a Maserati or on a Brompton, they behave exactly the same. At its worst, modern cycling in Britain has become as ugly as modern driving is.

But, at its best, cycling is still exactly as the author William Saroyan once described it. Saroyan's work has been going through a bit of a quiet moment over the past few decades, but in his heyday during the forties and fifties he was celebrated for his apparently guileless style and his conversational accounts of life in Depression-era California. He won a Pulitzer Prize, refused it, drank, picked fights with the wrong people, died with his critical reputation already fractured. He wrote fast – too fast and too prolifically, many readers suggested – to be any good. Like many writers before and since, he wrote to raise himself out of debt. More than anyone, he managed to articulate the bicycle's capacity to turn a journey from a simple progress from A to B into a state of grace.

Saroyan spent three years from the age of fourteen to sixteen working for the San Francisco Telegraph Company during the 1920s to support his three siblings and his widowed mother. He learned to type and then to courier, earning a reputation for himself as one of the speediest of all the Bay Area's messengers. Apart from the obvious hazards – wind, rain, melted tar, grit in his eyes – he loved the work. As he wrote in *The Bicycle Rider in Beverly Hills*, 'I was not yet sixteen when I understood a great deal from having ridden bicycles for so long, about style, speed, grace, purpose, value, form, integrity, health, humour, music, mathematics (but not numbers), breathing, and finally and perhaps best of all the relationship between the beginning and the end.'

Saroyan was taking nothing but messages – no packages, no heavy weights, just the sort of traffic that would now be communicated by email or phone. Most of the messages were business communications, but many were more personal; Saroyan particularly hated delivering what he knew were the 'death telegrams' informing families that their sons or brothers had been killed in war. To be a good messenger, Saroyan concluded, one had to do several things. You had to be fast, but not so fast you ran into accidents. You had to be knowledgeable, because otherwise you'd spend far too much valuable earning time checking maps. And you had to be conscientious. 'A man learns style from everything,' he wrote later, 'but I learned mine from things on which I moved, and as writing is a thing which moves, I think I was lucky to learn as I did.' Best and most precious of all, he notes, 'The action of the imagination brings home to the bicycle-rider the limitlessness of the potential in all things.' That sense of limitlessness is still there. It is still possible to go out along the roads of Britain and find when you return that some essential part of you has been restored. It is still possible to find yourself on your own flying machine. All that Saroyan asked of his bike and received in return is still there, at the stroke of a pedal. At its best, what a bike gives you is love, and *souplesse*.

🚲 🚲 🚲

GLOSSARY

Aero bars: Handlebars that extend horizontally ahead from the stem, supporting the rider's forearms and giving a more aerodynamic, 'tucked-in' position.

Aluminium: A non-ferrous metal used in framemaking useful for its stiffness and lightness, but often giving a harsher ride.

Audax: A long-distance event, either paced or unpaced, in which riders are free to go at their own pace but must remain within a time limit.

Bar ends: Extensions at right angles to straight handlebars, allowing different hand positions. Useful for climbing.

Bidon: Water bottle.

'Boneshaker': The earliest bicycles in general use, pre-penny farthing. The pedals and cranks were connected directly to the front hub, the rims were of either iron or wood, and tyres were solid.

Butted: Frame tubing which is thicker at the ends where the joints are and lighter in the middle, thus saving on weight but still providing a strong frame.

Cadence: The speed at which you turn the pedals. Measured in revolutions per minute.

Campagnolo: Italian manufacturer of cycle components.

Carbon fibre: A composite material popular in framemaking for its lightness, flexibility and strength. Frames can either be made as individual tubes and then (as with a steel frame) joined with lugs, or they can be formed as a single entity – a monocoque frame.

Cassette: A set of sprockets on a hub, arranged in decreasing order of size.

Chromoly (or chrome moly): A light and cheap high-strength steel alloy with a high percentage of carbon used in mass-market frame construction.

Derailleur: The mechanism which moves the chain from one sprocket to another on a multigeared bike.

Diamond frame: The conventional bicycle shape. The diamond form is shaped from the angles of the top tube, the down tube, the seat stays and the chain stays.

Drafting: The lead cyclist in a group is the one who is effectively making the hole in the air. Those cyclists directly behind him or her benefit by up to 40 per cent from that reduction in drag, which in turn reduces the amount of energy they need to expend. Hence the close formations which develop within road races. See also *Wheelsucker.*

Drivetrain: The parts of the bike which generate motion – pedals, cranks, bottom bracket, chain, derailleurs, sprockets and rear hub – and which are directly stressed by engagement with those parts.

Drop bars: 'Racing'-type handlebars. The bars' centre is the top point, the two ends curve out and down to the side. The point is both to allow several different grips and, when the rider is using the lower grip, to offer a more aerodynamic position.

Drop-outs: An open-ended slot into which the rear wheel hub fits. It allows the wheel to be adjusted or removed without having to disengage the chain.

Echelon: A line of road racers strung diagonally across the road. Used mainly in situations where there's a strong crosswind, the diagonal line gives each rider the chance to draft, but also to see ahead.

Eddy Merckx: Belgian racing cyclist. Often considered the greatest racing cyclist of all time.

Fixed gear: (or Fixie) A bike without a freewheel – when the wheels rotate, so do the pedals.

Fork: The two blades which together hold the front wheel axle in place.

Frameset: Generally, the frame and fork alone.

Freeride: A form of mountain biking often involving a course with several natural and artificial obstacles built in – jumps, drops, walls etc.

Granny gear: The smallest gear for the steepest hills.

Groupset: The parts of a bike which make it go – gearing, brakes, derailleurs, headset, chain etc. Generally defined as the drivetrain and brake components supplied by a single manufacturer.

Hardtail: A mountain bike with suspension at the front but not at the rear.

Headset: The components which connect the front fork to the frame and allow it to turn.

Mitre: In order to fit two steel tubes snugly and at an angle to each other, the end of one must be filed down to precisely fit the curve of the other.

Monocoque: A frame fashioned as a single hollow shell rather than as jointed tubes. More common with carbon-fibre frames.

Musette: The bag handed out to a rider during a road race containing food and drink.

North Road bars: Wide, semi-dropped handlebars shaped like a loose drooping 'W'.

Peloton: The main group or pack of riders in a road race.

Quill: The upright section of a handlebar stem. Or the part of a quill-stem that is inserted inside an older-generation threaded fork steerer tube and headset combination.

Rake: (or Offset) The angle or curve of the fork between the front wheel axle and the headset.

Randonnée: Not dissimilar to 'audax' although really you need to be French to get away with saying you're a randonneur taking part in a randonnée. Designed to test the rider's tolerance for discomfort, indignity and self-examination.

Recumbent: As it implies, a bike or trike designed to be ridden in a more or less horizontal position.

Road bike: Often used to describe a bicycle with drop-handlebars designed to be ridden in road races.

Roadster: The traditional utility bike, precursor of today's hybrids. Still used in India and the Netherlands.

Single-speed: One gear, freewheel, front and back brakes.

Single-track: A path or trail used by mountain bikers.

Souplesse: A French term incorporating the idea of suppleness and flexibility in motion, but conveying much more than that – grace, harmony, flow.

Sportive: (or Cyclosportive, or Sportif) Not a race, but an event equivalent to a marathon in which riders are individually timed along a particular course. The routes often follow a stage of a subsequent road race, as in the Étape du Tour. Usually set in beautiful surroundings. Participants choose a route based on distance and then try to beat the crap out of each other while trying to make it appear that it's no more than 'a fun day out'.

Sprockets: The toothed gears around the rim of a chain ring.

Tandem: A form of bicycle designed to accommodate two riders, one in front of the other.

Time trial: A race in which riders start one at a time in individual competition against the clock – the fastest rider is the winner. Team time trials involve four riders, each taking it in turns to lead and to draft. Again, the fastest team around the course are the winners.

Titanium: A metal used in framemaking for its lightness and toughness. Expensive to produce, and therefore not as popular as either aluminium or carbon fibre.

Touring bike: A touring bicycle is designed to be ridden for long distances and carry heavy loads. It is thus sturdy, comfortable and very stable, probably at the expense of speed or aerodynamism.

Track bike: A bicycle designed to be ridden in a velodrome. Track bikes have no brakes, one gear, no freewheel and steep angles.

Track standing: Balancing upright on a bike which isn't moving. Popular with fixies at traffic lights.

Tubular tyres: Tubular tyres were the original pneumatics. The outer layer would be stitched around the inner tube and glued onto the wheel rim.

Velodrome: A cambered racetrack for cyclists.

Wheelsucker: Someone who does more than their fair share of drafting and less than their fair share of leading.

LIST OF ILLUSTRATIONS

Colour inserts
All photographs © Bella Bathurst

Framebuilder Dave Yates in his workshop in
Lincolnshire.
Dave Yates with the newly brazed lug joining the head
tube to the down tube of the author's bike.
The author's completed bike frame in Richmond Park.
Alex Brown, head of the Scottish Vintage Cycle Club.
Jan Rijkeboer, founder and head of Azor bicycle factory
in the Netherlands
A station bike park in the Netherlands.
A cargo trishaw under the Howrah Bridge, Calcutta.
A hand-pulled rickshaw in Calcutta.
Noor Hussein and his rented tricycle rickshaw.
A standard-issue Indian roadster.
(Inset) Vinod Punmiya, the man who raced the *Deccan
Queen*.
Riders on the Ronde van Vlaanderen.
A sportive rider after the Ronde van Vlaanderen.
The 2009 Tour of Flanders.

The last few kilometres of the Tour de France, Champs-Élysée, Paris.

Andy Schlek, Alberto Contador and Lance Armstrong at the end of the 2009 Tour de France.

Charly Wegelius.

Graeme Obree.

Eva Ballin and Jim Young in Edinburgh.

Cyclo-cross near Glentress, Scottish Borders.

Dan, Rachel and Gee Atherton.

Pulling stunts on track bikes.

Danny MacAskill.

Nik Ford.

Love and Souplesse.

Integrated images

Page 8 Racing bike. *Gareth Plumb*

Page 22 Bike evolution.

Page 25 Scene in a Velocipede Riding School, 1869. © *Bettmann/CORBIS*

Page 33 National Clarion Cycling Club. *Courtesy of Ian Clarke, Secretary, National Clarion Cycling Club*

Page 36 Major Taylor by E. Chickering, c. 1900. *Courtesy of Major Taylor Associaton, Inc. (www.majortaylorassociation.org)*

Page 96 Watercycle race on the Thames, c. 1920. *Photo: akg-images*

Page 99 Zetta Hills. © *Hulton Archive/Getty*

Page 107 Women's Emancipation (Being a Letter Addressed to Mr. Punch with a drawing by a strong minded American Woman.) *Missouri History Museum, St. Louis*

BIBLIOGRAPHY

PAPERS, ARTICLES ETC.

Bicycle Couriers in the 'New' Economy, Benjamin Fincham, School of Social Sciences, Cardiff, January 2004

Cycling – Towards Health & Safety, BMA, Oxford University Press, London, 1992

Cycling & Vitality, anonymous author, *The Lancet*, vol. 2, 1892

The Dutch Bicycle Master Plan, Directorate-General for Passenger Transport, Ministry of Transport, Public Works and Water Management, March 1999

The Road Ahead: Traffic Injuries & Fatalities in India, Dinesh Mohan, WHO, 2004

The Asclepiad, vol. VII, Benjamin Ward Richardson, Longmans, Green & Co., London, 1890

Centenaire des Troupes Cyclistes 1891–1991, unknown Swiss army author, EIDG Militärbibliothek, 1991, Bern

Department of Transport, National Statistics, 2007

BOOKS

John Adams, *Risk*, Routledge, Abingdon, 2007

Lance Armstrong, *It's Not About the Bike*, Yellow Jersey Press, London, 2001

Geoffrey Bles, *Wheels Within Wheels: The Starleys of Coventry*, London, 1966

Geoffrey Boumphrey, *British Roads*, Nelson, London, 1939

Marlene Brill, *Marshall Taylor, World Champion Bicyclist*, 21st Century Books, Minneapolis, Minnesota, 2008

Johann Bruyneel and Bill Strickland, *We Might As Well Win*, Mainstream Publishing, Edinburgh, 2008

Mike Burrows, *Bicycle Design*, Snowbooks Ltd, 2008

Patricia Burstall, *The World-Wide Story of Cycling in the 1890s*, Little Croft Press, Marlow, 2004

Beryl Burton, *Personal Best*, Springfield Books, Huddersfield, 1986

Viscount Bury and G. Lacy Hillier, *Cycling: The Badminton Library of Sports & Pastimes*, Longmans, London, 1887

Martin Caidin and Jay Barbree, *Bicycles in War*, Hawthorn Books, New York, 1974

Lillias Campbell, *Handbook for Lady Cyclists*, Davidson, London, 1896

Paul Dimeo, *A History of Drug Use in Sport 1876–1976*, Routledge, London, 2007

Alastair Dodds, *Scottish Bicycles & Tricycles*, NMS Publishing, Edinburgh, 1999

Pryor Dodge, *The Bicycle*, Flammarion, Paris, 1996

F. J. Erskine, *Lady Cycling*, Walter Scott, London, 1897

Jim Fitzpatrick, *The Bicycle in Wartime*, Brassey's, Virginia, 1998

Jan Heine and Jean-Pierre Pradères, *The Golden Age of Handbuilt Bicycles*, Rizzoli, New York, 2009

David V. Herlihy, *Bicycle: The History*, Yale University Press, New Haven, Connecticut, 2004

George Herschell, *Cycling as a Cause of Heart Disease*, Baillière, Tindall & Cox, London, 1895

David Horton, Paul Rosen and Peter Cox, eds, *Cycling and Society*, MPG Books Limited, Bodmin, 2007

Paul Kimmage, *Rough Ride*, Yellow Jersey Press, London, 2007

Tim Krabbé, *The Rider*, Bloomsbury, London, 1978

R. Lloyd Jones and M. J. Lewis, *Raleigh and the British Bicycle Industry*, Ashgate, Aldershot, 2000

Jeanne Mackenzie, *Cycling*, Oxford University Press, London, 1981

J. A. Mangan and Andrew Ritchie, eds, *Ethnicity, Sport, Identity: Struggles for Status*, Frank Cass Publishing, Abington, 2004

James McGurn, *On Your Bicycle*, John Murray, London, 1987

R. J. Mecredy and Gerald Stoney, *The Art and Pastime of Cycling*, Mecredy & Kyle, Dublin, 1891

Graeme Obree, *The Flying Scotsman*, Birlinn, Edinburgh, 2003

Tony Oliver, *Touring Bikes: A Practical Guide*, Crowood Press, Ramsbury, 1990

Joe Parkin, *A Dog in a Hat*, Velo Press, Boulder, Colorado, 2008

Denis Pye, *Fellowship Is Life: The National Clarion Cycling Club, 1895–1995*, Clarion Publishing, Bolton, 1995

William Saroyan, *The Human Comedy*, Faber & Faber, London, 1944

— *The Bicycle Rider in Beverly Hills*, Faber & Faber, London, 1953

Charles Spencer, *The Modern Bicycle*, Frederick Warne & Co., London, 1877

Leigh Summers, *Bound to Please: A History of the Victorian Corset*, Berg, Oxford, 2001

Major Taylor, *The Fastest Bicycle Rider in the World*, self-published, USA, 1928

Willy Voet, *Breaking the Chain*, Yellow Jersey Press, London, 2002

Frances Willard, *How I Learned to Ride the Bicycle*, Fair Oaks Publishing, Fair Oaks, California, 1991

David Gordon Wilson, *Bicycling Science*, MIT Press, Cambridge, Massachusetts, 2004

John Woodforde, *The Story of the Bicycle*, Routledge & Kegan Paul, London, 1970

Les Woodland, *This Island Race*, Mousehold Press, Norwich, 2005

— *The Yellow Jersey Companion to the Tour de France*, Yellow Jersey Press, London, 2007

WEBSITES

Athertons: athertonracing.co.uk
Bike Radar: www.bikeradar.com
Bike Statistics: quickrelease.tv/?p=279
Brick Lane Bikes: bricklanebikes.co.uk

Canterbury Sports Science: www.canterbury.ac.uk/
social-applied-sciences/
sport-science-tourism-and-leisure/

Condor Cycles: www.condorcycles.com

Cycling history: www.jimlangley.net/ride/bicyclehistory

Cycling Women: www.procyclingwomen.com/Great-
Women.html

Dave Yates: www.daveyatescycles.co.uk

David Millar Diaries: www.slipstreamsports.
com/2008/03/21

Dutch cycling history: www.rijwiel.net

Glentress: www.thehubintheforest.co.uk

History of British Paratroopers: http://polarisreddevils.
tripod.com/id2.html

House of Pistard: www.houseofpistard.com

Lance Armstrong: www.lancearmstrong.com

Lucas Brunelle: www.digave.com/video.html

Moving Target: www.movingtargetzine.com

National Clarion: www.clarioncc.org

National Cycle Museum: www.cyclemuseum.org.uk

Official Rules of the Euro Cyclist: www.facebook.com/
group.php?gid=2258201150

Porteurs: www.blackbirdsf.org/courierracing/velos.html

Rapha: www.rapha.cc

Resonance FM's *The Bike Show***:** thebikeshow.net

Rough Stuff Fellowship: http://www.rsf.org.uk/index.htm

Sargent & Co. Bespoke Bikes: sargentandco.com

Scottish Cycling: new.britishcycling.org.uk/scotland

Sheldon Brown: www.sheldonbrown.com/organization.
html

Tour of Britain: www.tourofbritain.co.uk
Tweed Cycling Club: www.tweed.cc
Union Cycliste Internationale: www.uci.ch
Velo Archive: www.veloarchive.com
Velorution: www.velorution.biz/bikes
W. M. Robinson – Wayfarer: www.cyclingnorthwales.
co.uk/pages/wayfarer.htm

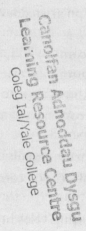

Canolfan Adnoddau Dysgu
Learning Resource Centre
Coleg Iâl/Yale College

ACKNOWLEDGEMENTS

Those who ride bikes and love them are in general a like-able lot, keen to share the knowledge they have and even more keen to communicate their passion. I was offered unstinting help by members of every one of cycling's many tribes. Their contribution to this book is so fundamental that it's difficult to know where their work ends and mine begins. I hope I made it clear to all of those I interviewed in whatever capacity that I was, and continue to be, immensely grateful. Without their help – either organised or impromptu – this wouldn't have happened.

In India, Mrinmayee Ranade helped with organisation and translation, Vinod and Indira Punmiya made us welcome and Ashok Captain acted as both interpreter and historian. As before, Tim Grandage at Future Hope made working in Calcutta a joy. In Belgium, Tim Harris and Jos Ryan opened up the world of European racing. In Edinburgh, Eva Ballin, Mike Napier and Jim Young showed me the messengers' way of seeing things, and in London Adrian Davies and Michael Barratt offered patience and knowledge. Over in Saltcoats, Graeme Obree was just astonishing. In Wales, the Athertons showed the best of themselves and their landscape. In Lincolnshire, Dave Yates shared the secrets of a lifetime of framebuilding and taught Graeme Symington and me how to build a bicycle. In London, Patrick Field turned the business of city cycling into an adventure and a masterclass in urban philosophy. And in Paris, Charly Wegelius was just very, very honest.

I've been hugely lucky to have been published and looked after by real enthusiasts – in every sense. It was as much Victoria Hobbs' interest in debating the minutiae of cycling etiquette (knobbly *v.* flat, mountain bike *v.* hybrid, whether several kilos of groceries have the same momentum on descents as a large, fat bloke in a hurry) which gave this book its reason for being.

I also drew on books, articles and websites from a huge variety of sources, including the blackbirdsf.org website for much of the information on the Parisian porteurs, and the CyclingNorthWales site for information on Wayfarer. It was a treat getting to know Alex Brown in East Lothian and a privilege to use his library. Pedalhead friends Harry Mount, Kevin Braddock and Chloe Hall all answered a lot of nerdy questions. Gavin, Nick and Laura Marshall made me laugh all the way round France. Erik Meek in Assen offered me friendship and insight into the Dutch way of doing things. Chris and Max Fraser offered hospitality beyond the call of duty, while Gus Garfield reminded me why and for whom I'm writing. Lucy and Flora provided love and Souplesse. And Dawn, Urièle and Marc dealt with all the things too big to name.